SAS PINK PANTHER LAND-ROVER

SAS PINK PANTHER LAND-ROVER

THE SPECIAL AIR SERVICE REGIMENT'S UNIQUE PATROL VEHICLE

ADRIAN HAYWARD-WILLS

FRONTLINE
BOOKS

SAS PINK PANTHER Land-Rover
From WW2 into the Cold War

First published in Great Britain in 2026
by Frontline Books
An imprint of
Pen & Sword Books Ltd
Yorkshire - Philadelphia

ISBN 9781036186470

A CIP catalogue record for this book is available from the British Library

Typeset by Lapiz Digital
Printed and bound in the UK by CPI Group (UK) Ltd,
Croydon, CR0 4YY.

Printed on paper from a sustainable source by
CPI Group (UK) Ltd, Croydon, CR0 4YY

The Publisher's authorised representative in the EU for product safety is Authorised Rep Compliance Ltd., Ground Floor, 71 Lower Baggot Street, Dublin D02 P593, Ireland.
www.arccompliance.com

For a complete list of Pen & Sword titles please contact
PEN & SWORD BOOKS LTD
47 Church Street, Barnsley, South Yorkshire, S70 2AS, England
E-mail: enquiries@pen-and-sword.co.uk
Website: www.pen-and-sword.co.uk
or
PEN & SWORD BOOKS
1950 Lawrence Rd, Havertown, PA 19083, USA
E-mail: uspen-and-sword@casematepublishers.com

CONTENTS

Abbreviations vi

Preface x

Introduction 1

Chapter One: The Land-Rover SAS Pink Panther: An Introduction and Brief History 4

Chapter Two: Pink or Green Boss? 23

Chapter Three: Equipment – SAS Land-Rover Series IIA Pink Panther 37

Chapter Four: Equipment Registration Marks SAS Land-Rovers 122

Chapter Five: The SAS Pink Panther in Popular Culture 131

Chapter Six: The Marshall of Cambridge Land-Rover 134

Chapter Seven: SAS Pink Panthers: A Celebration of Personal Ownership 141

Chapter Eight: Technical Data of *Truck, General Service (Utility), SAS, ¾ Ton, 4 x 4 Rover II* 144

Chapter Nine: The Final Destination of the Land-Rover Series IIA SAS Pink Panther 149

Index 167

ABBREVIATIONS

°	Degree
°C	Degrees Celsius
^{2}	Squared
AATDC	Army Air Transport Training and Development Centre
ABP	Ambi-Budd Presswerk
ADP	Automatic Data Processing
ADPCON	Automatic Data Processing Conversion
AFV	Armoured Fighting Vehicle
AKA	Also Known As
APC	Armoured Personnel Carrier
AR	Armalite Rifle
ARTF	Alkali Removable Temporary Finish
ASN	Army Serial Number
AUW	All-Up (Operational) Weight
BAOR	British Army of the Rhine
BBC	British Broadcasting Corporation
BCF	Bromochlorodifluoromethane
BER	Beyond Economic Repair
BP	British Petroleum
BS	British Standard
BMW	Bayerische Motoren Werke AG
cal	Calibre
CES	Complete Equipment Schedule
cc	Cubic Centimetre
CHOSC	Commando Helicopter Operating Support Cells
cm	Centimetre
cm^2	Centimetre Squared
CVDs	Central Vehicle Depots
cwt	Hundredweight
DC	Direct Current
DCI	Directorate of Cataloguing and Identification
DIS	Date in Service
DoE	Department of Environment
DPM	Disruptive Pattern Material
DPV	Desert Patrol Vehicles

DSO	Distinguished Service Order
DVLA	Driver and Vehicle Licensing Agency
ERM	Equipment Registration Mark
FFR	Fitted For Radio
FV	Fighting Vehicle
FVRDE	Fighting Vehicles Research and Development Establishment
GEC	General Electric Company
GMT	Greenwich Mean Time
GPMG	General Purpose Machine Gun
GS	General Service
HE	High Explosive
HEDP	High Explosive Dual Purpose
HEAT	High Explosive Anti-Tank
HM	Her/His Majesty's
Ibf	Pound Force
ICI	Imperial Chemical Industries
IFVME	Inspectorate of Fighting Vehicles and Mechanical Equipment
IMI	Imperial Metal Industries
IMPS	Invicta Military-Vehicle Preservation Society
in	Inch
in^2	Inch Squared
IoS	Item of Supply
IPB	Illustrated Parts Breakdown
IR	Infra-Red
IRR	Infra-Red Reflective
IWM	Imperial War Museum
JATE	Joint Air Transport Establishment
JLR	Jaguar Land Rover
KERR	Kinetic Energy Recovery Rope
kg	Kilogram
kgf	Kilogram Force
kgf/cm^2	Kilogram Force Per Centimetre Squared
kN	Kilonewton
kN/m^2	Kilonewton Per Square Metre
LAD	Light Aid Detachment
LAW	Light Anti-Tank Weapon
LRDG	Long Range Desert Group
LRHC	Land Rover Heritage Collection
LRP	Long Range Patrol
Ltd	Limited
LUP	Lying Up Position
LWB	Long Wheel Base
m	Metre
m^2	Metre Squared
MBE	Member of the British Empire

MCE	Marshall (of) Cambridge Engineering
MM	Military Medal
MoD	Ministry of Defence
MoT	Ministry of Transport
MT	Motor Transport/Mechanised Transport
NATO	North Atlantic Treaty Organisation
NBC	Nuclear Biological Chemical
NCB	National Codification Bureau
NDT	Non-Directional Tyre or Tread
NSN	NATO Stock Number
NVD	Night Vision Devices
OBE	Order of the British Empire
ono	Or Nearest Offer
PLCE	Personal Load Carrying Equipment
PPA	Popski's Private Army
PRU	Photo-Reconnaissance Unit
PSP	Pierced (Pressed) Steel Planking
PTO	Power Take-Off
Q or QM	Quartermaster
RAL	Reichs-Ausschuss für Lieferbedingungen und Gütesicherung
RAF	Royal Air Force
RAOC	Royal Army Ordnance Corps
RARDE	Royal Armament Research and Development Establishment
RCT	Royal Corps of Transport
REME	Royal Electrical and Mechanical Engineers
RHD	Right-Hand Drive
RMO	Regimental Medical Officer
RN	Royal Navy
RPM	Rounds Per Minute
RSM	Regimental Sergeant Major
SALOME	System for the Accounting, Location and Online Management of Equipment
SAS	Special Air Service
SCRDE	Stores and Clothing Research Development Establishment
SF	Sustained Fire
SLR	Self-Loading Rifle
SOE	Special Operations Executive
SP	Special Projects
SWG	Standard-Wire Gauge
SWL	Safe-Working Load
TP	Target Practice
TU-AAM	Tuning Unit, Automatic Antenna Matching
UK	United Kingdom
USA	United States of America
USAAF	United States Army Air Force

UV	Ultraviolet
VAOS	Vocabulary of Army Ordnance Services
VESPER	Vehicle Equipment and Spares, Provision Economics Repairs
VIN	Vehicle Identification Number
VRC	Vehicle Radio Communications
VRN	Vehicle Registration Number
VRN	Vocabulary Reference Number
VSN	Vehicle Serial Number
WE	Web Equipment
WV	Wheeled Vehicle

PREFACE

The Special Air Service (SAS) has a legendary reputation that commands admiration and awe across the globe. While there are many books written about the SAS Regiment, most cover a wide range of topics – including historical figures, specific patrols, or notable operations. However, this book is unique because it focuses solely on the Marshall of Cambridge SAS Land-Rover, also known as the SAS Pink Panther. A genre-defining special forces vehicle that served at the apex of military automotive triangles as the ultimate British Army predator for almost two decades, with the SAS Regiment.

The Land-Rover SAS Pink Panther is a testament to British engineering and an extraordinary machine; looking away is difficult. However, not everyone thinks alike, and opinions are as diverse as those of the vehicles themselves, especially in the world of military vehicles. Some military vehicle enthusiasts believe the sun rises and sets on the Willys MB (G503) and Ford GPW Jeep; in contrast, others believe it is the Long Range Desert Group's Chevy 30cwt 1533 x 2 – vehicles that are equally worthy and have bloodlines that get auctioneers and collectors breaking a sweat.

However, for me, it is the Marshall of Cambridge SAS Land-Rover Pink Panther. Its exposed open bodywork and ever-menacing weapons provide a superior and visually captivating package that simultaneously creates combinations of light and shadow, smoothness and angularity. And still has the capacity to flabbergast many decades later. Indeed, there are fewer synergies in the world of military vehicles than those of the SAS Regiment and the Land-Rover Pink Panther.

The Land-Rover Pink Panther is synonymous with the SAS as much as the SAS is synonymous with the Land-Rover Pink Panther; they go hand in glove and are intertwined. No other military vehicle enjoys such an exciting aristocratic connection to an army regiment. In short, perfection from the constant quest for the correct equilibrium between an alchemy of extremes and desired functionality. Everything dovetailed at the right time to produce an enticing blend of brutal beauty yet skillfully achieved and maintained a full spectrum of mobility dominance on the battlefield when required. A vehicle that arguably set a high-water mark for all other fighting vehicles to follow. Indeed, the SAS Pink Panther Land-Rover created a new stratosphere of templates for special forces vehicles to inhabit and dominate.

Moreover, the Land-Rover is an iconic yet accessible vehicle with heritage and DNA that lies firmly in the realm of the serious driver, even before its long association with the SAS. The detailed, ahead-of-the-curve, battle-ready refinements by Marshall of Cambridge took it to another level: predatory and silently waiting. It growls, purrs, bites, and possesses an intoxicating personality and a panache. It was destined to be a surefire winner, no matter how hostile and remote the environment and battle space it successfully operated in. Few military vehicle enthusiasts have ever seen an SAS Pink Panther up close and personal, let alone had the privilege to have driven one.

Other than a few magazine articles and a scant paragraph here and there, SAS Land-Rovers are covered little, and when they are, information is scarce, inaccurate, and repeated. This book seeks to rectify that status quo by tracing its development, encapsulating its technical features and exploring its operational context by carefully using rare and previously unseen photographic images. In short, this publication is the definitive story of the Land-Rover Pink Panther's association with the SAS Regiment.

It's worth noting, at this juncture, that the spelling of Land-Rover and the use of a hyphen differ from the modern spelling, which is Land Rover. In this book, I will predominantly use Land-Rover. It's my understanding that the hyphen was dropped *circa* 1978. Occasionally, you will see Land Rover; invariably, this will refer to later desert patrol vehicles (DPVs) or when the army publications referenced in this book have omitted the hyphen. On occasions, I have even seen it spelt LANDROVER in British Army publications; where this is the case, I have deliberately replicated the spelling.

Indeed, these spelling variations can be observed in official SAS documentation, where the company name of Land-Rover is spelt Landrover. Interestingly, this spelling is circled by a member of the SAS Regiment as a spelling mistake – nice!

While preparing to undertake the journey of writing and publishing this book, I benefited from a variety of open and closed sources of information, the first being the unique opportunity, while serving in the British Army, to have actually driven the vehicle and the second, having early unparalleled access associated with the Marshall of Cambridge Land-Rover, much of which had HM

Government – Ministry of Defence (MoD) – security classifications during its service life.

Moreover, I have had fortunate and unfettered access to members of the SAS Pink Panther Register. These 'hands-on' intrinsic and valuable inputs have immensely helped broaden my knowledge of the Land-Rover Series IIA and shape the book's structure, content, and style. I am confident that this eye-catching book, with its highly readable and digestible text – free of heavy academic flavour – stylish layout, immersive narrative and important historical images, will help satisfy even the most voracious of SAS Land-Rover Pink Panther appetites and become a catalyst for enriching the heritage of this most important of potent special forces vehicles.

Additionally, I hope that this book will serve as a powerful souvenir of time spent driving the vehicle in a hostile environment whilst watching the majestic theatre of an unchallenged sunset, punctuated only by the crackled voice transmissions in radio headsets.

This study is deliberately void of SAS tactics, techniques and procedures; it seeks only to demonstrate the vehicle's ability to remain relevant for nearly two decades, both in terms of application and, increasingly, through its flexibility and significance to the SAS Regiment.

Moreover, I hope that this publication will enhance your experience of making a simple yet satisfying plastic or metal scale model of the famous and addictive Land-Rover Pinkie, manufactured by such companies as TAMIYA, ITALERI, DRAGON or Kit Form Services, to display in your collection of other notable and historic military fighting vehicles.

My goals in writing this book are both simple and twofold. First, I want to paint a vivid picture by informing the reader of what the SAS Pink Panther was all about, what weapons and vital equipment it carried, how it drove, and how (perhaps) the retina-catching colour scheme came about.

Secondly, by demystifying the technical army and engineering jargon, I hope this book will provide real insight into the vehicle that will one day serve as a valuable resource for anyone wishing to get to know the SAS Land-Rover, particularly if they find themselves in the fortunate position of being a temporary custodian of one. Iconic vehicles such as the SAS Pink Panther are extremely useful for galvanising interest and inspiration – rather than being relegated to museum artefacts, their true purpose lies in inspiring innovation and igniting creativity for the future development of other special forces vehicle platforms. In short, this book was written to contribute a unique and definitive reference and preserve an image and memory of an SAS Pink Panther (and its early interpretations) before the vehicle fades into time's distance and obscurity.

With a project of this magnitude and complexity, there are many people to thank. Grateful as I am for all the assistance provided in the preparation and research of this book – of which there was much – I am especially indebted to the following: former SAS soldiers (Regular and Reserve, some of whom wish to remain anonymous), Patrick Baty, colour specialist and archivist; P.J. O'Connor for his photographs of in-country Land-Rovers; Eddie Jones, for numerous and early photos of Land-Rover usage with the Territorial SAS; Combat Joe for kindly supplying in-country photos of Unit Conversion Land-Rovers; and the RLC Museum Worthy Down, Winchester, for kindly allowing me access to the vehicle data cards.

Furthermore, I extend my most profound appreciation to Marshall of Cambridge and the esteemed members of the Pink Panther Register, namely, Sue Cummings, Steve Beasley, Johan 'Julf' Helsingius, Wayne Davies, Alan Bucknell and James Dixon. Their unwavering commitment, time, and unique historical resources have been instrumental in shaping this book. I trust this book will hold a cherished place in their collection of Land-Rover memorabilia, serving as a testament to the invaluable support of the Pink Panther Register and the past employees of Marshall of Cambridge.

Equally, I am deeply grateful to Louise Limb (https://www.louiselimb.com) for her exceptional contributions; she is a truly gifted artist, writer, photographer and talented illustrator from the Yorkshire Dales. Her bespoke imagery, in collaboration with the Pink Panther Register – captured with a deft touch – is almost tactile in its approach. Moreover, her superb 'pen and wash' illustrations of SAS Land-Rovers, 10 FG 56, 10 FG 57, and 10 FG 65 have significantly enhanced this book.

These additions make it a valuable resource for anyone interested in restoring or modelling their SAS Land-Rover. The inclusion of her contemporary photos captured throughout this book provides a highly visual element and is pivotal in ensuring an accurate representation of the Land-Rover Pink Panther. It simply would not be possible to write a history of the SAS Pink Panther without the willing assistance of those whose memories and knowledge contain the true nub, flavour and idiosyncrasies of the vehicle.

The unwavering support, guidance, and assistance provided throughout this book's preparation and research phases have been invaluable. To summarise, this project would not have been possible without their dedication, expertise, and encouragement. I am deeply grateful for their contributions and would like to extend my heartfelt thanks to each and every one of them.

SAS Pink Panther Land-Rover went through the disclosure procedure for both the photos provided and the manuscript submitted before publication. I accept full responsibility for any errors or inaccuracies, all of which are purely unintentional. The opinions and statements mentioned in this book are solely the author's own and do not reflect the views of Jaguar Land Rover (JLR), Marshall of Cambridge or the Pink Panther Register. The author takes full responsibility for the accuracy and content of the book.

Finally, and on a personal note, I wish to thank my family, be they near and far, particularly when I have been serving overseas. A special thanks goes to my wife and best friend for allowing me to indulge in my hobbies; marrying her was the best decision in my life. A huge debt of thanks also goes to our beautiful daughter, whose energised and intellectual free spirit serves as a daily reminder to all that life is truly a gift. *Carpe diem*!

INTRODUCTION

As SAS Regiment requirements evolved to address more advanced threats, the existing status quo of equipment being used in the theatre they operated in could no longer be acceptable.

Moreover, as a battle-proven leader in specialised mobility combat and in need of a revised tactical vehicle platform that could take an increased payload, provide more stowage, and a greater distance covered, the SAS Regiment tasked the Fighting Vehicles Research and Development Establishment (FVRDE) based at Chertsey, with several overarching goals and to come up with a vehicle that could replace the ageing ¼- ton Mk. 5 Land-Rover (that had remained in faithful service up until and including the late 1960s, without compromising the user requirements.

An excellent example of the SAS Mk. 5 Land-Rover (FV18006, Truck, Utility and contract number of 6/Veh/24950) is the Land-Rover with the registration plate – equipment registration mark (ERM) – of 66 BS 14 (Driver and Vehicle Licensing Agency (DVLA) civilian registration plate of 929 XUR), currently on display at the Dunsfold Collection, in Surrey. With a colourful history attached to 66 BS 14, it featured in such films as the British children's fantasy-adventure *Digby, the Biggest Dog in the World* (1973) and the British television science fiction series 'Quatermass' (1979). Later, the renowned and dedicated Land Rover enthusiast and collector Barry Pocock acquired it and displayed it for many years. Anyway, with a date in service (DIS) of 4 March 1957, the SAS Mk. 5 Land-Rover (66 BS 14, chassis number 111702993) was enhanced with uprated front and rear springs designed to accommodate ever-increasing heavier payloads demanded by the SAS Regiment. Moreover, the spare wheel was repositioned to the front, diverging from the traditional bonnet mount.

Additionally, two Jerrycans for fuel and water were located ahead of each wing. Interestingly, to optimise functionality and reduce weight, the doors and windscreen were omitted, while a searchlight, a sun compass, and a radio were included in accordance with the

Complete Equipment Schedule (CES). It's important to note that while the *CES* outlines specific equipment, it is not an exhaustive list, and items carried will/were often tailored to meet the particular demands of each mission or training exercise.

Moreover, the *CES* can and will include such items as cooking implements, extra Jerrycans, fire extinguishers, first aid kits, torches and other essential equipment. Indeed, early and recently discovered archive-quality photographs would confirm this.

Particularly noteworthy were the weapons carried, which included, at times, a twin-Vickers (K.303) machine gun to the front of the vehicle and a further machine gun to the rear. An additional machine gun was mounted beside the driver, and Lee-Enfield rifles were further located in stowage. It is generally accepted that approximately ten such Land-Rovers were configured to this special force's specification, although this figure has yet to be confirmed within SAS Regiment circles.

Readers interested in early SAS Land-Rovers, particularly 66 BS 14, I highly recommend an article that appeared in *Land Rover Monthly* (April 2021), entitled 'Rarest of the Rare', penned by Gary Pusey with photographs by Craig Pusey and the Dunsfold Archive Collection. Similarly, in the book *Special Operations Landies in Detail: Armed Land Rovers Used by Special Forces* by Jan W. de Boer, Aleš Kautsky and František Koran (Wings & Wheels Publications, 2012), there are some great photos of 66 BS 14 at a military vehicle show.

Interestingly, the prototype for this particular vehicle was converted by SAS and Royal Electrical and Mechanical Engineers (REME) workshops and was based upon a Mk. 3, 86-inch right-hand drive model from an earlier contract number of 6/Veh/20244. With the assigned ERM of 43 BR 70 (DVLA civilian registration plate of 176 YUP), it sold for £71,300 in September 2023 at the Bonhams' Goodwood Revival Collectors' auction. This particular Land-Rover (43 BR 70, chassis number 170601215) features extensively in the January 2024 edition of *Classic and Sports Car,* authored by Simon Hucknall and under the chapter heading 'SAS Land-Rover vs Belgian Army Minerva: Locked and Loaded', it makes for a great read.

The FVRDE was chosen because it provided an unrivalled location of excellence for benchmarking, demonstration, and setting the rigorous trajectory of the measurement of military vehicle mobility, capability, endurance and safety trials. Moreover, its geographical position allowed for high-complexity testing and evaluation, which met a wide range of development and military proving ground test scenarios. Moreover, deliver a low-risk, cost-effective solution that would rapidly provide a continued combat-overmatch capability for the SAS Regiment.

In short, a next-generation vehicle platform integrated to meet the ever-increasing challenges of special forces warfare and emerging threats across the globe, one that would be done by becoming lighter, more agile, more lethal and allowing SAS soldiers to be more expeditionary in their role of operating discreetly in a variety of complex and high-threat environments that were linguistically diverse and politically sensitive.

This empirical book seeks to follow in the mud, dirt and sand tracks of a motoring vehicle masterpiece, a significant milestone in military transportation. Indeed, the SAS Pink Panther is a special forces icon that has sparked more conversation and legend than there is metalwork and cemented its place in special forces history. Enjoy your personal journey to Samarkand, as this book explores and celebrates this iconic vehicle's legendary and enduring legacy.

Chapter One

THE LAND-ROVER SAS PINK PANTHER: AN INTRODUCTION AND BRIEF HISTORY

A shade of pink on a heavily weaponised vehicle is not an immediate thought a highly trained special forces soldier would think is appropriate while operating deep behind enemy lines, but it most certainly works, and in the methodology, the SAS crew deployed their desert patrol vehicle – a gem of a Land-Rover with many hidden facets and a diamond that still shines brightly to this day. Land-Rover vehicles have a solid reputation for successfully navigating various terrains and weather conditions and are commonly used as tools for agriculture and exploration.

Since the first Land-Rover (also known as the Series 1) was produced in Solihull, Warwickshire in 1948, they have been recognised for providing essential mobility, transportability, and survivability necessary for business and military missions.

The brainchild of Maurice Wilks, the head designer for The Rover Company Limited (Rover was founded in 1878) – of which his brother Spencer Wilks was the managing director, came from inspiration when he was using an old American-made Willys-Overland Jeep to do work at his farm in England.

To provide some context for the Marshall of Cambridge SAS Land-Rover, it may be helpful to briefly mention the history that led to the creation of the SAS Land-Rover Pink Panther. It is widespread knowledge that the SAS made excellent use of early Willys Jeeps while under the command of the late Lieutenant Colonel Sir David Stirling

DSO OBE and the late Lieutenant Colonel Robert Blair 'Paddy' Mayne DSO and three Bars. These daring exploits, conducted while they were junior British Army officers, have been well-researched and published over the years.

Indeed, during the early to mid-1950s, the SAS Regiment continued using the Willys Jeep and then progressed to the more broad-shouldered Mk. 5 Land-Rovers. Interestingly, there is mention of the use of Austin Champs in military collectors' circles by the SAS. However, this usage was limited. Sadly, photographic and written supporting evidence of Austin Champ's usage with the SAS Regiment is scarce.

However, the Austin Champ vehicles that were used were equipped with the Austin A90 four-cylinder 2,660cc petrol engine, and were used in an armoured capacity (FV 1801A/5) around 1952/53. These vehicles were marked with ERMs XX BE XX. Interestingly, the armoured aspect of the Austin Champ involved a bolt-on kit that could be added to the vehicle in-country. This information can be verified in official publications like the *CES*. However, it is important to note that these vehicles did not have side, rear, or roof armour protection and were primarily designed for a reconnaissance role.

The armoured plating equipment supplied for the Austin Champ comprised of a sizeable single-angled plate, which was mounted on the front, covering the vulnerable radiator extending just above the bonnet, the intention being that the plate would deflect rounds (projectiles) upwards over the vehicle or down to the ground.

While for those crewing the vehicle, two further rectangular shields were provided, with one for the driver and another for the front seat passenger featuring a cut out for various weapons platforms, including the 7.62-milimetre Browning Machine Gun (.30 cal), .303 Bren Light Machine Gun, a 106-millimetre recoilless rifle, and the .303 calibre (drum-fed) Vickers K (Gas Operated) Mk. 1, No. 1 Machine Gun. Weapon platforms that were identical to the earlier Desert and European Theatre SAS Willys Jeep.

Indeed, the SAS's use of armour-plating and extra equipment being towed on SAS vehicles was not new. This was particularly evident in the later stages of the Second World War (European theatre) while on active service with the late Major Roy Farran DSO MC and the late Harold Gordon 'Tanky' Challenor MM. Indeed, in his book *Tanky Challenor: SAS and the Met* (1990), there is a photo of Tanky and a Willys Jeep suitably named 'Little Tanky' on the front spare wheel, towing a trailer out of the village of L'Isle-sur-Serein in 1944.

Particularly notable is that the naming of SAS jeeps was not uncommon and can be evidenced in period photographs of the day and the published SAS War Diary. Examples of such names seen painted in white on SAS Jeeps are MARIE, MONICA and CONSTANCE with A Squadron, 1SAS.

Additionally, more photographic evidence of SAS Willys Jeeps with names painted in white can be found in numerous collections of SAS books. Examples being MARY, THE COMEBACK, and the German wording *'ZUTRITT VERBOTEN'* (translated as 'no entry') on the vehicle's passenger panel with an M2 Browning .50 cal at the front. Interestingly, the M2 Browning .50 cal was described by Major Roy Farran in the *SAS War Diary*, during Operation Tombola, as a 'simple, effective weapon'.

Another such example of painted wording is the word 'WEHR WOLF', a reference to the Nazi guerrilla force called the 'Werewolves' that was raised, organised and, at times, trained by SS Officer Otto Skorzeny, and further propagated by Joseph Goebbels to disrupt (unsuccessfully) the successful Allied occupation of Germany.

Armour plating was particularly vital when confronted by concealed snipers. This can be evidenced in operational reports of the day, where examples can be read that suggest that 'Jeeps were useless against concealed snipers when woods covered both our flanks'. These accounts – observed in the 'Lessons Learnt' – underscore the significant vulnerability that SAS troops experienced in terrain that provided cover for enemy shooters.

Another referenced example of armour-plating and equipment being towed is during Operation Wallace, where the SAS often towed extra equipment with Willys Jeeps. Major Roy Farran's best-selling book *Winged Dagger* (1948) confirms this practice. In addition to ammunition and rations, they carried an Ordnance ML 3-inch muzzle-loaded and drop-fired mortar. Interestingly, Major Farran did suggest the attachment of 'big iron racks' to the rear of vehicles (Jeeps) for carrying extra equipment. This prophetic recommendation could easily be argued as the catalyst for the rear panniers one sees on and around much later SAS Land-Rovers.

Anyway, this transition and utilising numerous vehicles (trucks) to gain much-needed synergy marked a significant shift in the military's use of vehicles, with the Land-Rover becoming a symbol of their adaptability and innovation and ultimately winning the MoD contract prize. Early Land-Rovers, with a confirmed SAS provenance, are not just rare; they are a testament to a unique era. Their scarcity is such that when they do appear at auction, they command a premium price. This exclusivity adds a layer of intrigue to the story, making the later Marshall of Cambridge SAS Land-Rover Pink Panther even more fascinating and making them a prized possession for collectors, museums and enthusiasts alike.

Mission-critical outcomes demand mission-proven talent and equipment. Few vehicles in military and automotive history underscore an era and define new concepts; the Marshall of Cambridge SAS Land-Rover is one such vehicle. Military production vehicles rarely possess the kind of presence or drama that the SAS Land-Rover does. It doesn't just draw your attention; it kidnaps your attention upon first contact. Walking away from an SAS Land-Rover without smiling or shaking your head wistfully is difficult.

I would love to know the mindset of the individuals – clearly those with remarkable intelligence and creativity – who created the SAS Land-Rover. They designed an impressive and accessible military vehicle that lacks any identity crisis and has a robust presence that is far from delicate. The entire design captivates and engages from the first encounter.

Simply put, it was groundbreaking and, in every sense, ahead of its time. Its initial impression on a casual observer is defined more by what is missing (the doors and roof) than by what is actually present. Indeed, it possesses more mettle than metal!

In short, form follows function, or is it, in this case, the other way round, function follows form? It is an excellent example, and a rare case, of design and engineering winning the same coin toss. Whichever way you decide to look at it, it works, and it works exceedingly well. But remember, one size doesn't always fit. Sometimes, that means that either form will win, or function will win – life would be boring otherwise, and the SAS Pink Panther certainly isn't boring by any stretch. Indeed, there can be no greater synergy than that of a specialised vehicle, such as the SAS Land-Rover Pink Panther, in the hands of a highly trained SAS Regiment soldier.

Simply put, the Marshall of Cambridge Land-Rover successfully connected the SAS to the terrain and environment they were operating in a direct, open and intimate manner. This total-fusion principle extended not only to the engine, seats and equipment but also to the on-board armaments. Moreover, it invites, provokes, and demands our closest attention upon first meeting; it's mesmerising in detail and execution. It's an analogue celebrity in a digital world.

Moreover, it's a confident-in-your-face head-turner, almost shouting at us from the very edge of the Jebel (mountain or hill) it dominates. This is still evident some five decades later, when the vehicle can be observed at military vehicle preservation shows. It's the go-to machine for the military vehicle historian and buff; simply put, it eclipses all other vehicles on the Regimental Sergeant Major's parade square!

Anyway, as a result of these extensive investigations and trials and over 500 miles of the FVRDE test track used, a number of detailed specifications were issued that included a variety of modifications to equipment, vehicle stowage areas, and overall performance. Minor modifications included some but not all of the following:

- Mirror mounting and location be improved.
- Rear Pannier to be redesigned and more secure.
- Radio Stowage bin mountings to be more secure.
- Shovel Stowage to be provided with rubbing padding.

The vehicle finally conceived, modified, and executed by the FVRDE was a Long Wheel Base (LWB) Land-Rover registered with the ERM (registration plate) of 18 DM 93, and some examples of the modifications on the prototype included the following:

- Heavy duty leaf springs.
- Bash guards for the differentials.
- General-purpose machine gun (GPMG) mountings for the Land-Rover.
- Installation of long-range fuel tanks (x 2).
- The removal of standard Land-Rover bodywork, windscreen, doors, etc.
- Electrically fired canister discharge barrels located to the front and rear.
- Relocation of the Spare Wheel carrier to the front of the fighting vehicle.

In official, original and fading documentation seen by the author, all of these modifications can be seen in a 1/8 scale blueprint (schematic). This detailed depiction of the modifications made provides valuable insight into the changes implemented during this period. Particularly noteworthy is how the sand channel has sixteen holes instead of the usual fourteen holes and the offering of an alternative mounting point for the Cole military Sun compass.

Although heavy-duty springs were NOT fitted to the prototype vehicle, the use of heavy-duty springs was recommended, as safety margins on both front and rear axles were such that some deterioration in reliability compared with the Standard Vehicle was inevitable.

The clever idea of the installation and shoehorning of two (auxiliary) long-range fuel tanks (80 gallons total) to the rear of the Driver and Navigator was inspirational; it was certainly not new – as this practice had been utilised in the later Second World War European theatre SAS Willys Jeeps – and was included to negate the use of carrying thirty-nine heavy metal Jerrycans of fuel between each patrol of two or three vehicles.

The long-range fuel tank idea is nicely yet briefly touched on in a contemporary magazine article published under the title of 'SAS Weapons and Equipment Organisation', where it discusses the SAS Land-Rover modified for operational use. And I quote,

> One of the few SAS projects to be completely homegrown is the SAS Land-Rover modified for use in Western Europe. No design met the 1000-miles-in-ten-days stipulation and all other requirements, so the Hereford motor transport pool built its own and it has been accepted.

Under the chapter title of 'Theory, Test and Practice', this statement includes an early photograph (with x 3 SAS soldiers) of a unit-modified Land-Rover, complete with a portable search light, a front-mounted spare wheel, and, perhaps just visible, a Type E2B compass. The picture is accompanied by the annotation 'A design for the standard SAS Land Rover close to the finally approved version. In the end, the unit produced its own blueprint for adaptation to the raiding role.'

It was therefore obvious to the vehicle's designers at the FVRDE, that it was vital for the longevity and operational effectiveness of an SAS Patrol, for the Jerrycans (plastic) to be utilised for drinking water rather than fuel (metal), as the fuel was now being stored/carried in the long-range fuel tanks.

Interestingly, a superb photo of 18 DM 93 is in Pat Ware's *A Compendium of British Soft-Skin Military Vehicles* (Volume 13, page 10, Military Vehicles Archive, 2023). What I like about this particular photographic example is that one can see the development stages the prototype is going through.

Some examples are that there are only two smoke discharges to the front of the vehicle – in contrast, there are three to the rear of the truck, the ERM is positioned slightly forward than usual, side mirrors positioned more forward of the vehicle, and differing GMPG mount handles. I particularly like the metal FVRDE sign affixed to the vehicle's front passenger side, where the bridging plate would typically be mounted.

To turn the concept into reality and to provide a special forces vehicle-centric focused lens to the problem, Marshall of Cambridge was commissioned to breathe a new lease of life into an existing standard Series IIA 109 Long Wheel Base Land-Rover under the contact number of WV7293, the 'WV' standing for 'wheeled vehicle'. Under this particular contract, Land-Rover were committed to a low-rate production run of just seventy-two vehicles.

Interestingly, the full contract number should read 'A/CTS/WV/7293/AC12(a)1'. However, and fortunately for Land Rover buffs, contemporary documentation and renowned historical references, the contract number (in most cases) is sensibly shortened to just WV7293. It is perhaps worth noting at this point that this particular contract number for the Marshall of Cambridge SAS Land-Rover, can often be observed on preserved SAS Pink Panthers, by use of an original and period plaque securely riveted to the lower exposed and visible bodywork on the commander's/gunner's side of the vehicle.

Marshall of Cambridge was founded in 1909 by David Gregory Marshall MBE with its first premises in Brunswick Terrace, Cambridge, as Engineers and in 1929, the Aircraft Division was established, followed in 1946 by the Vehicle Division, and in the early 1950s, the Vehicle Division was involved in contract work with the MoD. Working often in tandem with the then Royal Armament Research and Development Establishment (RARDE) based at Chertsey, the company was responsible for many of the specialised vehicles the British military was using at the time. Namely, ambulances, specialised assault vehicles, gunships, communications (Royal Signals) vehicles, and lastly, specialised DPVs.

Interestingly, the company went on to build special vehicles for the Queen's Flight and the RAF's Support Harrier Force; the first air portable containers for the Rapier Weapon System developed by the British Aircraft Corporation and engineering mock-ups of armoured command vehicles and armoured signal vehicles for the FVRDE in addition to other specialised and successful areas of business to the present day.

In correspondence from Marshall of Cambridge received by the author dated 10 July 2023, it was kindly confirmed that the correct title of Marshall of Cambridge is, in fact, Marshall of Cambridge rather than Marshalls of Cambridge (note the addition of the letter S at the end of Marshall) that for several decades now, books, magazines and e-books have erroneously added an S to the name.

Indeed, this detailed correspondence confirms the exact Marshall business (division) that received the orders for the SAS Land-Rovers was Marshall Motor Bodies Limited, which was created in 1948 as a sales company for the commercial vehicle bodies division.

Anyway, pairing a proven commercially available Land-Rover model with Marshall of Cambridge refinements played to their strengths and offered an enticing blend of engaging performance, a sweet-spot recipe and usability that lasted for almost two decades and set the benchmark (in my opinion) for all other special forces vehicles to follow and accomplished something extraordinary and all because they ventured everything and dared to pursue a challenge.

Specific additions included (2 x 40-gallon) fuel tanks, which allowed a (total) capacity of 100 gallons to be carried. Heavier-duty chassis, springs, sand tyres, guards to the differentials, and a specially front-mounted spare wheel was also fitted.

The doors and windscreen were removed to maintain a lower profile and increase all-round visibility coupled with carefully selected additions of general equipment and armament; which included two GPMGs, an anti-tank weapon (Carl-Gustaf), rifles, grenade holders, front and rear smoke dischargers and navigation equipment such as the Type E2B Illuminated Compass, a Watts Mk. 3 Theodolite and sun compasses (a Cole Mk. 2 Military Sun Compass), and when fully loaded with fuel, weapons and other kit, the vehicle weighed in excess of 3 (Imperial) tons (6,720 pounds).

Remembering that research, design, and development isn't always an upwards trajectory path and isn't always linear, the FVRDE conducted regular feedback sessions; this was done to ensure the next-generation fighting vehicle design of the Land-Rover met operational and functional special forces user needs. Interestingly, it was 10 FG 30 – the first one registered and, ironically, the first one to be disposed of and with a chassis number of 251-14139D, that was used for the acceptance and 'signing off' trials.

In a meeting that was convened on Thursday, 8 August 1968, at Marshall of Cambridge (Engineering) Limited (MCE) to discuss the pre-delivery and acceptance test checks of 10 FG 30 – with just under 150 miles (00141 miles) on the odometer. The meeting, with a total of eleven members present, consisted of the following diverse and important personnel:

- MCE
- FVRDE
- Inspectorate of Fighting Vehicles and Mechanical Equipment (IFVME).

The objective of the meeting, chaired by the IFVME was to inspect for conformance to specification and rectify several (minor) faults highlighted by operational members. For example, the grenade containers were initially lined with felt, but this resulted (quickly) in rusting, so rubber was installed for two reasons, one for noise reduction and the other to avoid corrosion.

Another example was the metal mounting for the Cole Sun Compass being too close to the gear stick when being put into third gear; this was an easy fix and was rectified by simply altering the gear change lever. It was also noted that if the Rear Pannier Bag was being used, it would be challenging to couple-up trailer leads to the available electrical sockets to the rear nearside of the vehicle.

Interestingly, I have seen preserved SAS Pink Panthers with a tow bar fitted, but these are civilian tow hooks rather than North Atlantic Treaty Organisation (NATO) hooks, which differ quite considerably and are used sensibly and safely to transport extra equipment when going to vehicle preservation shows, etc. You can find a helpful illustration of a NATO hitch and a civilian tow ball on a Land-Rover drop plate in the *Military Modelcraft International* magazine (September 1997). The example is featured on page 38 and is nicely showcased on the preserved SAS Pink Panther, 10 FG 69.

Further documentation reveals that a meeting was held at Marshall of Cambridge, where this time fifteen members were present. The group used the same Land-Rover 10 FG 30 as before, but the speedometer reading had increased to 00151.

These Minutes of the meeting confirm that action was taken on the points (minor faults) raised at the previous meeting and that they were quickly rectified or deemed 'operationally acceptable' by the inspecting team from the Regiment. Interestingly, the cost per vehicle was £3,300. What's notable in this paperwork is the mention of additional purchases of Land-Rovers, possibly a further 104 in the financial year of 1970/1971, and this is where it gets interesting, whether they were suitable for use in the European Theatre or not. The document also suggests that the Land-Rover Mk.8 Lightweight was being discussed.

Anyway, as a result of that meeting, preliminary contractual delivery of *Truck, General Service (Utility), SAS, ¾ Ton, 4 x 4, Rover II* was successfully made and the majority of converted vehicles under the Marshall of Cambridge contract arrived for duty at Bradbury Lines. Many, however, were kept at various Royal Army Ordnance Corps (RAOC) Central Vehicle Depots (CVDs) for several years before being delivered to the SAS Regiment; this is evidenced on the individual 'B' vehicle data cards (DOS Form 419B) by means of a handwritten entry, preserved SAS Land-Rover 10 FG 97 (chassis number 251-13968D) is a case in point despite having a DIS of January 1970, it wasn't delivered until several years later.

Moreover, it would explain why some SAS Land-Rovers had exceedingly low mileages recorded on their odometers when sold off. Interestingly, 10 FG 97 was later sold off at the British Car Auctions, Birmingham in 1986.

Through research, the FG range of ERMs were allocated to Class 'B' vehicles *circa* 1967/1968, and 10 FG 30 upwards were assigned to Hereford but were delivered from several CVDs, such as CVD Hilton (Derbyshire), CVD Irvine (Scotland) and CVD Feltham (Middlesex) in 1969 and 1970, and then even later in 1975. For information, here is a breakdown/explanation of British tri-service vehicle classes.

'A' Vehicle: Armoured Fighting Vehicle (AFV)

An AFV is an armed combat vehicle protected by armour, generally combining operational mobility with offensive and defensive capabilities. AFVs can be wheeled or tracked. Main battle tanks, armoured cars, armoured self-propelled guns, infantry fighting vehicles and armoured personnel carriers are all examples of AFVs.

'B' Vehicle: (Green Fleet)

A soft-skinned tracked or wheeled land use vehicle, self-propelled or towed, commercial or general service, which is not primarily designed for offensive purposes but which may in some cases be armoured for defensive purposes, and which is not otherwise specifically defined, in other words, *Truck, General Service (Utility), SAS, ¾ Ton, 4 x 4, Rover II.*

'C' Vehicle: Wheeled or Tracked

A wheeled or tracked item of earth-moving equipment, either self-propelled or towed; all self-mobile, self-steering, purpose-made cranes, cable laying ploughs; all industrial and agricultural tractors, and rough terrain forklift tractors, excluding warehouse tractors. Entering the British Army's inventory and in extensive service between 1969 and 1984 and with at least one mid-life rebuild with further changes/improvements during its lifetime.

With the Marshall of Cambridge SAS Pink Panther being retired in 1984 and later replaced with a newer vehicle that was altogether more brutal and packed with lashings of extra gear, it is the Land-Rover Series IIA that radiates a perfect blend of classic motoring, ultimate force and lastly, affection with members of the SAS and military vehicle enthusiasts.

Interestingly, out of all the Land-Rovers expertly built by Marshall of Cambridge, approximately only twenty or so examples are believed to have survived the two decades of dutiful service and are now either in private hands or museums, as many were sold over the years through Ruddington's Auctions. According to B vehicle data cards, several 'Pinkies' were lost to the desert, 10 FG 53 (chassis number 251-14094D), 10 FG 68 (chassis number 251-13984) and 10 FG 71 (chassis number

251-13982D) being excellent examples of being officially 'cannibalised and desert dumped' and other training areas, where other examples exist such as 10 FG 66 (chassis number. 251-13966D), 10 FG 77 (chassis number 251-14091D) and 11 FG 01 (chassis number 251-14161D) have been disposed of elsewhere.

In contrast, others were deemed unsafe for public consumption and scrapped for a few hundred pounds after thousands of punishing miles for their spare parts, 11 FG 00 (chassis number 251-14005D) being one such example, having been discovered in a scrapyard and sadly dismembered almost beyond recognition.

Another Pink Panther of note is 10 FG 54 (chassis number 251-14081D) – although standard green in colour and shod with Bar Grip tyres instead of the Dunlop/Bridgestone sand tyres – was 'struck off' during jump trials at Boscombe Down, Wiltshire, in the mid-1970s under the command of the Joint Air Transport Establishment (JATE) unit. JATE being the specialised unit responsible for the study, development, and service testing of techniques and equipment for airborne assault, aerial delivery, and air transport operations.

Interestingly, the load configuration of the SAS Land-Rover was specified by the JATE drawing number JATE 6323/AO. This drawing number covers all the lashing and rigging points for the parachute and main slings. The slings were constructed of nylon cord that had been stress-tested to 1,200 pounds.

In a widely available photograph, one can see the Equipment Registration Mark (10 FG 54), the Smoke Dischargers, a type E2B Illuminated Compass to the right of the driver, and lastly, other than a mangled Land-Rover, a No. 5, Mk. 1 Gun Mount for the GPMG. According to the vehicle data card, 10 FG 54 was reduced to scrap in late 1976.

ERMs – Chassis Numbers – NATO Stock Numbers and More!

Equipment Registration Numbers

The vehicle registration plates, sometimes known as vehicle serial numbers (VSN), vehicle registration numbers (VRNs), army serial numbers (ASNs), or equipment registration marks (ERMs) to give them their correct title, being allocated to the specially commissioned Land-Rovers, were 10 FG 30 to 11 FG 01, respectively. Interestingly, vehicle registration plates (ERMs) that were issued to the Land-Rovers do give a slight indication of the date of the vehicle – rather like civilian counterpart vehicle registration numbers via the DVLA based at Swansea.

Normally for tri-service (Royal Navy (RN), British Army and Royal Air Force (RAF)) registrations (ERMs) in this format and in the period we are studying, the middle letter pair indicates when it was purchased as it does in this case with FG, but sometimes, and deliberately, it does indicate the vehicle type or similar. A few Equipment Registration Mark examples being:

- XX CP XX = Construction Plant (*circa* 1982 onwards) – tractors and diggers etc.
- XX CV XX = Captured Vehicle (*circa* 1982 onwards) – Falklands War started this one!
- XX WH XX = White Helmets (*circa* 1982 onwards) – The Royal Signals Motorcycle Display Team.
- XX CC XX = Chassis Cabs (*circa* 1975 onwards) – Chassis Cabs purchased from manufacturers.

Anyway, getting back to Land-Rover and SAS Pinkies, stocks being held at the Land-Rover depot at Solihull – for some unknown reason – were never held in chassis serial number order. As a consequence, vehicle registration plates did not run numerically in line with chassis numbers issued. For example, the ERM 10 FG 46 was built on chassis number 251-14140D and 10 FG 47 used chassis number 251-13995D. This anomaly of serial number order is well-known within the Land Rover community and can be frustrating when tracing a vehicle's history.

It is perhaps interesting to note that the registration number plates (ERMs) – serial letters in this case, FG – indicate the financial year the Land-Rover was purchased. Vehicle registration plates (ERMs) were generally allocated at the time of the original contract and almost a year before contract completion and delivered at a nominated RAOC Central Vehicle Depot.

Also of note is that the Land-Rover model year at that time ran from September to the end of July the following year, August being omitted for the work's (factory) annual holiday and then getting the production assembly lines ready for the new lines coming through.

Moreover, during the inspection trials conducted by FVRDE of 10 FG 30, it was noted that the rear pannier number plate light mount required a 'top hat' profile to protect wires entering the rear of the lamp itself. British Army ERMs will be covered in greater detail in a later chapter.

Chassis Numbers

Land-Rover chassis codes built around this period had a three-digit identifying prefix in the chassis code, this would indicate the model type, steering position and other identifying features, such as a different carburettor, new instruments and a lengthened handbrake lever.

Using 10 FG 65's chassis Code 251-14095D as an example, 251 indicates it is a right-hand drive (RHD) vehicle and a 109 version. Interestingly, the letter D at the end of the series of numbers incorporated certain evolutionary production modifications to the vehicle's specification that may or may not have affected servicing and can often assist in identifying subsequent spare parts the vehicle may require. Therefore, the letter 'D' shouldn't be interpreted as a Desert conversion, as is sometimes wrongly suggested/quoted in overheard conversations and numerous automotive literature.

A vehicle identification number (VIN) is the identifying code for a specific vehicle, VIN plates, also known as chassis numbers or in the USA sometimes referred to as the VIN tag, are individual for each vehicle and is, therefore, much like a fingerprint.

The SAS Land-Rover Pink Panther has its unique VIN plate secured (pop-riveted) to the right of the inside bulkhead part of the vehicle and directly below the fire extinguisher and is both easily accessible and visible and reads as follows: *Truck, General Service (Utility), SAS, ¾ Ton, 4 x 4, Rover II.* Note the use of General Service rather than UTILITY.

Information covered on the (black and silver alloy) chassis plate includes the following essential details: chassis number (251-14095D); the contract number (WV 7318 – the original Land-Rover Contract, rather than the Marshall of Cambridge contract, which was WV 7293); vehicle number (left blank); code number (1725-0766). The publication code of the *CES* was (*CES* P/34178/1). And lastly, in a tabulated format, the class of repair, date, workshop number, and inspection. Ideally, these alloy chassis plates would have been etched by REME workshop personnel, but in reality, this never happened as by the late 1960s and early 1970s, paper/card and then a little later, computer records were (meticulously, not!) maintained.

Note that on some preserved SAS Land-Rovers, the letter D is stamped at the end of the chassis number in the space provided. This can also be seen (handwritten) on the individual B vehicle data cards. However, on occasions, the letter/suffix D is missing on the data card; this can more than likely be attributed to a clerical inputting detail rather than a deliberate omission.

In addition to the chassis plate on the SAS Land-Rover, there is also a small identification plate visible on the vehicle, which is securely riveted to the lower, exposed and visible bodywork on the commander's/gunner's side of the vehicle. However, this plate is attributed to Marshall of Cambridge, as their contract number (WV 7293) is clearly visible. Interestingly, it is the entire contract number on it: A/CTS/WV7293/AC12(a)1.

It is perhaps interesting to note that the hyphen used in these particular chassis examples and in future chapters, do not appear on the Land-Rover chassis itself; I have inserted the hyphen merely to make a clear definition between numbers etc. Land-Rover chassis codes can easily be observed on the instruction bulkhead gearbox/ transfer box information chassis plate/plaque for transfer gears.

Moreover, on many preserved SAS Land-Rovers, one can also see a distinct letter 'T' in the form of an engraved plate/plaque to the lower half of the vehicle just by the expansion tank; this letter 'T' simply means that any wood on board (slatted duckboards and sand channel (LH/RH) supports) had been Tropicalised, a standard treatment of wood at the time, done to preserve and prevent adverse weather conditions affecting performance and durability, etc.

Of particular note with regard to 'B' Class 'Tropicalised' vehicles and according to the FVRDE and, in particular, Specification 2012 (Painting Regulations) issued at the time. All vehicles should be accordingly marked in WHITE, with the letter 'T' of ¾ inch thickness, within a ¼-inch-thick ring 6 inches in diameter. This marking would have been to the nearside door or, where no front door exists, on the near side of the driver's position. Note how Marshall of Cambridge uses the metal plaque on the commander's side, almost anticipating the many layers of paint that would be applied to the vehicle during its operational lifespan.

Examples of vehicle chassis plates, contract identification plates, and the letter 'T' etc. can be seen in various publications, such as *SAS Panthers in Detail: SAS Pink Panthers of the Barry Pocock's and Another British Private Collection* by František Kořán and Aleš Kautský (Wings & Wheels Publications, November 2010); *Military Machines International* (April 2006), pages 45 and 46, and *Military Machines International* (July 2011), page 88.

An excellent photographic example of a chassis code can be seen on the Bonhams auction website for 10 FG 61 that came up for auction on 17 October 2020 Bonhams Goodwood Speedweek (2020), lot number 208, where, against its chassis code, one can clearly see 'stamped' on the metalwork 25113989D, note the slight gap between letter and numbers.

NATO Stock Numbers and Vehicle Data Cards

NATO, founded in 1948, (AKA, Not Able To Organise!) had devised a system to identify any military asset that, of course, includes military vehicles, and by 1962, after varying versions of asset codes that indicated the vehicle role, manufacturer, steering and chassis type, a new code and format was introduced. These new codes appeared on the 'B' vehicle data cards (a DOS Form 419B) in the top right-hand corner as a group of two, four-digit numbers.

For example, and being in the case of SAS Land-Rover, 10 FG 65 *Truck, General Service (Utility), SAS, ¾ Ton, 4 x 4, Rover II,* the asset code reads as 1725 0766, and this group of two four digit numbers was seen on its 'B' vehicle data card alongside its registration plate (ERM), Chassis number and Chassis contract number of WV7318. And lastly, according to the 'B' vehicle data card (DOS Form 419B) 10 FG 65's DIS, being recorded as July 1969 using a rubber date stamp entry.

What is perhaps interesting to note at this juncture and in this study of the SAS Land-Rover is that official MoD (British Army) records and documentation list the vehicle's nomenclature as *Truck, General Service (Utility), SAS, ¾ Ton, 4 x 4, Rover II.*

However, on the metal (alloy) chassis VIN which is secured to the bulkhead of the Land-Rover it reads 'TRUCK, GENERAL SERVICE, SAS, ¾ TON, 4 X 4, ROVER II'. It is also worth noting that on the 'B' vehicle data cards, the lettering GS (general service) is scored through (by hand in black ink), and a rubber stamp entry with the word 'UTILITY' is entered in its place.

For the purposes of this book, I will go with what was written on the vehicle data cards (UTILITY) rather than the vehicle identification chassis plate (GENERAL SERVICE). However, where the word UTILITY is used in official publications, it will be used rather than GENERAL SERVICE.

Vehicle Data Cards (DOS Form 419A and DOS Form 419B)

A vehicle data card is an excellent piece of military tri-service (RN, British Army or RAF) vehicle history, and they were used as an integrated accounting tool to inform higher authorities what and which vehicles they had on the ground (commanding officers and quartermasters) had on their books (AKA 'Charge'). There were two types of vehicle data cards produced there was the DOS Form 419A and the DOS Form 419B; the DOS Form 419B is the one we will concentrate on for the purposes of this book and for the study of the Land-Rover SAS Pink Panther.

The vital key to this vehicle data card (DOS Form 419B) is the ERM of the vehicle itself, for example, 10 FG 65. Interestingly, before 1949, military vehicles were administered by use of key cards, and these key cards held essential data such as the ERM, the engine number, the contract, and the type of vehicle.

However, post-1949 brought about a change in the methodology and maintenance of information, and the use of large format 'registers' was introduced to facilitate the recording of vehicle details and much later, saw the introduction of the more familiar DOS Form 419B associated with the SAS Pink Panther, which came about in the late 1960s.

As these cards were maintained by hand and clerical errors ensued. A classic example is that the letter 'D' was often missed off the chassis number of the vehicle entirely, 10 FG 44, 10 FG 46, 10 FG 59, 10 FG 61, 10 FG 63, 10 FG 64, 10 FG 65, being some examples. Particularly noteworthy from that collection is that 10 FG 63 is the SAS Land-Rover that TAMIYA uses for their scale model box artwork!

Interestingly, 10 FG 42's chassis number is 251-14907G; note the letter G at the end of the number; this is the only example, though. Moreover, on 10 FG 31's 'B' vehicle data card, there is clear evidence of white correction fluid being used over the chassis number, and rather than using an official rubber stamp, the words 'TRUCK GS SAS 3/4 TON 4x4 11' is written in hand. Interestingly, the letters GS were later scored out, and a rubber stamp entry with the words UTILITY was stamped underneath.

Anyway, these vehicle data cards hold a wealth of information to the military vehicle historian, ranging from its ERM (10 FG 65); DIS (July 1969); the Chassis contract number (WV 7318); its various locations/ units of the vehicle and its all-important chassis number (25114095) – (note the omission of the letter D!) and when and where it was sold/ struck/cast off (12 August 1976). When the vehicle was eventually 'cast' off the unit's inventory, a hand entry was made (in red ink), which included the following information: the date and location it was sold off, for example, Ruddington.

The vehicle data card did go through one notable revision in 1974. Examples seen by the author are those of 10 FG 77 (chassis number 251-14091D) and 10 FG 93 (chassis number 251-14078D). This update included the addition of an entry field for a civilian registration number if required, and the inclusion of an essential colour code box. Additionally, changes were made to the viewing orientation of the form (landscape/portrait etc.) and its title to Vehicle History Card.

As computerisation was gradually introduced into the military, the transference of the vehicle data cards was processed using the system that was known as 'VESPER' (Vehicle Equipment and Spares, Provision Economics) and then later 'SALOME' (System for the Accounting, Location and Online Management of Equipment).

These two computer platforms recorded all the essential details that were found on the DOS Form 419A and the DOS Form 419B, respectively. The confirmation of this input of information to the computer was recorded on the vehicle data card by using a rubber stamp with the letters ADPCON, which stood for automatic data processing conversion and a tick or user initials was entered against the letters ADPCON by hand to confirm it had been inputted on the computer system.

Fortunately for tri-service vehicle military historians, most of these important vehicle data cards have been held by museums around the country for decades, and DOS Form 419B cards associated with the SAS Land-Rover are currently being held by the RLC Museum, Worthy Down, Connaught Road, Kings Worthy in Winchester, England, UK. It's definitely worth visiting the museum's website for any Land Rover or military vehicle enthusiasts.

NATO Stock Numbers

Interestingly, the NATO stock number (NSN) for the *Truck, General Service (Utility), SAS, ¾ Ton, 4 x 4, Rover II* was NSN 2320-99-807-0075. This is confirmed in the RAOC Director of Ordnance Services publication entitled *Illustrated Spare Parts List for Body Used on Truck, Utility, SAS, ¾ Ton, 4 x 4, Rover II* (January 1970) (British Army code number 22128). Again, note how the title reads 'UTILITY' rather than 'GENERAL SERVICE'.

This is a beneficial publication for the restorer, vehicle historian, and model maker. As it gives every, and I mean every single NSN, item name, and designation for every nut, bolt, and washer for the BODY modifications only of the SAS Land-Rover that were undertaken by Marshall of Cambridge to convert the standard Series IIA 109 Long Wheel Base Land-Rovers under the contract number of WV7293 for modifications to the seventy-two vehicles. Moreover, there are seven pages of detailed architectural plates, drawings of the Auxiliary Fuel System and Searchlights, and the GPMG front and rear mountings.

Most of the publication of the *Illustrated Spare Parts List for Body Used on Truck, Utility, SAS, ¾ Ton, 4 x 4, Rover II* is written in British Army jargon. Interestingly, there is one page dedicated to British Army acronyms and abbreviations, with sixty-four abbreviations and acronyms being listed! Sadly, there isn't an explanation in the publication of some of the important acronyms; as at the time of publication, there was an understanding that the person (soldier, mechanic or storeman) demanding said item of stores would understand!

For ease of interpretation and help in the translation of this essential publication, I have expanded on these acronyms and abbreviations in the following few paragraphs. Moreover, of particular note at this point is that in the *Illustrated Spare Parts List for Body Used on Truck, Utility, SAS, ¾ Ton, 4 x 4, Rover II* the entire British Army catalogue number is always used for each individual item. This is evident and confirmed on page 2, paragraph 4, where it mentions that the following particulars must be quoted when demanding spare parts for the SAS Land-Rover.

A catalogue number, including VAOS Section (Vocabulary of Army Ordnance Services) and the item name of the equipment for which the part is required and informs the reader that when demanding spare parts or equipment, an Indent Form G.8136 (ADP) should be used. The 'G' in this instance stands for general, and ADP stands for automatic data processing. Copies of the *Illustrated Spare Parts List for Body Used on Truck, Utility, SAS, ¾ Ton, 4 x 4, Rover II* are readily available on internet platforms such as eBay.

When the catalogue numbers were used, they were to be converted to a VRN format. VRN stands for Vocabulary Reference Number; the VRN was eventually replaced with the NSN, still used today. So, for example, the catalogue number for the No. 1, Mk. 1 Searchlight for the SAS Land-Rover Pink Panther is LV6MT3/6230-99-803-2936 and should therefore read as per the Directorate of Cataloguing and Identification (DCI) publication; as 6MT3/6230998032936, the LV being dropped and the MT standing for Motor Transport.

This clearly indicates a modern army – RAOC in particular – changing with the times and migrating from simple data cards and issue and receipt store vouchers to a fully integrated computerised store system. Moreover, it would allow for 'fit for mission' readiness and enable parts and equipment for the SAS Land-Rover to be quickly indented and receipted by RAOC stores sections.

On the rare occasion when there were VRN or NSN anomalies, when demand for the stock was made, there was an opportunity to write a brief description of the item by the side of the vocabulary reference number or NSN. This was done using the illustrated parts breakdown (IPB) diagrams found in the *Illustrated Spare Parts List for Body Used on Truck, Utility, SAS, ¾ Ton, 4 x 4, Rover II.* This simple addition of further information would aid the demand being made by either the MT Department (Royal Corps of Transport (RCT)); REME Workshop (Light Aid Detachment (LAD)), or the Quartermaster's (SAS and RAOC) Department based at Bradbury Lines and then later renamed Stirling Lines, Hereford.

NSN are thirteen-digit numbers allocated by the (UK) National Codification Bureau (NCB). In summary, codification creates a detailed catalogue of everything the armed forces use on a daily basis, not just weapons systems and hardware, but spares, clothing, medical items, and anything else HM Armed Forces need to operate effectively and provides a common language of logistics.

For example, the first four numbers of the NSN for the SAS Land-Rover 2320-99-807-0075 relate to the Item of Supply (IoS) to the group and class of similar items or type of store, 2320 being trucks and truck tractors, wheeled and the second set of two numbers is the country of origin/manufacture, and in this case, 99 is the identification mark (country code) for the UK. And lastly, the final seven digits are randomly assigned, never duplicated, and uniquely identify the Item of Supply or store! It is common for a dash to be inserted at strategic points in the NSN (for example, 2320-99-807-0075); however, whenever an NSN is read in an ADP environment, the NSN will be represented in its true form (i.e. 2320998070075) as a thirteen-digit string.

Where NSNs have been identified in this book, they have been obtained from the publications described, namely, the *Illustrated Spare Parts List for Body Used on Truck, Utility, SAS, ¾ Ton, 4 x 4, Rover II* (British Army code number 22128), and the *Complete Equipment Schedule (Service Edition)* (British Army census code number 1725, 0766) (April 1969).

What is interesting to note on this particular edition is that there is a typing entry on the front page of the *CES* booklet for the 'TRUCK GS SAS ¾ TON, ROVER II, LHD (2320-99-893-2548)' typed directly below the right-hand-drive version.

Moreover, further NSNs are then taken from another *Complete Equipment Schedule (Service Edition)* booklet for the 'TRUCK UTILITY SAS ¾ TON, 4 X 4, ROVER II', British Army census code number 1725.0766 (this time dated April 1978).

Chapter Two

PINK OR GREEN BOSS?

'All Warfare is based on deception.'
Sun Tzu, *The Art of War*

The SAS Land-Rovers – FV18064 – the FV standing for fighting vehicle, were yet to be nick-named Pink Panthers, and were duly delivered under contract numbers WV7293 and WV7318 respectively, in the standard British Army deep bronze green (colour code BS 381C-224).

However, while the bronze green (AKA Land Rover bronze green LRC001) can look smart and protect the metal from the elements, it was felt that the shine from painted vehicles could not only identify them but also highlight and compromise their outline. The words 'Shape, Shine, Shadow and Silhouette' were mentioned many times – words that are familiar phrases to officers, soldiers, or troopers, from their basic training days!

After delivery and receipt, there was a growing concern that, tactically, it was not good to have a paint that could glint in the sunshine and define all the vehicles as British and, therefore, not advantageous. In contrast, NATO partners had switched to a matt finish form of camouflage sometime earlier.

It was also felt that it was not acceptable for confidence, as the paint scheme set back all the efforts made by SAS soldiers to camouflage themselves, their equipment and their positions. It is perhaps interesting to note that manuals of the era advised specialist advance and reconnaissance units that 'Shiny paint must be dulled using a mixture of dust and oil, mud or netting'.

As a result, the Army Strategic Command set up a comprehensive trial under what was called 'Project 212'. During this trial, numerous MoD vehicles (not SAS) were observed. They were photographed both from the ground and at altitude during exercises in various locations and climates, including the United Kingdom (and Northern Ireland), Germany (BAOR), Denmark and Cyprus. Of particular note is that paints at this time were not specially formulated for low infra-red (IR) reflectance.

As a result, British Army vehicles, aircraft, and equipment (trailers, motorcycles, etc.) could easily be observed by emerging technological advancements in night vision detection systems that were being field tested by specialist Army units at the time.

Anyway, the general conclusions of this trial set up by the Army Strategic Command were that:

- Painting should be of a non-standard, disruptive pattern.
- The painting should cover the entire vehicle, except the wheel rims.
- Using matt paint provides better concealment than the glossy paints currently in use.
- The interiors only need to be painted with a matt finish if the vehicles are permanently open.

As a consequence, British military vehicles and equipment at the time were gradually being painted in the manner of olive drab (BS 381C-298) with the familiar NATO black shadow/cloud camouflage for use in the North West European theatre, either on delivery of a contract or by local REME workshops and camp motor/mechanised transport) personnel.

There is indeed not one definitive colour green for an SAS (Marshall of Cambridge) Land-Rover that operated in European or other similar strategic environments during their period of service. This is borne out in the green-camouflage colour schemes in the remaining and preserved SAS Land-Rovers (AKA Green Dragons) in private collections.

At the critical time of delivery, changes were rapidly implemented to the colour scheme, shifting it to the more familiar Olive Drab (BS 381C-298). Moreover, there was also the gradual phasing-in of disruptive pattern material (DPM) to military service uniforms! Compounding these all-important changes was the painting of desert pink to the Land-Rovers for service in desert regions, making it a hectic and noteworthy period for SAS soldiers. Indeed, for the entire Green (British) Army as a whole!

Interestingly, due to the demand to keep pace with colour scheme changes, the availability of matt green paint to MoD units meant that, occasionally, matt black was applied over an existing deep bronze green. Unfortunately, this gives a very dark and unnatural appearance.

I have seen this combination in 'period' photographs and at military vehicle preservation shows of British Army vehicles. This is why, when acquiring a former MoD vehicle – such as an SAS Land-Rover – there will often be many layers of paint, all of which add to the patina and all-important background story and vehicle provenance.

Factors also include varying paint batch numbers, paint manufacturers of the time and storage conditions. This is perhaps why there are so many preserved Land Rovers – in fact, British military vehicles as a whole – with varying degrees of 'camouflage green and pink' one sees at military shows and museums.

Indeed, in correspondence and meetings with Patrick Baty, a colour specialist and an archivist, he suggested that the only accurate way to obtain an exact colour match would be to use a spectrophotometer. A spectrophotometer is an instrument that measures the full spectrum colour of a physical sample, producing precise data beyond that visible by the human eye.

However, finding a suitable SAS Land-Rover that hasn't been overpainted or light-damaged would be challenging. Unfortunately, this may be almost impossible to achieve decades after such specialised vehicles were deployed. With acknowledgement of his military career and knowledge, Patrick's invaluable advice and guidance in this chapter have been immensely helpful.

It is perhaps interesting to note that although vehicles were now being painted olive drab (BS 381C-298), new replacement parts – that had perhaps been in an RAOC storage depot for several years – were still being issued in deep bronze green (colour code BS 381C-224). So, it wasn't unusual to see an AFV in the newly recommended camouflage, with a glossy (bronze green) new stowage bin, vehicle bonnet, or mudguard. Very tactical!

To rectify the problem of the correct colour scheme to use when painting military camouflage on vehicles, units were given detailed published advice and guidance (over several decades) on how to paint them. These instructions appeared in a British Army publication entitled *Materiel Regulations for the Army: Painting of Army Vehicles, Aircraft and Equipment*, well worth a read if you get the opportunity!

For example, it stated that vehicles should be two-thirds green and one-third black. This will give the correct colour balance at extreme distances when observable and distinguishable patterns are no longer visible to the human eye. Moreover, wheel rims should be painted in just one colour, and tyres to remain un-painted, as the paint used was known to degrade the rubber and effectiveness of the tyre over time. This is perhaps interesting to note, as I have seen many colour photographs of 'preserved' SAS Land-Rovers (and scale models) with their tyres painted pink. Yet many of the 'period and in theatre' photos observed would suggest differently and, therefore, conform to British Army regulations.

Of particular note with regards tyres, a significant amount of British Army – indeed NATO as a whole – ground vehicles, the front, and side image profile consists of tyres. Historically and currently, these tyres are black in colour due to their constructed materials. This means that a significant portion of a vehicle is left unaided by camouflage and is often in complete contrast to the vehicle and its immediate environment. As a result, combat vehicles can be identified by the enemy and targeted more efficiently and at greater distances. The goal should have been to develop a durable coating, painting or construction method to reduce the contrast between the vehicle's body and its four or more tyres. Ideally, this would have improved the vehicle's overall visible signature reduction and ameliorated camouflage problems encountered by on-the-ground troops.

Anyway, where there is evidence of a pink tyre in an 'in-country' photograph, this was often due to an over brush or simply not following the publication of *Materiel Regulations for the Army: Painting of Army Vehicles, Aircraft and Equipment*. Where paint had been applied to the tyres, it would often flake off when in contact with the abrasive granular effect of sand. This was especially evident when the Land-Rover was driven at speed and in an abrasive environment like the desert.

Further advice and guidance directed that the bridge load plate (convoy plate) should be painted in the colour of the surrounding bodywork rather than the golden yellow (BS 381C-356) previously used and with the load class marked in the contrasting colour (for example, black on green or green on black). Similarly, stencilled tyre pressures on the vehicle's bodywork were no longer marked in white but the opposing colour.

The best example of an originally delivered – out of the box – Marshall of Cambridge SAS Land-Rover is 10 FG 80 (chassis number 251-14121D). Beautifully restored and meticulous in every detail by Dunsfold DLR and presented in the standard British Army deep bronze green (colour code BS 381C – 224) with a bridge load plate (convoy plate) painted in the correct golden yellow (BS 381C – 356) too!

The British Army colour code for deep bronze green was 72, the standard MoD paint code for green was seven (7), and the gloss paint code was two (2). Interestingly, I have seen the paint code 72 annotated on 10 FG 93's (chassis number (251-14078D) vehicle history card

(Rev 1974). Indeed, another British Army colour code I have seen is '00' on SAS Land-Rover 10 FG 77's (chassis number 251-14091D) vehicle history card (Rev 1974). '0' (zero) being 'multi'.

Note how both these examples are on the later vehicle history cards (where there is an entry box) rather than the early and differently named vehicle data cards that did not have such an entry field.

This can be confirmed by some of the RAOC British Army Junior Leaders with whom I served and still keep in touch, who informed me that when the exact colour of a vehicle was unknown, the preferred method of entry (which was computer-friendly) into the relevant field, was to use '00'. This zero / zero entry indicated that the colour code was unavailable, rather than deliberately leaving the field blank:

0: multi
1: red
2: blue
3: yellow
4: brown
5: black
6: orange
7: green
8: white
9: grey or silver

A: Army green
B: beige
C: Army commercial colour
C3: beige / stone
CH: champagne
G: gold
N: RN blue
N3: grey / green
NI–N / K: Northern Ireland
P: purple
Q: turquoise
R: RAF blue
S: sand
V: silver
Z: bronze.

1: matt
2: gloss
3: trade finish
4: disruptive pattern

5: distinctive pattern
6: IRR
7: disruptive pattern IRR
8: distinctive pattern IRR

In addition to the all-important change of deep bronze green (BS 381C-224) to Olive Drab (BS 381C-298) known as 'mean and green', many SAS Land-Rovers that had been delivered were later repainted by SAS members or, more often than not, support staff (admin staff) such as the elite RAOC, or REME, and RCT personnel behind the wire at the camp, in the pink colour we see today in preparation for future deployments in remote environments.

Over the years, there has been much speculation and conjecture as to the colour/camouflage (pink) paint scheme of the SAS Land-Rover. It is widely accepted that the shade used (a deeper rose colour than the mauve shade, known as Mountbatten Pink) was said to be a highly effective desert camouflage, especially at dawn and dusk (stand-to).

For example, as nighttime conditions appear, longer wavelengths (reds) of light will appear darker. In contrast, shorter wavelengths (blues) will appear relatively brighter. This means that red objects become more difficult to see at night than blue or green objects with similar reflectance values.

Indeed, one could argue that this is perhaps confirmed in the theories, observations and conclusions of the well-known Czech anatomist, polymath and physiologist, Jan Evangelista Purkyně (1787–1869). Known as the Purkinje effect – sometimes called the Purkinje shift – he argued that it is the changes in the brightness of colours, as light intensity decreases gradually at dusk and intensifies at dawn – that, shades of red are perceived to fade faster (to the human eye) than blue objects or the surrounding area of the same brightness.

In addition to the 'dusk and dawn' application of Purkyně's theory, the usefulness of the paint scheme was particularly evident on the flat panels of the Land-Rover, as it reflected the rising and setting desert sun, a similar colour of the granulated surface of the surrounding sand and rocks in areas of operation – remember that the desert is blessed with sands and gravels of many shades and granularity!

Please also note that on occasions, the colour scheme applied was often bright on initial application. However, the effects of sustained sunlight and adding several layers of dust to the equation do in fact quickly tone down the colour.

One immediate and apparent benefit of the colour change is that the recently coloured pink Land-Rovers, whilst on operations, would remain 'slightly' cooler to the touch than a green Land-Rover would do. The reason for this anomaly is that darker-coloured surfaces – such as a camouflaged green Land-Rover – heat up faster in the sun than light (pink) coloured ones because bright colours will reflect so much of the light wavelengths, as they absorb very little heat.

This is nicely evidenced in Anthony Rogers's interesting article on page 54 in the magazine *Combat & Survival*, Volume 1, Issue 9 (December 1989), where he goes on to quote the owner and restorer of 10 FG 97 'You also find that on a hot day ... you can touch the bodywork and its cold. Absolutely cold. The heat reflects right off it.'

Anyway, as a result of their colour, they became affectionately known as 'Pink Panthers' or just 'Pinkies' by SAS soldiers (I have often seen the spelling as Pinkys, too, but for the purposes of this book, the spelling I will use will be Pinkies). This nickname Pink Panther is generally accepted as a result of former RAF entertainment troupe member and famous actor/comedian Peter Sellers's (1925–1980) comedy film franchise of the same title, being popular at a similar time the vehicles were being introduced at Hereford and painted. Moreover, the animal and word 'panther' is appropriate for a specialised military vehicle that essentially would be going on the prowl. There is, however, much conjecture as to the narrative of why this particular form of camouflage and colour of paint was utilised.

First of all, the use of (rose) pink in wartime is not new. Indeed, German aircraft in the First World War (1914–1918) often used pink in the lozenge pattern on wings and fuselages. Indeed, Mark IV Panzers of the 21st Panzer and armoured cars of the 90th Light in the Second World War (1939–1945) were seen using pink interspersed with a drab grey hue. Interestingly, this is referenced in Colonel John Stubbs' article in a magazine entitled *Military Modelling*.

More latterly and undoubtedly many years later, during Operation Granby (17 January 1991–28 February 1991), the RAF operating out of Bahrain, painted some of their aircraft, notably Blackburn Buccaneers, an ARTF (Alkali Removable Temporary Finish) theatre-specific paint scheme. As the paint applied was temporary and operating in a particularly harsh climate, coupled with round-the-clock sorties, regular paint touching-up was required. Consequently, the aircraft's look became a three-tone pink hue rather than a two-tone shade of desert pink.

This painting of desert pink was also evident in the Land Rovers deployed by the RAF Regiment on security patrol to protect the

Buccaneers. Indeed, commando helicopter operating support cells (CHOSC) were also observed operating with 'tiger-striped' soft top Land Rovers near al-Jubayl, in the eastern province on the Persian Gulf coast of Saudi Arabia.

Allegedly, the effectiveness of this particular colour/shade was discovered by accident. The story goes that aerial navigators/spotters often used specific ground markers to aid navigation. Whatever they were, they had recently been repainted. Still, the only paint available at the time was a mixture of whitewash and red lead paint. Due to the extreme UV light of the desert and other environmental influences, the paint eventually reacted and underwent photo-oxidation, resulting in a particular and unique shade of pink.

Another story is that a crashed ex-RAF de Havilland Mosquito (the RAF's Wooden Wonder) from the Second World War, which was discovered in the desert in North Africa. Being of wooden monocoque construction, the canvas had been blown away over the years, revealing the wood. At the time, wood that had been painted with a red oxide preservative primer was a widespread practice in woodworking. Unfortunately, although the plane could be seen from the ground, the shade of red had weathered slightly to a pinkish hue, which duly blended in with the desert sand and couldn't be seen by aircraft.

Staying with the RAF during the Second World War, the colour pink was used extensively as camouflage by bombing assessment units and their brave pilots. Equipped only with a limited number of cameras (they were not armed) to increase speed and manoeuvrability. The Spitfires and Mosquitos were flown immediately after a bombing raid. Hopefully, when the target was ablaze and kicking up a lot of smoke and flames, the sky would be a shade of rose pink similar to that of the plane's pink undercarriage.

Known as PRU Pink, the PRU stands for photo-reconnaissance unit. Interestingly and not to be taken too literally, is the action *Commando* magazine, Issue 2,263 entitled 'Jet Pilot', where there is a great cover painting of a 'pink' Spitfire pitted in aerial combat against a German Messerschmitt jet fighter.

Also of note is that during the Second World War, there was a short-lived experiment using pink on Royal Navy warships. The colour was/is known as 'Mountbatten Pink' after Lord Louis Mountbatten, a senior British naval officer. 'Mountbatten Pink', also called 'Plymouth Pink', is/was a naval camouflage colour resembling a greyish mauve.

Having noticed a ship (a Union-Castle liner) under British escort that was still wearing her pre-war hull colour of medium lavender mauve grey in a flotilla disappearing from sight. Mountbatten decided to apply the colour to his ships, believing the colour would render his ships challenging to observe during dawn and dusk, similar to the train of thought for the SAS Land-Rover Pink Panther colour code.

Another example of the early adoption of pink camouflage, and perhaps one closer to home regarding special forces, would be that of the Second World War's famous Long Range Desert Group (LRDG). Where patrol vehicles used by the LRDG, such as the Ford F30, the Chevrolet WB 30cwt, and the ubiquitous Willys Jeep, were often painted in whatever colour scheme they saw fit and with whatever paint and local painting facilities were at their disposal.

At the time, there was little or no official policy for camouflage schemes, and Patrol commanders were given autonomy to paint their trucks to suit the operational need and area. So, for example, in sandy regions, the colour of desert pink was selected to blend in the sun's warm light, with pastel shades of light green, blue, and mauve/purple used to break up the silhouette of the truck.

Indeed, a fascinating quote on colour (pink) schemes in the LRDG and especially on the colour scheme adopted by the famed G Patrol – recruited from volunteers from the Household Division can be found in Alastair Timpson's (Major J.A.L. Timpson MC, MiD* Scots Guards) and edited by Andrew Gibson-Watt book *In Rommel's Backyard* (Leo Cooper/Pen & Sword Books, 2000) on page 78, where he goes on to say,

> Considerable latitude was given to Patrol commanders ... in the methods of camouflaging their equipment. In the last respect, 'G' Patrol adopted an original colour scheme. We took each of them off in turn to a helpful paint shop where it was sprayed the most glorious pink, yellow and green. If they did not elude detection from enemy aircraft, they would at least dazzle them. When first sprayed, they did look a little flashy. Corporal Inwood ... said he would not be seen in Cairo driving such a thing but discipline overcame embarrassment. ... I assured my troops that the colours would soon tone down and that the trucks would become as good as chameleons eventually ...

This is also nicely confirmed in the book entitled *G Patrol* by Michael Crichton Stuart, where there is a great and befitting quote that mentions rose pink camouflage 'Maclean noted that the bold colour scheme of the rose pink and olive green, oddly enough made them practically invisible against the desert ...'

Another popular resource perhaps to consider but this time for paint schemes of the LRDG rather than the SAS, is Robin Jenner and David

List's book *The Long Range Desert Group* (Vanguard 36) (Osprey, 1983). With colour plates illustrated by Peter Sarson and Kevin Lyles, it is an excellent painting guide for restorers and modellers alike, as many of the LRDG vehicles are painted with a hint of a certain and familiar desert pink! However, I would like to add a caveat to this statement, as these illustrations are a modern interpretation of the camouflage techniques used by the LRDG rather than an exact in-theatre and period colour match.

Indeed, as computer technology improves and colourisation (photo colour manipulation) of the original black and white photographs enter historical accounts (as I'm sure it will do for SAS Land-Rovers, to). It is important that the photo editor needs to have an intuitive understanding of how light works and how it affects our perception of colours – even more so in the desert – without sacrificing historical accuracy. Perhaps the photo editor (and book publisher) could add a discreet watermark somewhere to inform readers that photo manipulation (colourisation) has been done?

Moreover, in Ben Skipper's book *Land Rover: Military Versions of the British 4 x 4* (Pen & Sword Books, 2020), there is a colour illustration of a (left-hand drive?) SAS Pink Panther (10 FG 55) on page 21, which has a shade of paint similar to that seen on preserved SAS Pink Panthers.

Furthermore, Gavin Mortimer's book *SAS Combat Vehicles 1941–1991* (Osprey, 2021), illustrates an SAS Pink Panther (10 FG 45) with another shade of desert pink – this time not so vibrant – being used. What I particularly like about this interpretation of the pink desert camouflage, is that there is a definite shade of deep bronze green underneath the pink!

Perhaps a more accurate account of how pink was chosen for desert camouflage and in particular, for the SAS Land-Rover Pink Panther, as opposed to a deep bronze green camouflage is cited in Francis 'Geordie' Doran's (with Mike Morgan) excellent book entitled *GEORDIE* (Sutton Publishing Limited), where in Chapter 17, page 205 of his book *First Pink Panther Jeep* there is mention of a Long Wheel Base Land-Rover 'Fighting Vehicle', desert travel and the business of navigating towards and locating a crashed American United States Air Force crashed Liberator bomber by the name of *Lady Be Good*.

When the team finally arrived at their chosen destination, having travelled hundreds of miles in the desert, he describes what he saw of the *Lady Be Good* heavy bomber,

> the only noticeable change was on the upper surfaces, which had been burnished by twenty-odd years of unrelenting sun. The whole machine

had a pinkish hue, which was, I learned later, the colour used to camouflage most Allied planes in the desert during the war ...

The Lady Be Good was a United States Army Air Force (USAAF) B-24D Liberator that had unfortunately disappeared without a trace on its first combat mission during the Second World War. The plane was a long-range heavy bomber and was designed by the Consolidated Aircraft Company in response to a January 1939 USAAF requirement for a four-engined heavy bomber. It was powered by four air-cooled radial engines and had a spacious boxlike fuselage slung beneath a high wing, a tricycle landing gear and a twin tail assembly. Based with the 376th Bombardment Group (Heavy), it was believed to have been lost – with its nine-man crew – in the Mediterranean Sea while returning to its base following a bombing raid on Naples on Sunday, 4 April 1943.

Of note, a photograph and short article of the USAAF B-24D Liberator can be seen in James Taylor's article 'SAS Land Rovers' published in *Classic Military Vehicle* magazine (January 2017) on page 38. The wreck was discovered some 440 miles inland in the Desert by an oil exploration team from British Petroleum (BP) in November 1958, having flown pilotless until the fuel ran out and glided to the ground.

Investigations concluded that the first-time (all-new) crew failed to realise they had overflown their air base in a sandstorm 'haboob'. After continuing to fly south into the desert for many hours, the crew bailed out when the plane's fuel was running low. The survivors then died in the desert trying to walk to safety. All but one of the crew's remains were recovered between February and August 1960.

Interestingly, in Geordie Doran's book, he mentions how when the RAF flew over, the pilot could see the Land-Rovers but had difficulty in picking out the crashed wreckage of the Liberator and clearly states in his book, that as a result of these extensive trials, observations and submissions, the 'famed Pink Panther was conceived on our trial ...'

Moreover, Doran's account provides detailed insight into the modifications made to six Land-Rovers obtained from Long Marston. The article mentions that these vehicles were expertly modified to incorporate thirty-five crucial changes such as spare wheel mount, machine gun mountings, rear pannier, sand channel stowage, and sun compass mountings.

The modifications were carried out in double-quick time and were later deployed with a team of twenty highly trained personnel.

Indeed, according to the article, the Army Air Transport Training and Development Centre (AATDC) – based at Old Sarum, Wiltshire – managed to produce a tie-down scheme for the Britannia Aircraft in just two days for the newly designed pre-Marshall of Cambridge SAS Land-Rover.

Once established in-country, numerous field trials were conducted in the surrounding areas and at the conclusion of these field trials, and an approximate distance of 1,650 miles of all types of terrain covered, the article reveals that as a result of the colour of the *Lady Be Good* and the pervading colour of most of the desert area seen from the air was also a pink hue and that they (Geordie Doran) had not had the time to repaint the green Land-Rovers to the standard sand colour, the decision was taken at the *Lady Be Good*, that the next generation SAS Land-Rover would be painted pink.

The pink used on the SAS Pink Panther could be classed as a terrain-specific camouflage pattern and is indeed an excellent camouflage colour in the desert but varies from vehicle to vehicle; not all vehicles were painted at the same time or the correct mixture used. However, having the original colour of deep bronze green underneath – as if an undercoat – does give a huge dark shadow and therefore distinct signature underneath a freshly painted lighter colour.

Indeed, many SAS Pinkies were painted several years later, hence the colour variations seen. Moreover, when the bonnet (hood) catch is released and lifted to expose the engine block, one can often see the original colour of camouflage green underneath the bonnet and engine bay. Interestingly, on the vehicle data card assigned to 10 FG 92 (chassis number 251-14164D), there is a handwritten entry directly below the Body Contract Number that says in brackets 'COLOUR PINK'. Nice!

Moreover, there is a great photo of a deep bronze green (BS 381C-224) 10 FG 40 (chassis number 251-13985D) during the Lord Mayor's Parade of 1972, in Bishopsgate, London, along with numerous other Land-Rovers but they are painted in different shades of green, almost matt green; the colour variations are very obvious in this particular and widely available photograph. Interestingly, 10 FG 40 is now a well-known preserved SAS Pink Panther and is now over-painted in the appropriate and befitting desert pink. Those interested in making a 'replica' SAS Pink Panther, a scaled plastic model, or undertaking an original renovation should take into account many paint variances when considering undertaking a faithful and accurate renovation and whether or not they want a fresh-out-of-the-box look or as if painted by REME, RAOC or RCT and MT Workshop personnel back in the early to mid-1970s/1980s.

Additionally, one must also consider what is known in the modelling world as the Scale Effect on models. For the uninformed, the scale effect reduces the intensity of colour to replicate the appearance of the subject matter to the human eye at different distances. This can result in ratios that are different between the model's paint and the original colour of the subject matter being viewed.

When I painted my models over the years, I circumvented this problem by simply painting a light or dark base (undercoat) colour and then the final coat. For instance, when using a matt white as your undercoat, you produce a less intense version of the deep bronze green (BS 381C-224) seen on a Solihull factory-finished SAS Land-Rover.

Another general tip is to use lighter paint for smaller-scale subjects, as darker paint can obscure fine details and look less realistic. It's worth noting that many reputable paint companies have wised up to the paint anomaly and have incorporated the Scale Effect into their paint.

Sadly, there isn't a British Standard (BS) or RAL colour code for the SAS Pink Panther's colour scheme. The British Standards for colours are the standard colours in the United Kingdom, which is incorporated under a Royal Charter (National Standards Body) and the standard colours are used in identification, coding and other special purposes for building and decorative paints. The paint schemes (green and pink) one sees on (most of) the preserved SAS Land-Rovers of today, are those that have colour-matched (in good faith) with today's paints and these vehicle paint schemes are based on genuine paint chips/samples taken directly from the vehicle's 'period and in-service' applied paint of the day.

Anyway, the story goes for the colour scheme for the SAS Land-Rover is that the original mix was one tin (0.5 litres) of red oxide (primer) and one tin (5 litres) in an 'off 'matt white paint. Mixed in a drip tray to suit the eye and terrain, thinned with petrol, and finally hand-painted with a brace of Squadron Quartermaster's finest 3-inch brushes!

It is particularly noteworthy that British Army petrol is/was mixed with a red dye – this may have further enhanced the observed hues. Interestingly, several military paint specialists will mix an accurate representation of the colour. Both in a tin format (brushable) and as spray paint (aerosol), it is known as 'Pink (SAS – Pink Panther, Military Vehicle Paint) BS 381 C Matt Finish'.

Under the title of 'Paint for Vehicles', a communication published some years ago, there is a suggestion in the letter that the paint used was 15 gallons of undercoat brushed light cream. The reason for this unusual request was, and I quote again, is as follows 'The unit states that other paints (shades) are not available in obtaining the desired effect'. In other similar documentation, again seen by the author, there is mention of another paint colour, and I quote,

> 1 (one) Part Paint priming Red Oxide of Iron/Zinc Chrome brushing. These official and period communications would neatly align with the long-held beliefs of Land-Rover enthusiasts and the SAS Pink Panther custodians as to the shade of pink used on desert Land-Rovers.

To conclude, I would like to submit that this article should not be considered as a definitive 'Gospel of SAS Land-Rover camouflage' but rather a helpful guideline to the reasons why and perhaps more importantly, how the pink came about. Moreover, I would like to add and finally close that of the colour photographs that do appear of Regiment Land-Rovers, manufacturers of colour film and printing methods of said photos varied considerably in their interpretation of natural colour and colour saturation and this will have an adverse effect on how the colour of the Pinkie is perceived by the viewer.

Moreover, when viewing on a computer monitor – where pixel numbers make a considerable difference and depending on the hosting platform of the picture – seeing an SAS Land-Rover on your mobile phone, will look remarkably different to that on your wide-screen computer monitor or television! Factors of consideration in colour diversity on the SAS Pinkie can also be attributed to the initial light source of the photograph, be it sunlight or artificial light.

To close on the subject of paint, the initial contract called for painting the vehicle to stringent FVRDE specification paint regulations. Therefore, only the parts fabricated and fitted by Marshall of Cambridge would be painted, and galvanised parts would not be overpainted. As a result, the SAS Land-Rover presented an irregular and distinctive appearance due to the varying shades of paint used. Remember, if every vehicle is painted in the same colour and the ERM is obscured, then opposing forces on 'Road Watch' won't be able to gauge and keep track of vehicle numbers accurately!

Chapter Three

EQUIPMENT – SAS LAND-ROVER SERIES II (A) PINK PANTHER

'Whoever said the pen is mightier than the sword obviously never encountered automatic weapons.'
General Douglas MacArthur (US Army)

The French aristocrat, aviator and writer Antoine de Saint-Exupéry (1900–1944), concluded in his memoir *Wind, Sand and Stars*, a book that involves an incident in the Sahara Desert: 'perfection is achieved not when there is nothing more to add but when there is nothing left to take away …' These few pertinent words (where he barely survived along with his mechanic-navigator André Prévot) so neatly encapsulate the very ethos behind the creation and onboard equipment of the SAS Land-Rover Pink Panther and the requirement to get everything right and fit for special forces purpose – an excellent and truly fitting example, of a symbiotic relationship between the soldier, the equipment and the desert.

Indeed, in order to ensure that everything carried in the SAS Land-Rover was just right, the SAS went to great lengths to document the weight and quantity of each individual item. For instance, to ensure that everything was properly prepared for the SAS Land-Rover, the SAS meticulously documented every item that was to be carried, along with its weight and quantity. For instance, when it came to navigation equipment, they even recorded the weight of six HB pencils (2 ounces), one large soft rubber (2 ounces) and one 9-inch circular protractor (6 ounces). This level of uber attention to detail and planning is a testament to the dedication of the SAS Regiment in achieving their desired aims and outcomes.

With all the extra mission-critical equipment on board and the Marshall of Cambridge additions designed to sustain small-scale activities, the Land-Rover Pink Panther was never going to cede to any new-fangled notion of aerodynamics, weight reduction ideas, or an increase in speed. Indeed, it was quite the opposite, especially in the desert – potential Lockheed Marin F-35B Lightning fighter jet pilots need not apply!

Remember that this is a heavy 'truck' – and this is before all the extra equipment is loaded. The steering is heavy and cumbersome; don't expect this vehicle to be free from scuttle-shake, especially on uneven roads or ground; it does flex noticeably. Indeed, you need to force yourself to work harder to manoeuvre the vehicle around an obstacle. It certainly doesn't dance delicately around the corner as a modern Land Rover does; you must place it where you want it to go and hope for the best.

However, when you do, it's incredibly satisfying. It produces an open-air driving experience of ephemeral thrills that many find hard to describe, even when using a thesaurus! Moreover, now that the Series IIA Land-Rover hales from another motoring era and decade, it demands that the driver keep both hands on the steering wheel every inch of the journey. It certainly isn't a one-finger-on-the-wheel limousine driving experience by any stretch.

This is perhaps why Pink Panther Register owners avoid waving at other Land Rover owners; they're too scared to let go of the wheel! Even when at full throttle and you've explored all the (limited) torque available by unceremoniously crunching your way through the gears. This vehicle isn't going to win any awards for top speed, nor narrow your field of vision like a cheap B-movie special effect!

Indeed, what empirically happens when you drive at speed is that everything vibrates violently. If it's not strapped down, it will fall off with a rhythmic regularity similar to that of the regimental march of the SAS Regiment! Indeed, as a result of earlier FVRDE trials, improved quick-release fasteners for equipment were introduced.

Anyway, moving on. Undeniably, there is a certain amount of theatre and scepticism attached to driving an open-top vehicle such as the SAS Pink Panther Land-Rover. However, once you've settled behind the spoked steering wheel, all this neatly disappears as the metal-framed dials spring to life as you start the engine, wrestle and engage first gear and corral all the available ponies and commence your journey into the sandstorm.

The gearbox wasn't (isn't) sweet or tight by any stretch. With its long movements and sticky engagement, but once warmed up, it loses its agricultural feel and has a sturdy (almost) mechanical quality about it. A kind of rifle-bolt precision and feel as you select the gears – an appropriate action that suits and still does, the character and feel of the SAS Pinkie. However, the SAS Land-Rover is all about how it operated in hostile environments to allow them the opportunity to execute the most effective actions (ways) in the most efficient manner (means) relative to achieving the desired impact on the problem (ends) and helped retain the overall battle-space winning initiative desired by the SAS Regiment at the time.

Because the Series IIA SAS Pink Panther tactical wheeled FV was already based upon a pre-existing high-volume, commercially available production Land-Rover vehicle platform, it benefited from a shared industrial base. Which included, on the military side, a research and development facility (FVRDE) at Chertsey and, on the commercial side, a successful supply chain of spare parts either at Land-Rover in Solihull itself or at Marshall of Cambridge.

Consequently, this mutual and beneficial commonality allowed for a unique and much-needed capacity to meet surge demands where necessary and support the sustainment of parts through recognised British Army (RAOC) and civilian (Land-Rover, Lucas, etc.) channels.

As previously discussed, the basic equipment on the SAS Pink Panther is standard and per the civilian Land-Rover Series IIA, but it has several additional specialist pieces of equipment fitted and in place for the exigencies of modern and desert warfare. For example, two slatted duckboards were fitted to the floor of the rear compartment. This provided extra grip when standing and for the stray 7.62-millimetre spent cartridge cases and link to fall between the wooden slats for later collection.

A publication of the period shows the reader a total of thirty-four pages that are divided into four sections with a total of nine illustrations and include a handy pull-out wiring diagram and an IPB for the auxiliary fuel tanks and portable searchlight); this (light green) softback booklet provides a wealth of detail-specific and technical information for the SAS Land-Rover.

This booklet is scarce and hard to find. Indeed, I have only ever seen one edition sold by P.A. Blanchard and Co. of Shiptonthorpe in York in July 2021 via the internet auction site eBay. Interestingly, the book lists the SAS Land-Rover Pink Panther as 'TRUCK, GENERAL SERVICE, SAS, ¾ TON, 4 X 4, ROVER II' in its text rather than making use of the word 'UTILITY' as used in other contemporary publications, official record-keeping documents/cards, etc. Whereas it should read 'UTILITY' as per the 72 'B' vehicle data cards. Interestingly, these 'B' vehicle data cards are now being held for posterity at the RLC Museum, Worthy Down, near Winchester.

Measuring approximately 13.7 centimetres (W) x 21.2 centimetres (H) and running to a total of thirty-four pages and divided into four sections with a total of nine illustrations, including a handy pull-out wiring diagram and an IPB for the auxiliary fuel tanks and portable searchlight); this (light green) softback booklet provides a wealth of detail-specific and technical information for the SAS Land-Rover.

Section One (pages 6–23) covers the general description of the vehicle, ranging from vehicle structure to seating and from pyrotechnics to duckboards. Section Two covers the vehicle's operation, ranging from the auxiliary fuel system to the fire extinguisher, and covers just one page (page 24). Section Three (pages 26–29 is the user servicing adjustments and covers seating to armament and navigation equipment to lamp replacement. And lastly, Section Four (pages 31–33) covers the all-important destruction of equipment to prevent enemy use. Subjects covered include the degree of damage to be inflicted on the vehicle and equipment, the priorities for destruction, and the authority required, through to methods of destruction to deny the enemy the asset.

Of particular note is that the SAS Land-Rover used in this (HM Government restricted) publication is 10 FG 35 and, in one instance, with its ERM just visible in the photo, 10 FG 31; both are particularly well-known and now more recently preserved SAS Pink Panthers.

Note also that at the time of publication (August 1969), the vehicles are indeed shown in their original deep bronze green colour as they were when they originally left the production line at Land-Rover in Solihull and later in the workshops at Marshall of Cambridge.

The vehicle (10 FG 35) is shown in a three-quarter front view on page 6 and a three-quarter rear view on page 7, accompanied by indicating lines showing where and what item it is and where each item is located. Then on page 8, we see a (smaller) detailed photograph of a Land-Rover engine compartment, showing oil can storage and the oil can securing strap. On page 13, with a semi-plan view (overhead) of the SAS Land-Rover – this time 10 FG 31 – we see in great detail where (thirty-six) items such as grenade stowage, to sun compass mounting(s) are located, and fire extinguishers to cooker and dixie stowage locations are positioned.

Moreover, on page 16, we see the dashboard photograph of an SAS Land-Rover (ERM not visible) showing where a total of eleven items are positioned, ranging this time from the signal pistol stowage to binocular stowage and locations of the type E2B compass and inter-vehicle starter socket. Other illustrations of use are line drawings and include items of interest, such as the differential guard and steering damper located near the front axle and the auxiliary fuel system and portable searchlight components.

According to its 'B' vehicle data card, 10 FG 35 with a chassis number of 251-13970D, arrived at the RAOC Central Vehicle Depot (CVD) Ashchurch on 22 May 1969, it was then transferred back to the RAOC CVD at Ashchurch, near Tewkesbury, Gloucestershire on the 5 August 1975, only to be disposed of (sold-off) at Ruddington in July 1976. Ruddington (Nottinghamshire) was the site to enable the MoD to auction off redundant ex-military vehicles and equipment.

It is perhaps interesting to note that 10 FG 35 is then further used in another official MoD publication, namely the *Technical Handbook for the Truck, General Service, SAS ¾, Rover II* (February 1970) where on page 4, there are two photographs used, both in the style of a three-quarter front and rear view.

Moreover, the other Land-Rover used (page 13) in the publication *SAS Landrover (Desert Version) User Handbook* (August 1969) is well known SAS Land-Rover Pink Panther 10 FG 31 and, according to its 'B' vehicle data card, 10 FG 31 has the chassis number of 251-14116D, which also arrived at the RAOC CVD Ashchurch on the 19 May 1969. Its DIS is recorded as July 1969.

Additionally, on its vehicle data card, there is (what appears to be) a minor clerical error with regards to its chassis number entry; this has been amended by the use of correcting fluid and then overwritten and reads as 2511.4116 D, note the dot between the 1 and 4 and the spacing between 6 and D.

Of particular note with regard to 10 FG 31 is that it also appears in the *Wheels & Track*, Issue 9 magazine entitled 'SAS Land Rovers, The SAS Pink Panther and Its Predecessors' on the back page and in full colour to – sadly, the only colour photograph of the entire article. However, it makes for a great renovation or modelling subject, as the picture is superb and has a crisp-like definition and detail.

Additionally, against its 'Designation', instead of a standard rubber-stamp entry for the words 'TRUCK GS SAS ¾ TON, 4 X 4, ROVER II' they are written by hand and then (presumably) later, the GS has been scored through, and a rubber stamp entry for the word 'UTILITY' entered – as with the other seventy-two vehicle data cards. A handwritten entry is also used for the chassis contract number; perhaps the rubber stamp emblazoned with WV7318 was missing on that day, as other vehicle data cards examined clearly make use of a (correct) rubber stamp entry.

Anyway, 10 FG 31 was then later transferred back to the RAOC CVD at Ashchurch on 5 August 1975 – along with several other Pinkies – having served like 10 FG 35, only to be unceremoniously disposed of (sold-off) at Ruddington in July 1976. The final entry, as with 10 FG 35 – again written by hand – just confirms the vehicle was sold with a date of 12 August 1976; interestingly, also amended by the use of correcting fluid!

Vehicle Structure

Despite Land-Rover's already unparalleled cross-country performance both in the commercial and military markets, it was felt that the vehicle's suspension should be further strengthened by the fitment of heavy-duty springs, coupled with drop-shackles and hydraulic telescopic shock absorber improvements.

The already proven and renowned box-section frame chassis was also given attention by being reinforced at known critical stress points and was done to enable the vehicle to operate successfully and, above all, reliably, not only in diverse climatic and topographical conditions worldwide but also within areas of interest and responsibility; moreover, the abnormal risk and excessive rigour the vehicle would be experiencing.

The Land-Rover underwent some minor structural modifications that were specific to the vehicle. These modifications helped to improve the overall efficiency and operational needs of the vehicle. For instance, the two top outer sections of the front bumper (bumperettes) were not fitted. In fact, there is no evidence of any bumperette holes on the existing bodywork, which suggests that a new bumper was fabricated for the vehicle. Additionally, the doors were removed, as well as the windscreen, windscreen pillars, hood frame and hood, in order to maintain a lower profile. Lastly, the sills were also removed from the vehicle.

The differential housings of both front and rear axles were provided with steel guards (AKA bash plates or underbody protection plates) carried on the cross members secured to the spring U-bolts and provided much-needed vital protection against the accidental hitting of rough/hard ground such as exposed rocks etc. – the desert isn't always fine sand! Indeed, protruding sharp boulders, which can become embedded in the sun-baked compacted sand, often presented problems to the Land-Rover's exposed chassis.

Interestingly, in addition to excessive engine temperature caused by over-use, the often thicker underbody paint would occasionally soften just enough to bond with the fine sand, leaving a concretion that proved challenging to remove and wipe clean upon returning to a camp that was many degrees colder.

The steering system was the same steering components used on a standard Land-Rover but was modified to accommodate the retrofitting (by Marshall of Cambridge) of a hydraulic cylinder steering damper across the front end of the vehicle between a bracket welded to the front transverse drag link and a bracket bolted to the left-hand side chassis member.

The damper system installed provided for a smoother, more tamed, and composed stable ride by inhibiting the undesirable and uncontrolled movement (or oscillation) of the vehicle's steering mechanism; this wobble was very evident at higher speeds (over 30 miles per hour!) and over rough terrain with an increased (very top-heavy) payload.

It is perhaps interesting to note that when the SAS Land-Rover was sitting stationary, and you turned the steering wheel from lock to lock, most people couldn't feel any difference; it was when the Pinkie was being driven at high speed, and you buried the pedal (regardless of which tyre was fitted) that was when you noticed the difference – you could almost feel the rod and piston pushing through the oil as it corrected the vibration (oscillation) through the steering wheel.

On the SAS Land-Rover, there is a switch called the 'Normal Ignition only switch' that is worth mentioning, for it has two positions and is located between the Speedometer and Instrument cluster. You can easily spot it because it says, 'IGNITION ONLY'. When the switch is in the 'IGNITION ONLY' mode, all electrical circuits are isolated except for the coil, starter, choke, fuel gauge, oil pressure circuits and smoke generators (No. 8 Mk. 8).

And lastly, where Marshall of Cambridge bespoke fabricated components were installed, these items were assigned a specific Marshall of Cambridge (Engineering) Limited code number and were stamped on such items, amongst others, as the metal bracket for the (dashboard) sun compass, the Land-Rover bulkhead grenade holders, the radio power plugs, and the metal clamp for the canvas cover on the ammo tin, which was secured by six screws.

These code numbers consisted of two letters (FV) and then proceeded by six numbers; an example being FV636380 (sun compass bracket) and the letters of MCE standing for Marshall Cambridge Engineering (Limited). These unique code numbers correspond to the original blueprints and refer to the FVRDE drawing number.

Photographic examples and illustrations of these underbody protection plates (bash plates) and steering damper can be seen in the *Truck, General Service, SAS, ¾ Ton, 4 x 4, Rover II* booklet (August 1969), page 8; *Wheels & Track*, Issue 9 'SAS Land Rovers' page 9; *Land Rover Owner International* (August 1995), page 160; *Military Modelcraft International* (September 1997), page 38 (front and rear views); *Land Rover Enthusiast* (November 2000), page 30; *Military Machines International* (April 2006), page 46 (with front and rear views); *SAS Panthers in Detail; Military Machines International* (July 2011), page 89 (again, with front and rear views).

Auxiliary Fuel Tanks and Expansion Tanks

In addition to the standard main tanks (x 2), which held (Imperial) 10-gallons (45.46 litres) of fuel each, there were two 40-gallon (181.84 litres) auxiliary fuel tanks fitted to the SAS Land-Rover, on either side of the forward end of the rear compartment and fuel (petrol) is fed via two screw valves through reinforced (transparent) plastic piping to the two main fuel tanks positioned under the driver's and commander's front seats.

The sheet steel tanks were fabricated and hot-tinned internally to enhance corrosion resistance. Inside the tanks, baffles were fitted to ensure stability by preventing fuel from shifting around as the truck moved. Baffles are inner walls that prevent sloshing and increase the durability and strength of the tank. Fuel is dense and can rapidly shift from one side of the tank to the other during sharp turns if the tank is half full. The baffles help keep the fuel in a stable position to prevent accidents. Finally, the fuel tanks were covered with asbestos cloth secured by adhesive. The asbestos lagging came in 40 x 40 inches x 1/16-inch sheets. Both fuel tanks sit firmly on rubber mats and are covered on top of the tank by a Sapele plywood decking hinged at the front to the top of the bulkhead and secured at the rear by a toggle fastener. Sapele plywood is a highly resistant wood with high tolerance against indentation, bending and shock resistance.

At the outer forward part of the tank top, there is a screw-in calibrated dipstick – for measuring the depth of the petrol – in the tanks and is accessible through the hole in the hinged decking. Each tank was fitted with an airtight screwed (brass) filler cap at its outer end, and the filler cap was securely anchored to the tank using a retaining chain.

Additionally, two 5-gallon (22.73 litres) expansion tanks are fitted, one on each side outboard of the left and right of the main chassis member and forward of the rear wheels. It is interesting to note that the main fuel tanks could be filled either via the auxiliary fuel tanks or through the main tank filler cap. These tanks were topped up regularly and formed part of the daily vehicle checks (routine) and chores.

Of note, is that during fuel transfer, it was necessary – for safety reasons – to inwardly vent the auxiliary fuel tanks by removing the dipsticks or filler caps. Moreover, when these tanks were subject to a rise in ambient temperature, the expansion would cause an increase in unwanted pressure, a relief valve would open, and fuel would flow into the expansion tank if and when the tank was full. When the tank was not full, the air would pass through the atmospheric vent pipe. When the auxiliary fuel tanks became full, it was a case of simply manually draining the tank through the use of the fitted drain cock.

However, it became a good practice to periodically do this for safety reasons. Interestingly, there needs to be more height clearance beneath the SAS Land-Rover to place a Jerrycan safely and decant from the expansion tank!

There are excellent official illustrations of the Auxiliary Fuel System in a number of MoD publications, namely the *SAS Landrover (Desert Version) User Handbook* on page 25; the *Illustrated Spare Parts List for Body Used on Truck, Utility, SAS, ¾ Ton, 4 x 4, Rover II* on plate H2 and the *Truck, General Service, SAS, ¾ Ton, 4 x 4, Rover II* (February 1970), all of which show both the 40-gallon auxiliary fuel tank (1 of 2) and the expansion 5-gallon tank (1 of 2) in their descriptions.

These official 'technical' drawings, in the format of an IPB, were an important source of information, particularly for ordering specific support equipment parts for the SAS Land-Rover, as they provided vital information necessary to identify a part number. IPBs provided cross-reference data to enable supply (RAOC) and maintenance (REME) personnel to identify and order replacement parts for equipment that can be used when the prime item requested did not have a NSN allocated or the item was deemed to be not considered for replacement. The *Illustrated Spare Parts List for Body Used on Truck, Utility, SAS, ¾ Ton, 4 x 4, Rover II* publication is a direct case in point, as every single nut and bolt (with sizes – Imperial) is catalogued and location identified.

There are numerous photographic examples in published magazines too; namely, *Land Rover Enthusiast* (August 2003), page 106 (Project Pink Panther – renovation of 10 FG 88); *Military Machines International* (April 2006), page 47 and *SAS Panthers in Detail.*

General Purpose Machine Gun – GPMG (x 2)

Two GPMGs (or 'Gimpys' or 'Jimpys' as they are often called), are used on the SAS Pink Panther Land-Rover and immediately punctuate the look and flow of the vehicle's lines and quickly accentuate the need to appreciate that this beast of a vehicle from the outset packs a powerful punch.

Moreover, it serves as a clear indication of its formidable firepower and needs to be taken seriously and with extreme caution, as it emits its fearsome arsenal of onboard weaponry. The GPMG's primary task is to provide protective fire in defence and support fire in the attack.

The GPMG is a versatile firearm that can be deployed as a light machine gun, firing from the shoulder, or in the sustained fire (SF) mode installed on a mount, such as the No. 5 Mk. 1 Mount fitted on the SAS Land-Rover Pink Panther. The GPMG is vital in the SF role, providing crucial fire support.

With the ability to deliver SF to the enemy for extended periods, its rapid rate of fire makes it an ideal option for overhead or flanking fire to assist advancing troops in an offensive strategy against enemy strongholds.

Using a mount increases the weapon's effective range to up to 1,800 metres. However, it is challenging to spot strikes at this range because the tracer rounds 'linked' in the ammunition belt often burn out at distances over 1,100 metres.

The GPMG was brought in after the Second World War to replace the Vickers Heavy Machine Gun and Bren Light Machine Gun. Indeed, the GPMG has also been successfully modified extensively for vehicular, naval and helicopter platforms, demonstrating versatility on land, sea and air – even to this day. Not bad for a weapon that has been in service with HM Armed Forces for many decades.

With a rate of fire (belt-fed) of up to 750 rounds per minute (RPM), the GPMG provided a chunky punch with superior penetrating power and could splinter swathes of jungle in seconds. Moreover, the GPMG barrel can be removed and replaced within seconds. Of particular note, the barrel quickly heats up, necessitating its replacement after 200–400 rounds of continuous fire; once cooled down, the barrel can be reused. Spare barrels and cleaning kits were carried on patrol and stowed in the Land-Rover. When not being used or transported, the GPMG was covered in a canvas cover to protect it from the elements.

With a weight of 13.85 kilograms (including a 50-round belt of 7.62 millimetres rounds), a muzzle velocity of 538 metres a second, and a total length of approximately 1.23 metres, the GPMGs are mounted on the SAS Land-Rover using two No. 5, Mk. 1 Mountings (NSN 1005-99-809-1903) one on the left-hand side of the dashboard and the other, in the rear compartment of the Land-Rover. However, although the top mountings are visually similar, there are differences; namely, the lower mounting structure and the live ammunition containers (AKA bin, ammunition, steel) are completely different. For example, the rear-facing mount has a deep narrow, rectangular box (NSN 1005-99-810-1961) with a bespoke curved ammunition belt guide at the top. This rectangular container can hold at least four belts (200 linked rounds per belt) in the box.

In contrast, the front-facing GPMG derives its (belt-fed) ammunition from a standard ammunition box, known as the H82, 7.62-millimetre ammunition box. Ammunition was/is supplied in belts of 200, a belt of 200 rounds of ammunition fitting neatly inside the H82 box. The 7.62-millimetre ammunition belts (usually) are issued as follows: four ball and one tracer round (4B/1T). The belts are of metal disintegrating links and can be readily broken or joined to give belts of any length – in other words, daisy-chained together.

When the GPMG is being fired, it is the firing action of the GPMG that draws out each round in turn to fire, and as each round is pulled out, a link falls free – disintegrating the belt into its constituent parts. This sound, alongside the spent cartridges falling to the ground, coupled with the smell of cordite, is so universally loved by all in the British Armed Forces.

The ammo box ammunition 'makeup' is clearly annotated (stencilled) on the H82/H84 box, alongside a large orange explosives label and the markings indicating a box holding 200 rounds of 7.62-millimetre ammunition in mixed link of four ball rounds to one tracer rounds. Approximate measurements of the Ammo Box are 25.5 centimetres long, 8.5 centimetres wide and 18.5 centimetres tall.

A frequent MoD ammunition contractor of the day was Radway Green. Their initials would be seen on the cartridge case surrounding the primer and sometimes stencilled on the box alongside the NSN and lot number.

The top of the ammo box has a large pull-out handle that allows it to be carried, and a large catch is fitted to one side of the can to secure the lid. This also allowed the box to be mounted alongside a GPMG when used aboard a vehicle in a special mounting. The H82/H84 ammo box is an exceptionally robust box.

Indeed, over the years, I have seen cases of intense fire on later Land Rovers and other specialised vehicles, where ammunition boxes have been stored, and those rounds (7.62 millimetre link) on the GPMGs have been cooked off, but the ammo stored in either H82 or H84 boxes have remained intact and unscathed, despite the swelling of said box.

The front GPMG mounting designed by the FVRDE (Turrets and Sights, Chobham Lane) and the Royal Small Arms Factory, based in Enfield, is fitted to the top of a square-section telescopic tubular column (AKA pedestal, gun- mounting NSN 1005-99-810-2279) and was 37 inches in length, and the bottom half of the column is bolted at the top to the dashboard structure and at the bottom to a chassis cross-member below the metal floor. A metal compression helical spring (NSN 5340-99-810-2278) is fitted into both inner and outer tubes. It acts like a shock absorber at the bottom and presses against blocks secured to both tubes to counter-balance the weight of the weapon and its mounting.

The rear-facing GPMG is securely mounted to the vehicle employing a metal base pedestal (complete with turntable and column clamp NSN 1005-99-810-2274), to which it is braced by four welded tubular legs. A heavy-duty rectangular plate is welded to the outer tube below the floor. It is secured to a chassis cross-member by a clamping plate, bolts, nuts, and distance pieces. Two alternate heights can be set at 9 inches apart by using a captive quick-release metal pin fitted through the two sections of the tubes. The rear compartment floor, where the rear GPMG was mounted, has slatted (sapele) duckboards that allow spent cartridge cases and metal disintegrating links to fall between the gaps in the wood.

The No. 5 Mk. 1 mounting provides a weapon elevation of 800 mils (45°) and a depression to 178 mils (10°); the GPMG can be locked in any intermediate position by a hand-wheel operated clamp on the right-hand side of the mounting (NSN 1010-99-199-0292). The mounting also provides three ranges of traverse by simple operation of a lift-and-turn knurled knob (hand-wheel NSN 1010-99-199-0284) in the front part of the mounting's platform.

For example, with the knob in the highest position, the gun can be swung through 6,400 mils (360°), and with the knob in the lowest position, a traverse of 2,133 mils (120°) can be obtained. For greater accuracy and stability, the GPMG can be locked at any angle by use of a simple clamping mechanism. Excellent photographic examples of the No. 5 Mk. 1 GPMG mounting can be evidenced in *SAS Panthers in Detail* on pages 47, 48 and 49. The GPMG is secured at the front end of the mounting by a quick-release pin (NSN 5315-99-199-0298) passing through two lugs on the mounting and two lugs on the weapon itself.

The two triggers are part of a spring return sliding frame (AKA trigger assembly NSN 1010-99-199-0275), which carries a spring-loaded sideways-moving lever to engage the trigger of the gun. A firm weapon grip is provided by two rearward extending tubular arms (AKA cradle assembly or gun mounting NSN 1005-99-810-1958) with two rubberised pistol-type handgrips (NSN 5340-99-199-0307).

A handy spent-cartridge case and empty link box is secured to the right-hand side of the mounting by two spigots (stoppers) and a knurled knob. A link chute is attached to the weapon, and a flap at the bottom of the box – held closed by a bent rod handle sprung over cam-shaped lugs – provides for quick removal of spent 7.62-millimetre cartridge cases and empty metal links.

Interestingly, these later GPMG mounts designed by the FVRDE were field tested by the SAS Regiment in 1967; documentation of the period states that the FVRDE invited Regiment members to attend firing trials along with a nominated gunner. Moreover, this documentation noted that under the working title of 'European Rovers', the SAS Regiment was finding it increasingly difficult to design a cover that would keep the weapon clean and dry yet allow it to be fired without removing the cover. The main obstacles were the unobstructed feed and ejection of clips, rounds, and cases. It was, therefore, decided to design a cover with a quick-release device.

Eventually, the GPMG was issued with a foul-weather canvas cover. This canvas cover, with a quick-release device, can be seen in many period photographs and provides for protection from sand and water ingress. Moreover, a dedicated GPMG cleaning kit was also issued. This canvas or later issued nylon wallet/roll cleaning kit, secured and stored various components such as an oil bottle, flannelette, cleaning rods, and the obligatory pull-through.

There are many books and magazines that show detailed photographs of the mounted GPMGs, some with 'period' wooden stock GPMGs and others, are of the modern black plastic stock; those magazines include the following published editions: *SAS Panthers in Detail*; *Land Rover Owner* (August 1995); *Military Modelcraft International* (September 1997); *Land Rover Enthusiast* (November 2002); *Classic Military Vehicle* (July 2002) and *Military Machines International* (July 2011) and *Special Operations Landies in Detail*.

Self-Loading Rifle and SLR Storage

Stowage for the L1A1 self-loading rifles (SLRs) was sensibly located in arm's reach for both the commander and driver of the Land-Rover, respectively, and are bolted to the outside surface(s) of each front mudguard. The L1A1 SLR was a gas-operated, tilting breechblock and slide, powerful semi-automatic weapon and was the British version of the Belgian FN FAL rifle.

The SLR is/was regarded as a reliable weapon with battle-proven exposure in all environmental conditions and is generally accepted as one of the most successful combat rifles ever produced. With an effective range of 1,640 feet (500 metres; 547 yards), the L1A1 SLR was a hard-hitting, magazine-fed semi-automatic rifle with a twenty-round (pressed steel and a separately attached floor plate) detachable box magazine (and, on occasions, the slightly curved, thirty-round L4A1 (Bren Gun – LMG) magazine) that saw service for nearly thirty years with the British Army.

The SLR used the same round as the SAS Land-Rover mounted GPMGs. That round, the 7.62 x 51 millimetre NATO (official NATO nomenclature 7.62 NATO round), is a rimless, bottlenecked rifle cartridge still used by British military personnel on mounted and crew-served weapons that are mounted to vehicles, aircraft, boats and ships to this day.

The SLR has significant recoil, which could affect the shooter's accuracy and cause fatigue during extended firing sessions. In addition, while the SLR is generally considered reliable, it can be prone to jamming in certain conditions, such as when it is dirty or improperly maintained. In conclusion, and from personal experience, it must be noted that the SLR was undeniably a rifle of exceptional user-friendliness and reliability, capable of firing an impressively powerful cartridge.

If you would like to learn more about the L1A1 SLR, I suggest reading the *SLR 7.62mm User Handbook*. It's a book that is still available from Green Machine Supplies and contains over sixty illustrations. The chapters cover the operation and servicing of the rifle and the book is A5 in size.

Anyway, the stowage of the SLRs consisted of two long tapering (steel) boxes (NSN 2540-99-809-0709 and NSN 2540-99-809-0710) positioned on either side of the vehicle and secured above the front wheels with a canvas cover to the rear end, which in turn is secured by the use of straps and toggle fasteners. The canvas cover protected the weapon from sand, grit, and other foreign objects that could inhibit immediate use of the weapon and kept it in place.

These fabricated metal storage holders (AKA holster assembly) were later given drain holes and sealant to protect the weapons and the integrity of the storage containers. Moreover, Sapele wood blocks were again used, this time inside the holsters, to hold the rifle securely and provide a 'guide' for the barrel of the weapon.

There are numerous books and magazines that show detailed photographs of the stowage for the SLRs, some with excellent 'period' wooden stock SLRs and others, are again of the modern black plastic stocks similar to that of later issued GPMGs seen on preserved SAS Pink Panthers. The Imperial War Museum (IWM) digitised weapons and ammunition collection shows examples of wooden and black plastic stock SLRs.

Readers interested in either the GPMG or SLR weapon, would be well advised to read the original HM publication (British Army code number 70498) of *Battle Handling (All Arms) Infantry Training, Volume 1* (1969). This detailed and now open-source pamphlet (Number 11) provides all the information you need about the GPMG and SLR, particularly firing from other positions, close-quarter battle and fire control orders. Available on most internet auction platforms.

A random sample of magazines that feature the SLR and SLR storage, includes the following published editions: *SAS Landrover (Desert Version) User Handbook* on pages 6 and 7; *Land Rover Owner* (August 1995); *Military Modelcraft International* (September 1997); *Land Rover Enthusiast,* June and November 2002; *Classic Military Vehicle* (July 2002); *Military Machines International* (April 2006); *SAS Panthers in Detail* and *Military Machines International* (July 2011); *Special Operations Landies in Detail* and *Classic Military Vehicle* magazine (February 2022). The list is endless, as are the pages they feature on!

Indeed, there isn't perhaps one publication (magazine or book), moreover, an internet example of a SAS Pink Panther Land-Rover that doesn't show these iconic weapon storage containers; they are intrinsic to the vehicle and no matter what angle you look at them, they are there, in your face!

Carl-Gustaf®

In addition to the GPMG firepower installed on the SAS Pink Panther, another potent weapon was also supplied, namely the Carl-Gustaf® 84-millimetre recoilless weapon. The L14A1 (M2 variant) Gun, 84 millimetre, Infantry Anti-Tank Weapon, known as the Carl-Gustaf or 'Charlie G', was the standard medium hand-held anti-tank weapon of the period. I have seen on numerous websites, the Carl-Gustaf recoilless rifle, spelt Carl Gustav, for the purposes of this book, the spelling will be Carl-Gustaf. Note also the use of the hyphen.

Cleverly utilising a rifled barrel for accuracy, the Carl-Gustaf employed a recoilless system to allow for a heavier propellant to be used. Thus, increasing range, accuracy, and ultimately power. Equipped with two hand-grips and a basic optical sight, it could puncture 400 millimetres of armour plate at ranges up to and including 700 metres. Adopted by British Army infantry units towards the end of the 1960s in its M2 variant, the 'Charlie G' as it became known, was a reusable weapon ready for any situation, including close combat, neutralising armoured tanks, clearing obstacles and engaging the enemy in buildings.

The Charlie G (M2 Variant) consisted of the main tube with a breech-mounted Venturi recoil damper, with two grips towards the front and a shoulder mount. The weapon is fitted with iron sights but can accommodate a telescopic sight and can be fired from the standing, kneeling, sitting, or prone positions. It can also be fired from a fire trench. However, it's at this point that you lose your hearing and require plasters for your blood blisters earned through closing the Venturi!

A handy bipod (gun mount) can be attached in front of the shoulder piece, and 'round 'selection included the following: 84-millimetre High Explosive Anti-Tank (HEAT – L40A3), high explosive (HE), high explosive dual purpose (HEDP), smoke, illumination (Para – L44A1), target practice (TP).

Stowage for the Carl-Gustaf (M2 Variant) was fitted across the front end of the rear compartment on top of the decking over the auxiliary fuel tanks. The stowage consisted of fabricated shaped blocks on a mounting board to which the weapon was secured employing straps and buckles. The mounting was secured to the decking using wing nuts, washers, and studs. A canvas cover was also supplied and fitted to the gun cover board, alongside tools and spare parts bag, carrying sling and No. 1 Mk. 1 cleaning kit.

Further ammunition for the Carl-Gustaf weapon was stowed in the rear compartment of the Land-Rover beside the rear part of the rear wheel arches and as per layout in the *SAS Landrover (Desert Version) User Handbook* on page 13. The stowage(s) consisted of open-top steel boxes – rather like a cage – with straps secured by toggle fasteners and close to hand at all times.

If you want to learn more about the Carl-Gustaf 84 millimetre recoilless (M2 Variant) weapon, I suggest reading the *User Handbook* (1968) by the Inspectorate of Armaments, based in Woolwich. With a British Army code number of 14985 26/MANS/4103, and with over eighty pages and forty-one illustrations, this (HM Government restricted) handbook covers the operation and servicing of the weapon and comes highly recommended. As does a quick trip to the UK Veterans Hearing Foundation, based in Hinckley, Leicestershire!

In August 2023, the Tank Museum, based in Bovington, Dorset, announced its acquisition of a Carl-Gustaf L14A1 (M2 variant) infantry anti-tank weapon. I highly recommend watching the accompanying video on their website, as the 13-minute presentation goes into detail about the weapon and handling skills required. Great for SAS Pink Panther owners and model makers, as during the informative narration, the camera gets up close and personal to the weapon and the rounds it fires.

Numerous photographic examples of the 84-millimetre Carl-Gustaf in magazine articles include the following: *Military Modelcraft International* (September 1997); *Land Rover Enthusiast* (June 2002); *Military Machines International* (April 2006 and July 2011).

Ammunition Stowage

Stowing ammunition aboard any vehicle requires thought and space availability, but more importantly, ease of immediate use. It should be fastened firmly and securely when it is not handled or used. A total of three ammunition stowages – consisting of open top boxes divided into compartments – were provided on the Marshall of Cambridge SAS Land-Rover, one between the two front seats (Driver and Commander) and one on each side of the rear compartment immediately to the rear of the twin auxiliary fuel tanks over the wheel arches. The front ammunition stowage consisted of a steel box container – x 8 compartments – with a canvas cover (NSN 2540-99-809-0715) secured by press studs.

The ammunition container is secured by a lip underneath the box that engages with a further lip on the vehicle's structure and at the front, by a toggle fastener. Of note is that front ammunition stowage is quickly detachable but the rear ammunition stowages were both bolted to the vehicle structure itself.

Various photographic examples of ammunition stowage appear in the following magazine articles, *Military Modelcraft International* (September 1997) in addition to *SAS Panthers in Detail.*

In the June 2004 edition of *Land Rover Enthusiast,* there is an interesting article in the Project Pink Panther section that covers the fabrication of ammunition stowage on 10 FG 88 and includes some great pictures. It is well worth a look, if not just for the photos.

Blackout Driving Light

The Blackout Driving Light (No. 1 Mk. 1) or Curfew Light (NSN 6220-99-808-1855), as it is sometimes referred to, is a standard Land-Rover headlight (No. 3 Mk. 1) but uses a light restricting shroud and the standard commercially available Lucas light unit. The light is securely mounted on the front of the right-hand driver's side mudguard and is a feature that is synonymous in SAS Pink Panther recognition, be it in green or desert pink in colour.

The shroud – like the column for the E2B Compass – was manufactured from glass fibre with a blank front face and an internal blank diaphragm and is secured to the light rim by three screws through keyhole slots in the flange of the shroud itself.

The front face and accompanying diaphragm each have a horizontal slot near the top of the circumference, designed to allow a shallow beam of light in a forward direction. Moreover, it also protected the glass lens against flying debris and detritus when at speed.

The cylindrical part of the blackout driving light has a narrow slot in its periphery to provide a limited amount of downward light to aid driving at low light or in the dark and is used in place of regular headlights during blackout conditions. Moreover, the patrol vehicles must maintain concealment by limiting their ability to be seen by the enemy while in convoy.

Remember that these vehicles were designed and manufactured before the introduction of passive night goggles or night-vision devices (NVD), both of which are optoelectronic devices that allow images to be produced in levels of light approaching total darkness. It is interesting to note that the image produced is typically monochrome green. This was because it is considered the easiest colour to look at for prolonged periods in the dark.

The power supply for the blackout driving light is taken from the convoy lights supply and is controlled by a simple turn switch (rotary switch) located on the Land-Rover's dashboard. The rear convoy light – which shouldn't be confused with the blackout driving light – is a small light that fits behind the rear cross-member and shines directly onto the 'white painted' rear face of the differential housing. This allows the following vehicle to observe the vehicle in front, but it can't be seen from a spotter aircraft or an enemy on higher ground.

Several photographic examples of the blackout driving light can be seen on page 40 of the magazine *Off Road and 4 Wheel Drive* (March 1989); *Land Rover Owner International* magazine (August 1995), page 160 and on page 46 of the April 2006 edition of the *Military Machines International* magazine and the ever-reliable *SAS Panthers in Detail*, Craig Philip and Alex Taylor's publication *Inside the SAS* (Bloomsbury, 1992) on page 199. And lastly, in *Compendium of British Soft-Skin Military Vehicles*.

Of particular note with regards to plastic kit models is the ITALERI model of the SAS Land-Rover, this time in deep bronze green (but more a NATO green with black shadow) and in 1/35 scale (model number 258) displaying the registration plate of 10 FG 58, for some reason, doesn't have the narrow slot to allow downward light to aide driving shown on the box artwork.

Type E2B Compass

Navigation has been an ongoing problem for travellers, Pilgrims and warriors alike, and desert navigation is no exception. Since the dawn of creation, the methods used by Bedouins or nomads and perhaps for the Wayfarer where mobility is the most efficient strategy for exploiting scarce resources to find the way are as useful now as they were thousands of years ago.

The purpose of any compass, solar or magnetic, is to locate, as accurately as possible, the direction of true north. Once north is found, the current or desired bearing can then be reasonably determined. Positions are determined with dead reckoning, on a fixed visible landmark, or by close reference to a map. Knowledge of the bearing is critical for the compass user, as it avoids the possibility of going around and around in frustrating circles and getting lost.

The E2B compass that was installed by Marshall of Cambridge on the SAS Pink Panther was primarily used as a standby compass and was mounted in a hollow square-section fibreglass post, to the right-hand side of the driver and is a variant of the E2A compass that was extensively used by the RAF (the Vulcan bomber and the de Havilland Vampire being two such examples) the difference being, that the E2B compass incorporated direct lighting of the compass bowl via a 12-volt non-magnetic red bulb.

Interestingly, during the several meetings held at the time with Marshall of Cambridge, it was noted that the compass mast containing the E2B compass, should have an aluminium bracket fitted to the mast and bulkhead, this was done to make it stronger and to avoid excessive 'wobble' of the mast as the vehicle travelled at speed.

The light was easily activated by a simple 'on/off' toggle switch located on the pillar, and below the compass bowl; the compass being secured to an aluminium plate close to the top of the mast itself. Annoyingly, this 'on/off' switch was often liable to water ingress. When the red light was on, it was ideal for low light or nighttime operations as the driver could easily see the compass card through a clear Perspex aperture near the upper part of the fibreglass column and at a handy eye level for the driver. Of note, is that the protective column on the SAS Land-Rover was manufactured in fibreglass. This was done so as not to affect compass operational effectiveness, as fibreglass is non-magnetic.

The magnetic compasses of the E2 series are precision miniature instruments developed for emergency or standby compasses where lack of space or opportunity precludes the use of a larger, more accurate compass. The compass bowl was filled with silicone fluid, chosen because it had no detrimental effect on the material of the bowl and because its temperature/viscosity changes are small, a particularly useful feature with the extremes of temperature when traveling in the desert. In addition, they were very lightweight, perhaps not much heavier than a cotton reel.

The cardinal points (N, E, S, W) of the Type E2B Compass are marked by the appropriate letter. The compass card is graduated every 10 degrees with figures every 30°. The compasses were designed to give a bench accuracy of ±½°and an operational accuracy of ±10°. However, under favourable conditions and a stable heading indication, interpolation may be comparable to bench accuracy.

A great photographic example of a mounted Type E2B compass (NSN 6605-99-104-8857) on an SAS Pink Panther can be seen in the April 2000 edition of the magazine *Land Rover Owner International* on page 55, where the four screws can be observed in the mast's top plate and on page 46 of the April 2006 edition of the *Military Machines International* magazine, this time clearly showing the on/off switch.

Of particular note, it is these four screws that need to be periodically removed to enable the compass deviation checks to be made by use of a 'compass adjusting key' in the keyholes near the top of the compass bowl; having completed these deviation checks, a final check was completed by the navigator using the master compass. Another great and detailed photographic example of the compass mast is in the November 2000 edition of Land Rover Enthusiast, page 31.

The use and field trials of the E2 Range of the compass are evidenced in numerous pieces of documentation seen by the author; these articles mention how the E2A aircraft compass was mounted on a shaft secured to the Driver's front door post and where using the theodolite and the Cole Mk. II sun compass mounted on the dashboard, night position fixes were achieved to an accuracy of 200 yards. Interestingly, commercial (and ex-military) variants of the E2A Compass manufactured by Kelvin and Hughes, are still used in rally cars today and offer a reasonably accurate ready-reckoner if the GPS is down.

Cole Sun Compass Mk. II

The Mk. II Cole (Military) Sun Compass was a heavy – and still is – bulky item; beautifully engineered to avoid the ingestion of sand and dust and were issued two per vehicle and mounted above the vehicle's dashboard and on the auxiliary fuel tank. Scaled to operate between latitude 40° north and 40° south of the equator, it incorporates the changes in shadow angle for date and latitude on an adjustable time and latitude scale. Once the instrument has been aligned in the vehicle, it requires no further preparation.

Most reference photos show just one compass mounted on a metal bracket (MCE number FV636392) above the dashboard (front bulkhead), which makes it easy for the navigator or driver to use. However, a second compass can be mounted above the auxiliary fuel tank behind the driver. This alternative mounting point is confirmed in the original documentation seen by the author, namely, the July 1966 (1/8) scale schematic used by Marshall of Cambridge for the fabrication of the SAS Land-Rover.

The front mounting bracket for the sun compass consisted of a strip of steel fabricated to form a horizontal surface, which was secured to the vehicle's structure above the instrument panel and the horizontal arm had a U-slot to take the sun compass attachment. The rear mounting bracket was a more robust feature.

It consisted of a slotted, hinged member to which was attached a sliding member secured employing a bolt, nut and plate. The outer end of the sliding member was at a right angle and incorporated a slot for the sun compass attachment. When used, the bracket was raised to the vertical position, and the sliding member extended.

Many photographs depict SAS Pink Panthers with two compasses mounted. This could be perceived as correct, as two such compasses appear in the *SAS Landrover (Desert Version) User Handbook* (British Army code number 22205). Indeed, they are both evidenced in this handbook in the text and in a photographic plate on page 13, where the mount brackets (x 2) are clearly shown.

However, only one Mk. II Cole (Military) Sun Compass was issued and is noted on the *CES*. The presence of two compasses in the photographs merely suggests possible locations for the compass to the end user.

Interestingly, Models by TAMIYA and ITALERI of the SAS Pink Panther do not include the second compass. This was perhaps done as a cost-cutting exercise, or they might have thought the model would look too cluttered, or maybe the original vehicle used for artwork and reference (10 FG 63), only had one fitted at the time. Indeed, when you look at the TAMIYA instructions that are included in the box, there appears to be only one sun compass fitted on the original 10 FG 63.

Indeed, in an early modelling magazine dated December 1972 and January 1973 and titled *Military Modelling*, Colonel John Stubbs writes a detailed article on the SAS Pink Panther, and the reference photos used are of 10 FG 63 (chassis number 251-13948D) showing only the one compass.

As there were only so many photos around of SAS Land-Rovers, especially in 1972, it is perhaps logical to assume that these early and very detailed photos may have been used as a reference for the TAMIYA version of the SAS Pink Panther released only a few years later in 1976. The very same year, some early Pinkies were being sold off at Ruddington Auctions.

Anyway, back to navigation! For use, a Universal Sun Compass needs only a watch (or chronometer) set to a local solar time or perhaps a BBC short wave radio broadcast to obtain GMT and then (locally) adjust; as the Cole military compass carries on it all the information required to operate it and comprises of a pointer, to which the angle of travel (direction) is set, the bearing to be set is shown around a rotatable plate from 0° to 360° (not in mils/mili-radians) and a vertical stylus/needle/pin (AKA gnomon) in the groove of the sliding date scale.

This type of compass is not suitable for continuous navigation. However, it was particularly good when a long distance was covered on a single bearing. Therefore, spare (and sometimes) differing-length gnomons, were kept in the wooden storage box. Indeed, I remember seeing some with a dab of luminescent paint on the top of the gnomon to aid navigation in times of poor visibility (sandstorms). Moreover, keeping a small cork on top was a good practice or, better still, placing the stylus/gnomon in the tray beneath the compass when not in use.

Ideally, regular compass bearings should be taken, as even a small error in compass readings at the outset will translate into a huge inaccuracy after a 100-mile (dead-reckoning) advance to battle. Factor in the Land-Rover's odometer might be broken too but above all, remember that terrain, weather, and war have scant regard for British Army equipment!

However, the sun compass is a useful and simple instrument for keeping a vehicle on a straight pre-ordained course or on a fixed observable distant feature, such as a mountain (Jebal), never a dune, as dunes are highly movable in the desert wind. Desert navigation is a learned skill, and SAS Veterans often referred to being in the desert as 'on the blue', comparing the desert to the featureless ocean.

Another navigational aid used on SAS patrols was the British Army prismatic compass. This handheld device was made of brass and had a mother-of-pearl compass card (dial) that glowed in the dark and floated in oil. Issued initially to British Army officers, it was probably one of the finest compasses in use at the outbreak of the Second World War. As with many military compasses, it could be read in degrees or mils.

Storage for the British Army prismatic compass was in the 1958 pattern small square and padded pouch (NSN 8465-99-973-6960). Padded with felt to help protect the slightly delicate compass from shocks and bumps associated with desert travel. The rear of the P58 pouch had a single metal 'C' hook and a transverse webbing loop to allow the 1958 pattern yoke to be slotted through.

On a safety note, many prismatic compasses use radium for the luminous paint markings on the dials. With time, these markings go brown but are still releasing Gamma and Beta radiation. Beta radiation is contained inside the case, but the Gamma radiation does leak out. Avoid excessive handling, and don't carry them regularly in your pocket. The prismatic compass was often used in tandem with the Cole Mk. II Military Sun compass in navigating the vast deserts, the SAS Regiment operated in.

Interestingly, and as every good soldier knows, as there was/is no insulation from magnetic distortion, it was always advisable to stand away from any vehicle or generator with the prismatic compass to avoid navigation errors caused by metal / magnetic interference emanating from said vehicle. Or, on occasions, the very ground (minerals) your map/ compass was resting on! The ITALERI model of the SAS Land-Rover, this time in deep bronze green (but more a NATO green with black shadow) in 1/35 scale (model number 258), displaying the registration plate of 10 FG 58, (chassis number 251-13983D) sadly doesn't have the Cole Sun Compass on the box cover artwork nor in the contents of the box.

Indeed, there is no reference to this important piece of equipment at all. However, on page 46 of the April 2006 edition of the *Military Machines International* magazine, there are two great close-up photographs of the Mk. 2 Cole Pattern, one in the centre of the front bulkhead and the other on top of the auxiliary fuel tank. Sun Compasses like the Mk. II Cole (Military) Sun Compass rarely appears for sale on the internet. However, one such opportunity arose in March 2024 when a rare example of a sun compass was auctioned. After receiving 20 bids, the compass finally sold for £910.

Photographic examples of not only the Sun Compass but the mounting brackets (front and rear) as well, can be seen in Tony Geraghty's (pictorial) book *This is the SAS* published in 1982 on page 120, plate 301 (pre-Marshall of Cambridge) and in numerous magazines notably the *Land Rover Owner International* (August 1995), page 160; *Military Modelcraft International*, September 1997; *Military Machines International* (April 2006), page 46; November's 2000 edition of *Land Rover Enthusiast*, page 31; *Land Rover Enthusiast* (June 2002), page 8; *SAS Panthers in Detail, Military Machines International* (July 2011), page 87.

Theodolite and Tripod

Each SAS Land-Rover was equipped with a theodolite and tripod, and the requirements of the theodolite ranged from robust manufacture to having enough tools for field adjustments. In total, fourteen operational requirements were asked of the Theodolite, and three manufacturers' names were considered for the project: Tavistock, Wild and Watts.

The theodolite finally used on the SAS Pink Panther was the Watts Mk. III Theodolite (Surveying, Microptic No. 2); it was produced in small numbers but was quickly superseded by the Mk. IV. The Watts Mk. III was and still is a precision-made optical instrument for calculating angles between designated observable points in the horizontal and vertical planes. The robust theodolite consisted of a telescope mounted on a base, further mounted on a supplied wooden tripod. Interestingly, examples have been observed on operational and preserved SAS Pink Panthers, where the tripod was made of metal.

The military theodolite (AKA surveyor's transit) issued to the SAS Pink Panther works by combining optical plummets (or plumb bobs), a spirit (bubble level), and graduated circles to locate vertical and horizontal angles in navigating. An optical plummet ensures the theodolite is placed as near to exactly vertical above the survey point. The internal spirit level makes sure the device is level to the horizon.

The telescope has a sight on top that aligns the target or destination, and the instrument has a focusing knob that is used to make the object clear. In addition, the telescope contains an eyepiece that the navigator looks through to find the target or destination being sighted. Also carried were chronometers and star charts (star maps) as there was always a good vault of stars at night due to nil light pollution in the desert.

Chronometers were carried, as getting a star-fix called 'shooting the stars' is very difficult to obtain a correct bearing, as a star-fix has to be precisely timed. Consequently, daylight navigation by SAS soldiers was preferred as 'shoot(ing) the sun' is an easier task and far more accurate. To 'shoot the sun' is to ascertain the sun's altitude to determine the latitude.

When not in use, the theodolite tripod was stowed on the external bodywork of the Land-Rover. The stowage consisted of two strip steel brackets to which the tripod was secured by straps, adjusting buckles, and toggle fasteners. Secure stowage space for the Watts Mk. III theodolite and hard-shell case, with leather strap, was provided forward of the rear gunner's seat back. And lastly, a handy canvas bag (navigation bag) for the stowage of navigation equipment was fitted to the front surface of the rear compartment forward bulkhead behind the front left-hand seat. Interestingly, the fasteners (turn buttons) used to attach the bag to the vehicle are the same ones fitted to the Austin Champ.

On occasions, preserved SAS Land-Rovers can be seen with the tripod secured on top of the bonnet, this was done when the radio communication setup had been retrofitted, and equipment extension plates were fitted over the wheel arch, 10 FG 51 (chassis number 251-13990D) is one such excellent example and can be seen proudly representing the Pink Panther Register at military reunions and shows around the country.

Finding a period-issued and perhaps used by the SAS Regiment theodolite tripod is particularly difficult; this would explain why so many styles, makes, and colour variances are seen on preserved SAS Land-Rover Pink Panthers. The Royal Artillery and Royal Engineers were/are – for obvious reasons – prolific users of the theodolite and corresponding tripod; this would make a great starting point to locate such an important piece of equipment for your SAS Land-Rover renovation.

Books and magazines that have published photographic references of the mounted theodolite include the following published editions: *Military Modelcraft International* (September 1997), page 36; *Land Rover Enthusiast* (November 2000 and June 2002) editions. Of particular note is the *SAS Panthers in Detail; Land Rover Owner* (August 1995); *Military Machines International* (April 2006 and July 2011). And lastly, *Special Operations Landies in Detail.*

Portable Searchlight

Military vehicles need a whole range of creative lighting solutions to perform effectively during nighttime operations. The SAS Land-Rover Pink Panther was no exception. Portable searchlights were required to not only function reliably but must also be resistant to shock and vibration, as well as being rugged enough to work in an adverse battlefield environment such as the desert in the 1970s.

The portable searchlight (or portable spotlight), as it was sometimes referred to that was fitted to the SAS Pink Panther, was the British Army's standard No. 1, Mk. 1 portable searchlight. Incorporating a commercially available two-filament pre-focused Lucas Light Unit, it was used extensively in the British Armed Forces for many years on vehicles such as the Ferret Scout car, Alvis Saracen, and the FV432 armoured personnel carrier (APC) to name but a few. It was vehicle mounted with a swivel capability to allow for traversing across the field of view and would instantly illuminate, identify and track a person or target of interest.

The Searchlights (NSN 6230-99-803-2936 or NSN 6230-99-803-2278) depending on which official reference you use came complete with approximately 28 feet of twin-core flexible power cable (black in colour) and a plug which was plugged in for use into the standard socket which was located on the vehicle's instrument panel. When not in use, the flexible cable was coiled around the outside of the light, where it was held in place by the top attachment of the control handle, an angle bracket at each side of the metal light housing assembly itself.

The *SAS Landrover (Desert Version) User Handbook* on page 30 makes excellent use of an IPB to show the parts of the light, ranging from the rim to the two-pin plug; this is then repeated on Plate H6 of the *Illustrated Spare Parts List for Body Used on Truck, Utility, SAS, ¾ Ton, 4 x 4, Rover II* and in the *Technical Handbook for the Truck, General Service, SAS ¾, Rover II.*

Interestingly, the 'dip' filament facility of the Portable Searchlight is not used; this is confirmed in several official publications; namely, the *SAS Landrover (Desert Version) User Handbook* (August 1969), pages 20 and 29, and the *Technical Handbook for the Truck, General Service, SAS ¾ Ton, Rover II* (February 1970).

However, a simple on/off switch – which was fitted in the top curvature of the lamp body – allowed for ease of use when illumination in the field was required. Moreover, there was also a socket located to the Spotlight handle to allow for safe storage of the plug.

The portable searchlights were located in the following strategic places: on the top of the vehicle's dashboard structure at the right centre and to the sides of the Land-Rover, above the sand ladders, and over the rear wheel arches and again, clamped securely to the vehicle's bodywork.

A steel strip handle is secured to the upper outside of the light bowl/body, allowing for the searchlight's ease of movement. It was noted that during the trials with the FVRDE, the spotlight clamp often worked loose.

Interestingly, in the later stages of the Second World War European theatre campaign, the SAS Willys Jeeps that were 'dropped in' were equipped with searchlights. However, insights from the now-published *SAS War Diary*, particularly in the section titled 'Lessons Learnt', reveal that these searchlights were occasionally removed. This can be further evidenced in period and in-country photos published in the *SAS War Diary*. The decision stemmed from their perceived ineffectiveness and lack of utility during active operations. This illustrates the constant evolution of tactics and equipment in the field.

Several preserved SAS Pink Panther Land-Rovers have two (x 2) portable searchlights fitted. The second one is fitted to the middle of the vehicle's instrumentation panel and clamped to the upper bodywork between the Cole sun compass and steering wheel above the ignition key switch, 10 FG 34; 10 FG 45; 10 FG 55; 10 FG 59; 10 FG 80, 10 FG 93 and 10 FG 94 being some such examples. Moreover, 10 FG 97 in the November 2000 edition of *Land Rover Enthusiast*, page 28, and 10 FG 61 in the Bonhams Auction (lot 208) of October 2020 can each be seen with three such Searchlights fitted.

Lastly, on page 46 of the April 2006 edition of the *Military Machines International* magazine, there are two great close-up photographs of the portable searchlight, all with approximately 28 feet of flexible power cable in the picture. Nice!

Smoke Discharger Units

The smoke discharger units, or smoke grenade launchers as they are sometimes referred to, were specifically designed and developed for the SAS Land-Rover, as pre-existing units in the British Army were unsuitable due to their weight and mounting arrangements. They are a synonymous visual identification point for the SAS Land-Rover Pink Panther.

Indeed, this particular smoke-dispersal (obscurant) feature has been carried through to numerous other special forces vehicles as standard kit. The Smoke Dischargers – electronically activated by a four push-button control box (NSN 2920-99-803-6144) located below the centre of the vehicle's instrument panel – are strategically located at each end of the four corners of the Land-Rover and were the primary means of generating tactical smokescreens and evading enemy observation. Smoke is a combat multiplier that can enhance the SAS commander's ability to concentrate combat power at a critical time and place. Indeed, the correct use of smoke is a far more significant battlefield factor than ever on flat desert terrain where little cover and concealment is available.

Used as a defensive countermeasure against an enemy and usually discharged individually or in salvos by the navigator or driver. The smoke grenades issued were slow-burning, high-volume, continuous-discharge grenades designed to last a few minutes. Deployment of said smoke would be accompanied by vigorous evasive manoeuvring by the driver and effective returned machine gun fire by the rear gunner using the vehicle-mounted 7.62mm GPMG.

Each set comprised three smoke discharger units (AKA smoke pots) welded to a mounting bracket set at a fixed elevation of 25 degrees (445 mils), but each tube was set with a different traverse angle. The outer tube was set at 30 degrees (533 mils) outwards, the centre tube at 15 degrees (267 mils) outwards, and the inner tube parallel to the vehicle's centre line. The closed end of each tube is fitted with an electrical firing pin and has an effective range of approximately 262 feet (80 metres).

Of particular note regarding the smoke pots, the units were initially conceived to be two barrels and anchored to each of the front corners and then three to the rear of the vehicle, but extensive trials revealed that three barrels fitted to each corner gave better arcs of coverage. It was also necessary to remove the front bumper (standard specification) over-riders – previously designed to allow one Land-Rover to push start another without damage – to allow this specialised, essential, and later iconic fitment.

The Smoke Dischargers (NSN 1040-99-809-0719 and NSN 1040-99-809-0720) are controlled by one of the (four) press-switches (push buttons) on the control box (AKA switchbox, smoke, grenade firing) that were clearly labelled for ease of use by either the driver or commander with the set of three smoke dischargers it controlled.

At the end of each canister / tube or barrel, there was a retaining chain and rubber cap fitted to the discharger; upon firing, the cap (AKA cap and chain assembly) would remain anchored to the vehicle as a result of the chain, thus allowing for further smoke grenades being fitted and protected from the elements.

Interestingly, during the fiftieth anniversary of the SAS Land-Rover in 2019, Alan Bucknell, a member of the SAS Pink Panther Register and former custodian of 10 FG 57, had a conversation with employees at Marshall of Cambridge headquarters. While I was researching this book, Alan shared with me that he found it fascinating to learn from the Smoke Pots fabricator that the MCE employees manufacturing these vehicles were only informed about the purpose of their work at the end of the process. It was only during the final assembly that the employees at Marshall of Cambridge came to know what exactly they were building and for whom it was being built.

In the August 2003 edition of the *Land Rover Enthusiast* magazine and under the 'Project Pink Panther' renovation progress report by Neil Mitchell and Barry Pocock, there is a short but interesting write-up by James Taylor on the replica smoke discharge units that were specially commissioned and fabricated for preserved SAS Land Rover 10 FG 88, with the chassis code number of 251-13956D.

Indeed, on page 40 of the magazine *Off Road and 4 Wheel Drive* (March 1989) by Roger Jones, there is a close-up photograph of the Smoke Dischargers and retaining chains. Moreover, on page 48 of the April 2006 edition of the Military Machines International magazine, there is a great close-up photo of the black plastic cap covers and retaining chains that fit neatly over the Smoke Discharge Units. Of particular note is the *SAS Panthers in Detail*, where there are many photographic references to the Smoke Discharger Units and the all-important Smoke Discharger Control Box and lastly, *Special Operations Landies in Detail.*

Sand Channels or Sand Ladders

The SAS Land-Rover Pink Panther was issued with two metal Sand Channels or Sand Ladders, as they are often referred to. They were mounted to the side of the vehicle using a secure bracket (cleat) at either end and as per *Illustrated Spare Parts List for Body Used on Truck, Utility, SAS, ¾ Ton, 4 x 4, Rover II* plate number H1. Similar Sand Channels – not to be confused with sand mats were extensively used by special forces vehicles during the Second World War.

In particular, by the LRDG, Popski's Private Army (PPA), Greek Sacred Squadron, Indian Long Range Squadron and the SAS. It is interesting to note that Sand Mats were sometimes used by SAS patrol members, and these tended to vary in design, length, and materials and were rolled up and stowed when not in use on the Pink Panther.

The sand channel, sand ladder, or more appropriately entitled, pierced (pressed) steel planking (PSP), is a standardised, perforated steel material primarily deployed for the rapid construction of temporary landing strips or runways. In the First World War, they were initially designed to provide engineers with a simple, effective, and strong material for trench and bunker systems. In addition, the hole pattern for the PSP was produced to allow easier transportation by reducing the weight and for improved grip and added traction.

Interestingly, in the publication by the RAOC's director of ordnance services entitled *Illustrated Spare Parts List for Body Used on Truck, Utility, SAS, ¾ Ton, 4 x 4, Rover II* (British Army code number 22128), the sand channels are correctly titled 'Pressed Steel Planking' and measured 16 x 60 inches or (40.64 x 152.4 centimetres) and were 10 SWG = 0.128-inches /3.251 millimetres thick – (standard-wire gauge (SWG)). Indeed, the title 'Pressed Steel Planking' is also used in the *SAS Landrover (Desert Version) User Handbook* (British Army code number 22205).

There is much conjecture and discussion about when and where sand channels (PSP) was first used by special forces, particularly the LRDG and SAS units. Indeed, many widely published photographs show slightly differing designs (unit modifications and local purchase points) of sand channels on such specialised desert vehicles. Moreover, on LRDG vehicles, sand ladders were sometimes seen mounted on the front bumper or tailgate rather than the side of the truck.

Indeed, one such early example of special forces' use is that by the well-known desert explorer Brigadier Ralph Alger Bagnold (3 April 1896–28 May 1990). The famous desert explorer, geologist, professional soldier, and principal founder of the Long Range Patrol (LRP) Unit but later named the Long Range Desert Group.

In his book *Sand, Wind, and War: Memoirs of a Desert Explorer*, he describes how, in a Cairo junk shop, steel channels intended for use as roofing dugouts during the First World War were found and were adopted and skilfully redeployed for use on his vehicles to save the problem of travel and recovery of vehicles on the sand. Whatever the catalyst was, it was a natural progression for the SAS Regiment's new fighting vehicle to have the sand channels (PSP) fitted as standard for a new decade. The sand ladder/channels that can be seen on SAS Pink Panther Land-Rovers had three rows of fourteen equal-sized holes and helped distribute the wheel weight and therefore prevented wheels from sinking into the sand or soil underneath. Thus, assisting the truck in getting traction and momentum after being stuck in the sand or mud.

For example, once a vehicle was stuck in the sand, the sand channels would be placed in front of the embedded wheels that provided the traction. As the wheels turned, the metal sand ladders would be fed underneath the wheels, which would then displace the truck's weight over a larger area and unstick the vehicle. It sounds easy in practice, but it was extremely labour intensive. Of particular note with regard to sand ladders and as a result of extensive FVRDE trials, the PSP (tropicalised) mounting sapele board(s) located behind the Sand Ladders and affixed to the Land-Rover's bodywork, were carefully designed to be shaped to contour the wheel opening of the bodywork to facilitate fitment (and puncture repair) of the rear wheel(s).

Interestingly, the sand ladders issued were notorious for being particularly difficult to mount and dismount on the hooks provided. Especially when the smooth side of the sand ladder was facing out and if they had been there for a while. Moreover, if they had received a lot of chassis and body 'movement' caused by rough driving, in other words, as a result of scuttle shake, also of note, is that well-used sand ladders, were often damaged in use. Which in turn would distort the shape and sometimes cause metal fatigue from the frequent flexing under the Pinkie's extreme load.

Indeed, period documentation would suggest the possible introduction of a 'slide plate'. The idea of the slide plate was to make it quicker and easier for the Land-Rover's crew to debog from a mound should the wheels (x 4) be totally off the ground. The trials involved the Land-Rover being driven into position on a mound of hard earth, unable to move under its own power with the vehicle's full weight resting on the slide (rover belly) plate. According to the report, the Land-Rover was successfully debogged in approximately thirty seconds by three men pushing the truck and with no engine power engaged.

When another vehicle (SAS Land-Rover) was placed on the same mound, but this time without the belly plate, the crew failed to debog by pushing AND towing. It was only winched clear with the use of the Tifor and having enlisted a fourth man to assist – time to de-bog, twenty minutes. The trial was conducted at Bradbury Lines.

Further trials were conducted using two SAS Land-Rovers, but this time up to full operational weight, one with a slide plate and the other without. Each vehicle went over the same mound/obstacle, but the results differed. The vehicle with the slide plate had no visible damage to the underside and was always easy to debog. The vehicle without the slide plate sustained moderate damage to the chassis and cross members and was not easy to move once bellied down.

The trials and report concluded that the belly plate was better than nothing, but it would become badly buckled over more extended periods. It was recommended that future slide plates be made using the same pattern (FVRDE), but thicker ⅛ steel plate as opposed to 1/16 as tested.

Various photographic examples of PSP sand channels can be seen in the majority of publications that have featured the SAS Land-Rover but in greater detail, can be found in the magazine *Military Machines International* (April 2006) and the book *SAS Panthers in Detail* and lastly *Special Operations Landies in Detail*.

Inter-Vehicle Starter Power Socket

The SAS Land-Rover's inter-vehicle starter power socket (or socket inter-vehicle starting panel) is located on the exterior surface of the driver's side of the vehicle and in line with the vehicle's dashboard. A fantastic close-up photograph of the inter-vehicle starter power socket, showing this location and still with its original retaining clip attached, can be seen in *Military Machines International* magazine, April 2006, on page 49 and with further photographs but with less detail, on pages 44 and 45 and lastly, *Land Rover Enthusiast* magazine (June 2002), page 7.

This simple but effective electronic method of starting vehicles was a helpful addition, as it was often required to 'jump-start' other vehicles that had been drained of power for several reasons. For example, climate variances, parasitic draws, or the battery wasn't charging correctly. The socket assembly was of a heavy-duty type, consisting of a single-pin receptacle surrounded by safety insulation contained in an externally machined metal housing.

When not used to start up other vehicles drained of power, the plug/socket is protected by a screw-on cap; the electric cable (NSN 2590-99-815-6019) is a handy 15 feet long and had plugs/sockets at either end to link with the other vehicle. According to the official publication *Truck, General Service, SAS, ¾ Ton, 4 x 4, Rover II* by command of the Defence Council, entitled *Electrical and Mechanical Engineering Regulations* (February 1970) for the SAS Land-Rover, the cable should be stored in the compartment located under the forward ammunition container.

Although this would have been personal preference and should only be taken as guidance. There are photographic examples of preserved SAS Land-Rover Pink Panthers, where stowage for the cable is under the Commander's seat. This can be evidenced with 10 FG 94 (chassis number 251-14087D) in the June 2002 edition of *Land Rover Enthusiast* on page 9.

Interestingly, some SAS Land-Rovers were prone to battery failure due to the cold of the desert night, degrading the vehicle's battery or the starter motor playing up. Therefore, storage of the inter-vehicle starter power cable was (temporarily) moved to be wrapped around the side wing mirror for ease of access while on operations or exercise. This empirical vignette would make an excellent addition to a scale model display.

The inter-vehicle starting power socket (NSN 2590-99-910-9946) is connected to the battery terminal of the starter solenoid, and to provide safety for the Land-Rover's crew, the Earth plug is connected to the vehicle structure at the dashboard. The inter-vehicle starter power socket provision was a much safer, more reliable, and more sophisticated option than using jump leads with the bonnets up in the dark of a hostile desert environment.

When doing a renovation of an original SAS Pink Panther, these inter-vehicle starting power sockets, can prove difficult to locate on the open market. If the vehicle failed to electronically start using the power cable, there was always the vehicle's trusty starting crank, which was provided and located underneath the front two seats, using metal clips on the vertical side face of the structure. Photographic examples of the 'crank – hand starting' (NSN 2805-99-850-0903) can be seen in *SAS Panthers in Detail* – an excellent reference point for collectors, renovators, and modellers alike and in *Military Machines International* magazine (April 2006) on page 49.

Battery Charger and Radio Sockets

Two power supply sockets, one for the Type A43 radio battery and one for the power supply to the Type A123 radio, were mounted on the forward face of the rear compartment to the right of the commander's seat. The battery charger power supply socket has five-pin receptacles, with two utilised, and the Type A123 radio power supply socket has four-pin receptacles, with two utilised. Of particular note, weather-proof rubber covers were provided to blank off the sockets when not in use.

Tyre-Bead Breaker

The tyre-bead breaker or tyre stripping tool as it can often be referred to and that was issued to the SAS Land-Rover – as punctures caused by thorny desert vegetation were a common occurrence – was a tool specifically used for separating the tyre from the standard 15-inch metal rim. The innermost diameter of the tyre that interfaces with the rim of a wheel is known as the tyre bead. Interestingly, it was not uncommon for an SAS Patrol to instead brace (where possible) the Land-Rover. This was done so it wouldn't sink further and dig a hole under the bad tyre rather than attempting to jack up the vehicle in unpredictable sand.

The bead is a thicker piece of rubber on the Pink Panther's sand tyre and is strengthened with braided steel cables called the bead bundle. The surface of the bead creates a tight seal between the tyre and rim on radial and bias-ply tyres. Often, the bead can become stuck to the rim having rusted, requiring the use of a bead breaker for the tyre to be safely removed.

The tyre bead breaker (AKA separator bead assy) (NSN 2540-99-809-0721), was stowed away when not in use on top of the SLR tapered steel stowage container, which was located on the outside of the commander's side front wheel arch and as per *Illustrated Spare Parts List for Body Used on Truck, Utility, SAS, ¾ Ton, 4 x 4, Rover II* – plate number H1. Perhaps it is worth noting that this particular piece of (period and in-service) equipment is now scarce to find and, consequently, quite expensive. Of note is that the SAS Land-Rover's bumper had a reinforced hole for the bead breaker's nose to engage into, thus allowing for greater purchase etc.

Interestingly, the vehicle was also issued, alongside the tyre-bead breaker, the following tools, a screwdriver, spanner (crescent-shaped), pliers, tyre levers (x 2) and a tyre pressure gauge. Fortunately, a 4-ton vehicle jack (NSN 5120-99-201-4907) was also supplied with the SAS Land-Rover.

Of particular note regarding scale model making, the 1/35 scale Tamiya model of the SAS Pink Panther (military miniature model number 76), with an ERM of 10 FG 63, describes this particular tool on its instruction sheet as a 'ground anchor'. Indeed, this mention of a 'ground anchor' and accompanying close-up photograph is also (wrongly) confirmed in the reference book *SAS Panthers in Detail* on page 22! Galvanised steel ground anchors are a reliable solution for extricating yourself from sticky situations in sand or mud when combined with a winch. They are not intended to be used as a tyre-bead breaker! Magazine photographic references for the tyre-bead breaker include *Land Rover Enthusiast* (November 2000) and July 2002 editions; *Military Machines International* (April 2006); *Classic Military Vehicle* (July 2002).

Sand Tyres

Terrain accessibility is a vital characteristic of an effective fighting vehicle such as an SAS Pink Panther Land-Rover. The whole raison d'être of such vehicles is to give the ability to project force and influence to any point within the theatre of operations.

As fighting vehicles are terra-based, their operating ability depends on the immediate topography. Soft terrain, such as sand, can cause excessive sinkage and damage, rendering the vehicle (truck) immobile. Therefore, the terrain must be able to support the vehicle's weight. The vehicle's suspension, overall weight, and tyre design also play a significant role in terrain accessibility, affecting the ground pressure on rough terrain and the vehicle's ability to navigate obstacles. Therefore, game-changing special forces trucks require game-changing tyres.

The SAS Land-Rover was equipped with 6-ply rating ribbed tread sand tyres (NSN 2610-99-804-2840) that measured 9 inches by 15 inches and had 'SAND TYPE' written (raised lettering) on the side wall. These pneumatic tyres, sometimes referred to as 'balloon tyres', were designed to have low-pressure and high floatation, making them ideal for use in the sand/desert.

Their tread pattern was specially designed to prevent soil disturbance and avoid cutting into the softer sand. To maximise their effectiveness, sand tyres should be smooth and almost slick to prevent digging into the sand. Additionally, tyres with larger diameters, greater widths, and more flexible, stronger side walls allow for better deflated contact area and will enable the tyre to scrabble for traction.

Having low-pressure tyres can significantly increase the tyre's footprint (AKA contact patch/area) on the sand, so you have the same weight of the vehicle spread over about twice as much rubber and, therefore, half the weight per square inch.

For information, the contact patch (tyre footprint) is governed by the vehicle's weight, the construction and tread of the tyre, and tyre pressure but not necessarily the tyre's dimensions. In layperson's terms, the contact patch/area is dictated by the air pressure in the tyre and the downward force caused by the weight of the vehicle itself.

Couple this with an already proven 4-cylinder, 2¼- (2,286cc-) litre liquid-cooled petrol engine, an efficient well designed terrain-specific tread, and remembering the old adage of 'low ratio, second gear, go anywhere' made for ease of use in the harshness of the desert terrain. Moving vehicles in the desert produce dust and distinctive tyre tracks; the slower the speed, the less dust is produced.

However, the need for speed must be balanced against the amount of dust, tracks, and sand clouds that may be produced; some sand areas will be covered by a surface crust caused by chemicals in the ground cementing sand particles together. In many cases, it was possible to drive on top of this crust and minimise the dust signature and the chance of bogging down. Interestingly, the best time to operate on sand is at night or early morning when the sand is damp, and traction is at its best.

Operating a manual gearbox fitted with low-pressure sand tyres demonstrated a high level of proficiency, almost a precise tactical interplay between SAS driver and machine. Balancing the operation of the accelerator, clutch, gearbox, and brakes takes focus and skill. It took practice, time, and complete mastery, especially when driving such a weight at speed – factor in the harsh desert conditions and all your soldiering skills, too.

At this juncture, it is essential to understand that the tyre's air holds up the weight of the vehicle and contents rather than the tyre itself. The rubber tyre merely holds the air in place by acting as a vessel for the pressurised air. If the air is doing the work of holding up the weight, then the air pressure dictates the characteristics of the interface between the tyre and sand – that was the idea anyway, and it didn't always work, hence carrying the all-important sand channels!

Sand tyres can easily be re-inflated once the harder ground is found, but it is perhaps interesting to note that the combination of heat and the continual grinding surface of the sand, coupled with lower tyre pressure, will mean that there is a dramatic reduction of tyre life. Tyres were often replaced as a matter of course upon return from operations or exercises, regardless of wear and tear. Of particular note regarding sand tyres, is that during the vehicle trials by the FVRDE on the vehicle training area in Bagshot in Surrey, the sand tyres were prone to punctures and were replaced with alternatives to allow the tests to continue.

Also of note is that the practice of driving at speed over sand dunes and the idea of lowering tyre pressures in a sand-rich environment were both techniques pioneered by Brigadier Ralph Bagnold, moreover, the author of the critically acclaimed landmark book *The Physics of Blown Sand and Desert Dunes* (1939). Indeed, period documentation would suggest that driving on sand tyres supplied by the FVRDE on the dunes ranging in height from 50 to 250 feet high was akin to skiing at 50 miles per hour!

Anyway, the sand tyres (9.00 – 15 tread) seen on Land-Rover Pink Panthers were manufactured by either Dunlop or Bridgestone, depending on where and when required. They were designed to suit the 6L x 15-inch, five-stud hole, well-base rims rather than the standard 16-inch Land-Rover type of well-base rims. Moreover, the tyres produced had to cope with the ever-changing heat and dust of a desert summer, periodic freezing, and thawing. In addition to, other climatic changes, such as flash floods, etc., constrain a vehicle's movement. Interestingly, the 15-inch rims used on the North American specification vehicles from 1968 onwards would correlate with Land-Rover Pink Panther production dates.

A well-base rim is a wheel with a central channel or recess into which one side of the tyre bead can drop; the other side can then be forced over the rim for fitting or removal. Land-Rover wheels with well-base rims are commonly used because they enable easy installation and removal of the tyre; the seats of the rim on which the tyre sits (rim flanges) have a 5° taper so that, as the tyre is inflated, the beads are forced up the taper to give a wedge fit and a good seal for tubeless tyres.

However, standard 'bar-grips' were used in other theatres of operation. Bar-grip tyres or 'NDT' (non-directional tyre or tread) in US military parlance, is an early tyre tread pattern developed for off-road use. Bar-grip tyres are characterised by a solid rubber circumferential centre strip, with large solid cleats alternately to either side, spanning the entire width of the tread.

Once 'spooned' on and pointing in the right direction on the road and scrubbed in, these bar-grip tyres provide good feedback and grip on various surfaces with predictable, stable turn-in. These bar-grip tyres are the ones that have a distinctive 'whirring' soundtrack when driven at speeds above 40 miles per hour. Indeed, when these tyres had some mileage on them, they were known as 'HiMilers', made even more noise and were known as 'Yowlers'.

Period documentation of the day suggests that discussions were being held at a commanding officers' convention that shed light on the ongoing trials for 'studded' tyres at FVRDE for the SAS Land-Rover. These trials assessed the tyres' effectiveness in winter conditions, and SAS personnel eagerly awaited the results. The documentation highlighted the significance of these trials and indicated that they could play a crucial role in enhancing the mobility of military operations during harsh winters.

Most of the known preserved SAS Pink Panther Land-Rovers are now 'shod' and drive with the standard 9.00 x R16 'bar-grip' tyres (as per the 101 Forward Control Land-Rover) fitted to a standard 5.5 x R16 Land-Rover steel rim; this was done for two reasons.

The first reason is that, from operational experience, the smaller tyres and rims were soon found to be unsuitable for the terrain they were operating in, and now, more recently, to satisfy (in-country) road legal requirements of the present day and the fact that most Pinkies are on display in a field or museum rather than on active duty in the desert!

However, when you do get to see a Pinkie shod with desert tyres, enjoy it; it is a credit to the owners and restorers that they have gone to the effort in not only changing the tyres at the show but also allowing the Pink Panther to be observed with the correct rubber attire fitted!

To give extra clearance for the larger tyres and to increase articulation of the leaf-springs when under adverse stress, such as traversing indentations in the rock and sand, coupled with deep fissures and sudden drops that could impede vehicle movement, the Marshall of Cambridge Land-Rovers were given a heavy-duty 'drop shackle' suspension. However, the body height rise from these more extended heavy-duty drop shackles also affected the front-steering angle and caused increased and uneven tyre wear, in addition to affecting the vehicle's steering stability at higher speeds.

Bend the SAS Pinkie through a series of demanding curved roads, and you will soon feel a tiny bit of pitch, roll, and occasional dive, don't worry, though; it's just your dance partner gently reminding you and sharing information about road and track conditions ahead while you keep driving! Photographic examples of the 'drop shackle' suspension can be seen in *Land Rover Owner International* magazine (August 1995), page 160; *Military Modelcraft International* magazine (September 1997), page 38; *Land Rover Enthusiast* (December 2002), page 81, (Project Pink Panther – renovation of 10 FG 88); *Military Machines International* dated 2006, page 46 and perhaps the best example, *Classic Military Vehicle* (January 2017), page 38.

Moreover, the 'drop shackle' suspension can also be seen in Ray Kirkpatrick's limited edition (250 copies) watercolour painting (2003) of an SAS Land-Rover. This artwork showcases the artist's exceptional attention to detail and unmatched observational skills. It has a history of selling quickly on online auction sites such as eBay. I recommend purchasing it if you come across it.

In addition to the extra clearance for the larger tyres provided by the 'drop shackle', the forward part of each rear wheel arch had been cut away at an angle to accommodate the larger section (sand) tyre. This fabrication anomaly is confirmed in the *SAS Land Rover (Desert Version) User Handbook*, section one, page 9, paragraph 5.

Punctures were a regular occurrence in the desert from camel shrub thorns – which look like six-inch nails as, at times, the only thing between the bottom of the Land-Rover and the desert floor when speeding along was a lonely prickly cactus – as a consequence, the need for a quick tyre change was essential. Fortunately, the majority of patrol vehicles would also carry a sixth (second spare) wheel on the bonnet of the vehicle as the space was available; preserved vehicles 10 FG 35, 10 FG 69 and 10 FG 84 are often seen with a second spare wheel mounted in this fashion and covered with a scrim net.

Indeed, in the areas of responsibility where the Regiment was deployed, protecting the spare wheel from the harsh elements was essential. Therefore, it was customary to cover the spare wheel with a scrim net to prevent premature ageing and cracking of the rubber (AKA crazing) caused by excessive heat and UV exposure, not necessarily for camouflage purposes. However, it was discovered that having the second covered spare wheel mounted on the bonnet made it challenging to access the engine bay quickly if needed.

Spare inner tubes (NSN 2610-99-825-8526), complete with TR150 valves, were kept by all vehicles. The TR150 valve issued was a tyre valve that was manufactured straight but could be bent by hand to the desired angle of inflation and was often taped over to avoid ingress of foreign matter into the valve cap and possibly creating a continuous air leak. As tyre pressures were important for this vehicle, each Land-Rover within a Patrol was issued with one tyre pressure gauge and two tyre levers.

Excellent published and colour examples of the scrim net placed over the sixth (second spare) wheel on preserved SAS Land-Rovers can be seen on the front covers of the British Army's magazine entitled *Soldier* (8 August 1988) (10 FG 69-Q33 CPE) and on the front cover of *Off Road and 4 Wheel Drive* magazine (March 1989) also 10 FG 69. Both these magazines have become sought after Pinkie memorabilia.

Indeed, frequent tyre punctures are mentioned in Geordie Doran's book (with Mike Morgan) *Fighting Legend of the SAS* (Sutton Publishing Limited 2007), where he goes on to say,

> and most nights, we had a puncture to mend. Our Rover was fitted with huge balloon tyres, which were OK on sand but because they had very little tread, were highly susceptible to penetration by camel scrub thorns and sharp rocks ...

While on exercise, it was good practice that one Pinkie would be designated as a 'spanner wagon' or just plain 'Q' (the Q standing for quartermaster) and would carry essential spares such as inner-tubes, coils, filters or starter motors as when they did break down, it would typically be in an isolated and remote part of the desert.

Interestingly, the preserved vehicle 10 FG 61 (chassis number 251-13989D) is often seen displaying a PTO-driven drum and cable winch fitted to its bodywork and with its spare wheel bolted to the bonnet. Power take-offs (PTOs), are mechanical gearboxes that attach to mounting faces provided on truck transmissions. They transmit power from the truck's engine to other auxiliary components, such as a winch in the SAS Pink Panther's case. However, the PTO winch displayed on photographs of the preserved vehicle 10 FG 61 seems to be a retrofit, as early (in-service) photos suggest it wasn't fitted while in service.

The spare wheel was fitted to a specially designed and angled 'spare wheel mount' (AKA spare wheel bracket) to the front of the vehicle. This 'wheel mount' allowed 360° access around the entire wheel rim to pull or reinsert a new inner tube. Moreover, it allowed the wheel to be out of contact with the sand for the change and provided a complete visual inspection of the tyre and rim. Of note, the spare wheel was clamped down with a quick-action spinner rather than the usual strapped or bolted methodology of securement.

Interestingly, a brief article on refurbishing the spare wheel bracket appears in the magazine *Land Rover Enthusiast* on their Project Pink Panther series. Dated October 2003, these and other similar articles provide insightful details about refurbishing the 'special to role' components used in the SAS Pink Panther and are a valuable resource for enthusiasts, modellers and professionals alike. Highly recommended. Indeed, it was later discovered that a slight improvement was noted in the radiator's cooling efficiency. Moreover, this mount could also be used as a solid base to change a tyre, an admin area or other running repairs when time allowed. Occasionally, it could also be used to push another vehicle.

Lastly, and particularly interesting to note, is that the Lockheed Hercules (C1-30) Tie-Down Scheme (serial number 132A, issue 2) has specific instructions relating to the spare wheel and the mounting bracket in that they should both be removed and stowed on the vehicle. Indeed, it is also noteworthy that the vehicle should be reversed up the aircraft ramp and into its required load station and that a copy of the Tie-Down Scheme be attached to the vehicle.

Moreover, the total weight limitations of the Tie-Down Scheme were listed as (both conditions) Rear Axle, 4,000 pounds and Front Axle, 2,500 pounds, giving a combined (AUW) weight of 6,500 pounds. AUW stands for all-up (operational) weight. Several great photos of the spare wheel mount are nicely shown in the following magazines, namely, *Military Machines International* April 2006 page 47 and *Classic Military Vehicle,* Issue 249 (February 2022), page 52.

Several excellent open-source colour photographic examples of sand tyres fitted to SAS Pink Panthers can be seen in the following books and magazines: *SAS Panthers in Detail,* page 60; *Land Rover Enthusiast* (June 2002) and *Military Machines International* (April 2006), page 50.

Shovels and Pickaxe – (Pioneer Equipment)

The SAS Land-Rover Pink Panther was equipped with two shovels and one pickaxe (AKA pick axe or pickhead); the Shovels (x 2), often described as a 'NATO service spade or shovel GS' – the GS standing for general service – were fastened to the driver's side front wheel arch and as per *Illustrated Spare Parts List for Body Used on Truck, Utility, SAS, ¾ Ton, 4 x 4, Rover II* plate number H1 and as per the layout in the *SAS Landrover (Desert Version) User Handbook* on page 6.

However, it is perhaps interesting to note that the original location first chosen for the Pickaxe was to be with the cammo net and placed across the Land-Rover's bonnet. Manufactured with a wooden shaft and a forged metal tip and topped with a T-shaped handle rather than a traditional garden 'D' shape. These shovels were often used to extricate vehicles trapped in the sand and are referred to along with the PSP and tow rope in the *SAS Landrover (Desert Version) User Handbook* as 'un-ditching equipment'.

The two shovels (NSN 5120-99-910-5934) are carried in a three-component stowage on top of the right-hand front mudguard. One stowage component is shaped to take the shovel shafts, the rear component is shaped to take the two shovel handles, and the third is a shaped rubber buffer under the shovel blades.

This buffer was to minimise the sound of metal on metal and to reduce damage to the bodywork and was a later modification as a result of trials by the FVRDE. And lastly, the shovels (both with a 28-inch handle) are secured in position by utilising a strap and buckle at the approximate centre of the shovel shafts.

Shovels GS were made by various manufacturers as military contracts were won and lost, so not all shovels on Pinkies will look the same during their active service. However, to the credit of preserved SAS Pink Panther owners and the Pink Panther Register, 'period' pickaxes and shovels are displayed where possible.

The Pickaxe (x 1) has a pointed end on one side of its head and a broad flat 'axe' blade opposite. It is noticeable by its gradual curve, characteristically spanning the length of the head. These two components can be separated for ease of transport. The shaft is tipped with an iron ferule to prevent the grain from splitting from the pick's impact on rocks or ice-hardened ground.

The pickaxe handle (AKA the 'pick helve'), has been used as a baton for riot control and camp patrol duty, and is typically made of ash or Hickory. Moreover, it must be precisely three feet (36 inches) in length, according to British Army tradition and regulation. This measurement was used in the field as it represents one yard or three feet, making it helpful in measuring trenches, shell scrapes or field targets.

Pickaxes could also be used for other purposes. Namely, rendering their vehicles useless by smashing the engines, radiators, etc., with them. Having smashed the engine, they would then be doused in petrol and set on fire.

The Pink Panther's pickaxe (NSN 5120-99-910-5473) and wooden handle (NSN 5120-99910-4746) were stowed on top of the SLR tapered steel stowage container which was located on the outside of the driver's side front wheel arch and as per *Illustrated Spare Parts List for Body Used on Truck, Utility, SAS, ¾ Ton, 4 x 4, Rover II* plate number H1.

Excellent photographic examples of the pickhead (pickaxe) digging chisel, can be seen in the following books/magazines the definitive *SAS Panthers in Detail; Military Modelcraft International* (September 1997); *Land Rover Enthusiast* in June 2002; *Military Machines International* (April 2006) and again in *Military Machines International* (July 2011).

Grenades

A grenade is an explosive weapon typically thrown by hand. It is used against enemy personnel or material at relatively short ranges. The grenade has been the staple of the infantryman's inventory ever since the invention of black powder. Grenades are designed for immediate use where artillery ammunition would be too slow, impractical, or dangerous to friendly troops.

Grenades were issued to the SAS Land-Rover and were stowed in specially designed containers (x 3) that were located on the outer parts (left and right) of the vehicle's dashboard structure and at the left-hand side of the vehicle adjacent to that of the rear gunner's position and were readily available should the need arise.

For safety during transit, the Grenade Boxes were lined with a thick (non-absorbent) rubber sheet (originally felt padding) and fitted with a push-on canvas cover, a cover similar to that of 1958 pattern webbing material and allowed for two grenades per compartment on either side of the dashboard.

A photographic example of the grenade stowage on either side of the dashboard can be seen on page 40 of the magazine *Off Road and 4 Wheel Drive* published in March 1989 and written by Roger Jones. Moreover, on page 48 of the April 2006 edition of the *Military Machines International* magazine, there is a great photograph of the grenades correctly stored in their metal (rubber rather than felt) lined stowage compartments

Additionally, I would advise looking at *SAS Panthers in Detail*; here, over many pages, one gets to see the grenade stowage compartments at various angles and against a backdrop of other specialised equipment. Lastly, in the June 2004 edition of *Land Rover Enthusiast*, an interesting article under the Project Pink Panther (Neil Mitchell and James Taylor) section covers the fabrication of grenade holders, rubber lining and placement of the side mirrors.

Bridging (Convoy) Plate

Ideally, all bridges in a military operational zone should be checked over by the Royal Engineers and the Royal Military Police and allocated a safe weight limit (per span) before vehicular access is permitted. The safe-working load (SWL) is written on a yellow disc and nailed to a post on either approach to the particular bridge.

In theory, military drivers of vehicles with bridging plates mounted on their vehicles should have their (gross) weight (rounded up to the nearest ton) written on their bridging plate. For example, 1, 2 or 3 and upwards, depending on the actual weight of the vehicle. The numbers represent the weight in tons of their respective vehicle. When they approach a bridge with a bridging plate on, for example, if the bridge had 1 on the plate and the vehicle approaching was a 2, then the driver should NOT proceed over if their vehicle is overweight.

Interestingly, the classification of bridges was also changed to take into account of the effects that particular vehicles would have on the bridge, and the load class number is based on vehicles travelling at average convoy speeds at a spacing of 100 feet.

Although carrying a Bridging Plate is not specific to the SAS Land-Rover, it was mandatory for all British military vehicles. However, in reality, only some units adhered to the ruling. While simple in idea, the actual classification is complicated by being based not only on gross vehicle weight but on whether the vehicle is wheeled or tracked, the number of axles, axle spacing, vehicle speed, the number of lanes the vehicle uses and whether or not the vehicle could be hauling a trailer.

The SAS Pink Panther's bridging plate is located (as you look at the front of the vehicle) on the navigator / observer / commander side of the vehicle above the smoke discharger units and is painted in the adjacent colour of the vehicle's bodywork.

Prior to 1977, the colour of the British Forces bridge plate was golden yellow (paint code BS 381C-356). In approximately 1980, infra-red reflective (IRR) paints were introduced. And their disruptive patterns of vehicles required the colour to be the same as the adjacent paintwork in most cases, that colour being olive drab (BS 381C-298), with disruptive matt black over the top.

There is much discussion and conjecture regarding the Bridging Plate on military vehicles. For example, what colour should it be? Should a number (weight) be written on it? How should the numbers be written? Is it made of the correct material? Many units in the British military never used – despite being fitted – the bridging plates, so regarding preserved vehicles of any military genre, I say it's up to the owner.

However, on SAS Pink Panther Land-Rovers, I would err on NOT painting the Bridging Plate, as I have personally never seen – in service – an SAS Land-Rover Pink Panther or any early or later DPVs with such markings. Other than 10 FG 80.

Indeed, preserved vehicle 10 FG 80 can often be seen in modern photographs displaying a golden yellow bridging plate. Indeed, in the official publication entitled 'Electrical and Mechanical Engineering Regulations' for the SAS Land-Rover, there are detailed (black and white) photographic views (x 2) showing 10 FG 35 with what appears to be a light-coloured (golden yellow) bridging plate. This repeat photograph of 10 FG 35 – in a three-quarter front view – also appears in the *SAS Landrover (Desert Version) User Handbook*.

Interestingly, 10 FG 89 can be seen sporting its bridging plate on page 80 in Pat Ware's book *Haynes Manual for Military Land Rovers* (2016), and with sand tyres. And again (same photo) in the excellent book by James Taylor and Geoff Fletcher entitled *British Military Land Rovers* (2015) on page 89, this early staged (repeat) photo – although in black and white – clearly shows a golden yellow bridging plate and without any numbers on!

Signal Pistol or Pistol Pyrotechnic

A standard British forces' No. 1 Mk. 5 Signal Pistol (NSN 1095-99-961-8490) was issued one per vehicle and was stowed suspended below the main instrumentation panel structure to the left of the engine clutch housing. The stowage consisted of a steel tube split in two longitudinally and lined with a thick rubber sheet, hinged along one edge and closed at the other edge by a toggle fastener.

For safety, the spare signal pistol cartridges stowage consisted of a steel box with a hinged lid secured by a toggle action catch. The stowage is located over the left-hand side of the clutch and gearbox cover below the dashboard structure.

The single-shot, break-action pistol was also commonly known as the 'Pistol Pyrotechnic, No. 1, Mk. 5' and the 1-inch (calibre) pistol signal remained standard issue with the British Army until the late 1980s and could still be found as part of the *CES* for the Sampson (FV106) Armoured Recovery Vehicle!

The No. 1 Mk. 5 Signal Pistol has a unique single-action movement and must therefore be cocked before each flare is discharged. It can be used to initiate an attack (rarely), help locate a lost member or patrol, assist in aerial or ground recognition of units, or various other signalling needs. Other markings indicated the cartridge type, the cartridges' lot number and, at the bottom, the manufacturer's name and dates of manufacture. Manufacturers of cartridges included Imperial Chemical Industries (ICI) and Imperial Metal Industries (IMI) – interestingly, both divisions of the same company in the 1960s. The base of the cartridge had a central percussion cap. Note also that No.1 Mk. 5 Signal Pistols were manufactured with a metal ring on the butt; this was done to allow a lanyard to be attached.

Interestingly, the signal pistol was no longer issued to SAS Land-Rovers by the mid to late 1970s and was no longer part of the *CES*. This is evidenced by handwritten entries in the *Complete Equipment Schedule (Service Edition)* (April 1978) on page 7, item 120. What it really means in terms of supply and demand by the elite RAOC and for the SAS Regimental Quartermaster's Department is that it would no longer be replaced/issued if that item had been lost, broken or removed. Of note is the pistol's distinctive and easily recognisable bell muzzle; this was cleverly designed to protect the operator's hands from burning powder grains upon firing/discharge of the signal pistol.

Flares (Signal) and Flare Box

The SAS Land-Rover truck was kitted out with various items that wouldn't be standard issue for a British Army Land-Rover of its day. A good example was the flares used with the No.1 Mk. 5 Signal Pistol. One of the dangers of travelling in the desert, whether in wartime or not, is being forced to ditch and possibly abandon a vehicle in a remote area. Indeed, once a vehicle breaks down, it is often hard to locate any survivors. Search teams need sharp eyes to spot figures/soldiers on the ground. To increase the chances of finding survivors, distress signals were packed and carried on board the SAS Land-Rover.

There are two types of flares: signalling and illumination. The signalling flare sends a distress signal or indicates a location for a rendezvous or possible supply drop. In contrast, illumination flares are used to light up an area at night to track enemy movements or to assist in search and rescue operations.

These two types of flares are easily distinguishable due to distinctive notches cut into the rim. These notches (serrations) indicate the flare type (usage) and the flare's colour. These centre-fire alloy cartridges, or on occasions, cardboard cartridges – depending on the available stock at the quartermasters – were often coded with a coloured band around each body and at the mouth of the cartridge, indicating the flare's (smoke) colour. For example, red, green, or white.

I have seen examples where the cartridge was both coloured and serrated. Where the serration has been seen, this was done to allow for correct identification at night by touch. This was particularly useful when firing in low light conditions, when it was difficult to see the colour code of the flare. The pistol could fire various cartridges to suit the different roles needed. Cartridges would have contained layers of chemicals to not only project the flare but also ignite it and make it burn as required.

The signal pistol cartridge stowage consisted of a steel box (with a hinged lid) located on the navigator/passenger side of the vehicle (below the dashboard structure) and to the right of the footwell and GPMG square-section telescopic tubular mount. The Flare Box, with circular rubberised inserts, contained nine such signal flares ready for immediate use should the need arise. Note also that there should be a toggle action catch for securing the lid.

In the September 2003 edition of the *Land Rover Enthusiast* magazine and under the 'Project Pink Panther' renovation progress report by Neil Mitchell and Barry Pocock, there is a short but interesting article by James Taylor on the stages in the fabrication of a replacement flare box that had to be specially commissioned and fabricated for 10 FG 88 (chassis number 251-13956D) as the original flare box was missing and presumed lost; perhaps removed because the No. 1 Mk. 5 Signal Pistol was no longer on the *CES* by the mid-1970s. Photographic examples of the flare box can be seen in *SAS Panthers in Detail*.

Machete or Machet

Each SAS Land-Rover Pink Panther truck was issued with a machete (NSN 5110-99-120-9242), and it was stowed behind the front seats in a specially designed carrier. A machete is a sharp, broad blade used as an agricultural tool similar to an axe or in combat, like a long-bladed knife. Also referred to (wrongly) as a Martindale No. 2 Golok in military circles. The *Golok* (an Indonesian word) was/is shorter and heavier than a traditional machete and tends not to get stuck in green wood as often as the longer issued machete.

Traditionally, each British military combat vehicle was issued with one machete, so the crew could clear an area in a wood to make an overnight camp and be used to chop bushes, and general shrub to camouflage the vehicle should the need arise.

Made from hot-rolled high-quality British Steel, the issued machete (AKA the metal tree beater!) had a unique cutting characteristic that was made for ease of use in the jungle when combined with the tool's weight. The 15-inch (381-millimetre) blade was an outstandingly sharp and well-balanced tool, but from experience, it needed to be oiled regularly to avoid rusting, etc., especially after leaving a humid environment.

The machete came with a simple heavy-duty, riveted canvas scabbard with hooks and belt loop making it compatible with 1958 pattern webbing. The scabbard constructed of webbing is better suited for hot and humid conditions than the leather scabbards used before – as those (leather) soaked up water and rotted quickly. Note also how the scabbard's throat is reinforced with metal to prevent the thin cotton from being damaged when the machete is inserted.

The double-riveted wood handle had a hole to facilitate the all-important lanyard attachment. The handle was often made from German beechwood, which should not split under normal circumstances because the timber is cross-sawn for maximum strength, durability, and stability. There are many examples held by the IWM in

10 FG 84 on Patrol, note the GPMG covered and road tyres.

10 FG 63 - The photo used for the TAMIYA 1/35 scale model.

Superb pen and wash illustrations by Louise Limb of three SAS Pink Panthers.

An incredibly rare Vehicle Record Book for 10 FG 49.

Equipment checking on a camouflaged SAS Land-Rover.

NATO camouflage paint on an SAS Land-Rover circa 1970s, note ERM obscured by netting.

10 FG 30 on Patrol, note the sand tyres and the weapons covered by hessian.

Willys Jeep 89 YH 96, note the RAF Goggles and Denison Smocks.

The Lady Be Good, a B-24D Liberator and early unit modified SAS Land-Rovers in the desert.

Willys Jeep 25 YH 69, note the No. 4 Lee-Enfield on the bonnet and the red and yellow flags.

Pink Panthers on parade - reminiscent of early WWII SAS Jeep photos.

Note the early wooden stock weapon and tripod for the Theodolite.

Early unit-modified SAS Pinkie, 49 EN 77. Note the shaped metal weapon holster.

Willys Jeep 66 BS 20 on parade for inspection, note Bridging Plate and large Radio to rear.

Note red fuel caps on the auxiliary fuel tanks and the Canary Yellow Bridging Plate on 10 FG 33.

Contemporary photo showing the Driver's view, equipment and vehicle controls.

Three Panthers, notably ERMs 10 FG 69, 10 FG 57 and a rare photo of a green 11 FG 00.

10 FG 61 with road tyres, note the different paint hues on the bodywork.

SAS Land-Rover showing standard 'bar-grips' tyres but missing other equipment.

10 FG 84 in use before disposal, note the camouflage netting strapped to the bonnet.

A selection of early SAS Land-Rovers, note the paint shine on the vehicle's bodywork.

10 FG 68 with sand tyres fitted and rare KERR towing equipment on spare wheel.

A rare photo of 10 FG 47, note the tentage stored over the Sand Channels.

A pink 11 FG 00 showing a canvas water vessel and netting draped over the bonnet.

Note Smoke Pots/ Dischargers, tentage and a rare spare seat on display.

Early Unit-Modified Land-Rovers, note sand tyres and ERM obscured.

A fully kitted out and Military Show prepared 10 FG 67, note the folding ERM mount.

A contemporary 10 FG 67 showing a KERR stored on top of the mounted spare wheel.

10 FG 31 and 10 FG 69 fitted with appropriate sand tyres (AKA Balloon Tyres).

10 FG 90 on the ramps, note water container bracket in the up position and sand tyres.

A nice side-elevation period photo showing SAS Pinkie fully equipped.

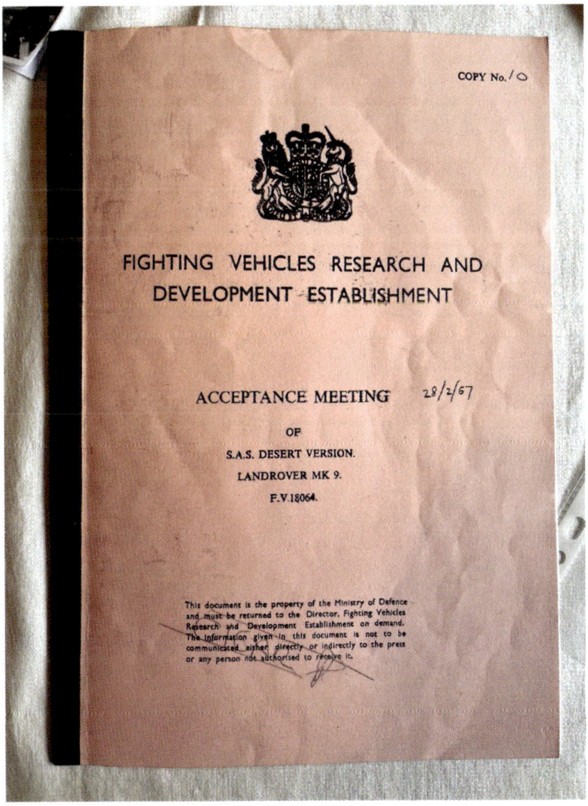

COPY No. 10

FIGHTING VEHICLES RESEARCH AND
DEVELOPMENT ESTABLISHMENT

ACCEPTANCE MEETING 28/2/67

OF

S.A.S. DESERT VERSION.

LANDROVER MK 9.

F.V.18064.

This document is the property of the Ministry of Defence and must be returned to the Director, Fighting Vehicles Research and Development Establishment on demand. The information given in this document is not to be communicated either directly or indirectly to the press or any person not authorised to receive it.

An Acceptance Meeting file for the SAS Desert Version LANDROVER - Note the spelling.

Contemporary photo showing the rear side of the SAS Land-Rover Pink Panther.

User Handbook, SAS Landrover (Desert Version) - Note spelling of LANDROVER.

their weapons and ammunition digitised collection, all with slightly different variations and styles manufactured.

Those readers interested in machetes or even a Kris would be well advised to read Martina Sprague's book *Machete, Kris and Throwing Iron* (2013). This book critically examines these weapons and the relationship between the soldier, his weapon, and the area of operation, including the tactics used in pre- and post-colonial warfare.

Photographs of the machete can be seen in *Land Rover Enthusiast* magazine (June 2002), on page 8 and page 49 of the April 2006 edition of *Military Machines International* magazine, where there is a scarce and great reference photograph of the machete correctly stowed in a metal scabbard. And lastly, in the July 2004 edition of *Land Rover Enthusiast*, an interesting article under the Project Pink Panther section covers the fabrication of a machete holder.

Depending on what radio was fitted, the location for the machete stowage varied from behind the rear gunner's seat to behind the commander's seat. When renovating a vintage Land-Rover such as an SAS Pink Panther, the bolt holes (fixing hole) can provide indications of previously installed equipment. These holes can often reveal vital clues about the types of equipment that were previously installed and can help you piece together the vehicle's past. By carefully inspecting these bolt holes and cross-referencing this important information with historical photographic records, you can better understand the SAS Land-Rover's unique special forces military story and the unique 'special to role' equipment issued.

Equipment Registration Mark – Vehicle Registration Plate

Under the contact numbers WV7293 and WV7318 to convert the standard Series IIA 109 Long Wheel Base right-hand drive Land-Rovers for desert duties and the vehicle data cards (DOS Form 419B), we know they were allocated registration numbers (ERMs) 10 FG 30 – 11 FG 01 respectively. As a contract background to this, in 1957, the MoD saw a dramatic change to the numbering system of vehicle registrations used by the British military for each class of vehicle.

In the official publication for the *Truck, General Service, SAS, ¾ Ton, 4 4, Rover II* entitled 'Electrical and Mechanical Engineering Regulations' and by command of the Defence Council (February 1970) for the SAS Land Rover. There are detailed (Black and White) portrait views (x 2) front and rear pictures showing 10 FG 35 clearing showing the rear ERM flipped down.

This was done because when the rear canvas carrier bag (NSN 2540-99-809-9030) was not loaded with essential equipment, the number plate could be flipped downwards towards the vehicle to allow for the pannier carrier board (AKA baseboard assembly pannier) to be secured to the rear of the vehicle should the need arise. This, in turn, would lessen the vehicle's visual profile and overall length.

There was also a discreet ERM light on the rear of the vehicle. It was fitted centrally on the rear edge of the pannier carrier board, illuminating the registration plate for normal driving conditions and road use. This particular piece of equipment can be seen in a close-up photograph of the July 2002 edition of James Taylor's article 'Pretty in Pink' where 10 FG 97's rear carrier board is in the folded down position, and the light can be observed. Another, perhaps less detailed example can also be seen in *Classic Military Vehicle* magazine (July 2002), on page 13. ERMs are covered later in another chapter.

Jerrycan – Fuel

Of the multiple jerrycans one sees on an SAS Land-Rover truck, some were cage-mounted inside the vehicle and used to supplement the two 40-gallon auxiliary fuel tanks. While others were stowed in the bespoke rear canvas carrier bag (NSN 2540-99-809-9030) alongside some spare/extra seating known as 'side seats'.

A jerrycan (AKA jerry can, jerrican or Jerrycan) is a robust liquid container manufactured from pressed steel or heavy-duty plastic. Interestingly, the term Jerrycan has grown to include a genre of cans differing in size, shape, and colour, but their essential function remains intact, that of carrying liquid. Several companies manufactured the pressed steel container, one example being Ambi-Budd Presswerk (ABP) based in Berlin.

ABP was a German auto-body manufacturing company specialising in pressed-steel technologies, notably BMW (Bayerische Motoren Werke AG) and Ford Motor Company bodies. When war seemed imminent, ABP switched operations to satisfy military needs, which included fabricating bodies for the now iconic and highly collectable Type 82 Kübelwagen ('Bucket-seat car') and its amphibious sibling, the Type 166 Schwimmwagen ('swimming or floating car').

Anyway, the Jerrycan was designed in metal and in Germany during the 1930s for military use to hold up to 20 litres (4.4 imperial gallon or 5.3 US gallon) of fuel. The development of the Jerrycan significantly improved on earlier British primitive designs, which required tools and funnels to facilitate ease of use, etc. These were often referred to as 'flimsy cans' and, due to their design and construction, often led to fuel wastage due to evaporation or leakage. This unwanted evaporation was caused by the fact that the lids were just pushed in rather than screwed – rather like a paint tin. Regular use would then result in leakage due to the lids not being secure.

Interestingly, the design of the 20-litre *Wehrmacht Kraftstoff Kanister* (AKA Jerrycan) incorporated a large air pocket above the fill line, enabling the can to float if immersed in water. Moreover, the design of the petrol can, with its three handles, allowed two people to carry a full can between them or pass one full along a line without changing grip.

Moreover, the clever design incorporated a centrally recessed weld that was protected by the two sides of the can. Additionally, a fitted gasket made the mouth leakproof, and an air-breathing tube from the spout to the air space kept the pouring smooth and consistent.

The British Army used cans captured from the Germans ('Jerries') - hence the name 'Jerrycans' – in preference to their own containers. After the second capture of Benghazi in the Mediterranean in 1941, large numbers of Axis jerricans were seized. This wartime requisition was sufficient to equip such units as the Long Range Desert Group, Popski's Private Army (PPA) and the recently formed 'L' Detachment, SAS Brigade.

Indeed, there is an excellent article entitled 'The Humble Jerrycan' on page 98 in Mike Morgan's book *Sting of the Scorpion: The Inside Story of the LRDG* (Sutton Publishing Limited, 2000) and is worth a read, as it discusses how vital the Jerrycan was/is to desert warfare. Moreover, in the magazine *Classic Military Vehicle,* Issue 266 (July 2023), there is a great article by Richard Pullen that focuses entirely on the Jerrycan. With excellent photographic examples and a concise history of the fuel container, this article is a joy to read and highly recommended.

Lastly, a superb book by Philippe Leger entitled *JERRYCAN: 70 Years and Still in Service* (Heimdal, 2008) is ALL about the Jerrycan. Surprisingly, given its ubiquity, very little quantity and quality has been written on the interesting subject of the Jerrycan over the years.

Regrettably, only a few articles published in military history or vehicle magazines have discussed the Jerrycan with any level of detail. This book is an invaluable resource for anyone interested in the history and development of this fascinating item.

Fortunately for collectors, this hardcover book by Philippe Leger relates the story of this ingenious container, bringing together documents and many colour photographs in one collection, all of which are particularly valuable to collectors of jerrycans. This is a book I highly recommend. Get the date correct on your Jerrycan, and the rest is easy when displaying your military vehicle; there is nothing worse than seeing a wrongly dated jerrycan on a vintage military vehicle.

Photographic examples of Jerrycans can be seen in *SAS Panthers in Detail*, and over many pages too! And lastly, *Special Operations Landies in Detail*.

Jerrycan – Water

The two black plastic or, on occasion, green colour water containers one sees fitted to the outside of the SAS Land-Rover – one on either side – contained water rather than fuel. Green containers (NSN 7240-99-120-7252) have been seen in period and in-service photographs and were often a result of in-theatre resupply.

Several preserved SAS Land-Rovers can be seen with their black water storage cans (NSN 7240-99-120-7251) with white markings painted on the container's fabricated and strengthened recessed design symbol in the middle of the can - the white paint is applied using a stencil or by hand. This white recognition marking was done to ease identification and prevent accidental contamination of the can's liquid contents by mixing different fuels or fuel with water.

Interestingly, water storage containers such as those seen on SAS Land-Rovers and the smaller 1958 pattern water bottles should not be shared; this was done to avoid contamination and for crew members not to fall ill due to contaminated water.

Indeed, I have seen black water jerricans with an additional white patch painted under the carrying handles, too. A legacy of post-Second World War jerrican markings; this was done again to ease identification when being observed at a standing height - some were also date marked and had the words 'WATER' on, too, to make sure.

However, the word 'WATER' should not be highlighted / picked out in white paint. Notably, preserved vehicles 10 FG 69 (chassis number 251-14093D) and 10 FG 80 (251-14121D) have been seen with correct identification markings on their respective water containers. Note that operational requirements deemed it necessary to have jerricans of water divided equally between vehicles, depending on how long the Patrol would be out.

The water jerrican (AKA can, water, military) has two filling caps on the top, a large one and a smaller one; both are secured with a chain to prevent loss. The larger cap allows the container to be quickly filled and allows a rapid pour if needed. The smaller one is better suited for pouring into smaller containers such as a personal 1958 pattern webbing water bottle. It also acts as an air inlet valve to allow for a smoother flow / pour. A large handle is fitted across the top of the can to enable hand carrying.

Moreover, like its counterpart, the fuel jerrycan, the sides of the container have expansion grooves moulded into them. Of interesting note is that the material used for manufacturing the water jerrycans is the same material used to manufacture the black P58 pattern webbing bottles – both of which have proven reliable and robust in their design and have stood the test of time.

Photographic examples of these white markings can be seen on page 41 of the magazine *Off Road and 4 Wheel Drive* (March 1989); *Land Rover Owner International* magazine (August 1995), pages 158 and 159, respectively, and in the *Land Rover Genuine Parts* catalogue (June 1989).

The SAS Land-Rover came equipped with foldable metal frames to the vehicle's side, which could securely hold the heavy water containers using quick-release clips. When not carrying the jerrycan of water, for reasons of not being required – perhaps they had been jettisoned – then these metal frames could easily be folded away.

The two foldable frames had NSN numbers 2540-99-809-0713 and 2540-99-809-0714. In *Wheels & Tracks* magazine, Issue 9, you can see an example of 10 FG 90 (251-13967D) on the outside service ramps with its metal frame folded up.

Moreover, the water storage container should be placed so that the screwable (larger) lid (with chain retainer) is uppermost to avoid accidental leakage should the lid become loose whilst the Land-Rover operates at speed.

Anyway, in the *Land Rover Monthly* magazine (January 2002), there is an excellent article by Bob Morrison entitled 'Behind the Lines' where one can clearly see several examples of correct water storage containers being used and displaying the white markings on two preserved SAS Land-Rovers.

When the water containers and tent (AKA lean-to crew shelter) were fitted, the working width of the vehicle was approximately 76 inches (193 centimetres). And then, in January 2010, the magazine *Military Machines International* published an article by James Taylor, where there is a pre-Marshall of Cambridge Land-Rover photograph outside what appears to be MT Sheds with its water container correctly marked.

This photograph is later repeated in his book (co-authored with Geoff Fletcher in 2015), a history of Leaf-sprung Land Rovers in British military service entitled *British Military Land Rovers* on page 89 and in an article – also by James Taylor – in the magazine *Classic Military Vehicle* (January 2017), this time on page 37.

Moreover, in the *Wheels & Tracks* magazine, Issue 9, this time on page 12, there is a great reference picture of the original General Service RHD Land Rover – modified by the FVRDE – with the ERM of 18 DM 93 and the prototype from which the standard FV18064 was derived from, that has the white markings correctly displayed on the water container.

There is an excellent short video on the internet sharing platform, YouTube by John Sear entitled 'Pink Panthers' that shows green water containers in theatre. This video nicely captures period photos of members of the SAS in the desert and with their Unit Modified SAS Pink Panthers (23 EL 59) and a Marshall of Cambridge version, 10 FG 30.

Chagall – Natural Fibre Water Carrier

Operating in an environment where sand and dust cake on your face and invades your sinuses and heat bakes and saps the very moisture from your body with utter relentlessness, water, and lots of it requires a specialised type of container. The chagal, chagul or chagil, is one such container used extensively by members of the SAS Regiment.

A chagul is an efficient jute or heavy-duty canvas water bladder constructed using a continuous stitched binding along its edge to hold it firmly together. When left to soak for a couple of days, the natural fibres will swell up and prevent the water from leaking. The principle behind it is that the water inside slowly evaporates through the sides of the chagul, which helps keep the drinking water cool.

In the right conditions, the chagul could retain 85 per cent of its contents over a twenty-four-hour period. It was good practice to secure the chagul to the sides of the Pinkie, where condensation caused by the passage of air over the surface kept the contents a lot cooler than the other water containers on the Land-Rover.

The chagul is an incredible and simple piece of equipment that has been used by Arabs in the deserts of North Africa for centuries. It is an ideal way of carrying extra water, as once it is empty; it weighs almost nothing and can be easily stowed until needed again on the Land-Rover.

The shape of the chagul is reminiscent of a goat's stomach, on which the shape was copied. Interestingly, I have seen many examples of (early) chaguls held by the IWM in their digitised equipment collection, all with slightly different variations and styles manufactured.

Moreover, I have seen many preserved SAS Pink Panther Land-Rovers and plastic model interpretations carrying such bags at military preservation vehicle shows, scale model exhibitions, and in numerous magazines. Examples are *Land Rover Owner* (August 1995); *Military Machines International*, September 2001; *Military Modelcraft International* (September 1997); *Classic Military Vehicle* (July 2002) and *Military Machines International* (April 2006), to name but a few and for a superb plastic scale model example, I highly recommend Paul Hargett's TAMIYA model of the SAS Pink Panther, which can be seen in Scale Military Modeller International magazine (March 2018).

Another example of a 'chagul' seen on an SAS Land-Rover is that by the well-known military artist Ray Kirkpatrick in his watercolour picture (2003) that features SAS Veteran of twenty-three years, the late Pete Scholey, sitting in his SAS Land-Rover Pink Panther. The jute water containers, both brimming with water, are evident to the viewer and nicely draped over the sand channels and to the driver's rear.

Canvas Bucket Mk. 5

For many years, the British Army has relied on the humble yet durable collapsible canvas bucket (NSN 7240-99-943-8717). This versatile tool is commonly used to carry water and is constructed with a sturdy hessian cloth and a reinforced fabric rim to maintain its shape. You can spot it on SAS Land-Rovers and armoured recovery and repair vehicles, where it serves primarily as a washing bowl. Despite its simplicity, this tentage store item is highly effective. When wet, the fabric fibres expand, creating a barrier that prevents water from seeping through.

The canvas bucket is an exceptional piece of equipment that boasts durability, lightweight design, and practicality. It outperforms metal buckets as it won't get dented or squashed and can be conveniently stored and transported due to its ability to be easily folded flat. The top handle of the canvas bucket (AKA 'Buckets, Water, Canvas, Mk. 5') was/is made of a piece of rope and is attached close to the top of the bucket by heavy stitching.

I have often seen the canvas bucket on preserved SAS Land-Rover Pink Panthers hanging to the vehicle's rear, this was routinely used to keep tools off the ground (especially sand) when working and conducting vital on-the-go vehicle repairs. Moreover, it was often used to hold the oil and grease containers. Of note, when folded and stored, it wouldn't split like a plastic washbowl. Excellent photographic examples of the canvas bucket can be seen in numerous open-source publications, but in particular, *SAS Panthers in Detail*.

Fire Extinguishers

The fire extinguishers (x 3) (NSN 4210-99-881-4724) that were fitted to the SAS Land-Rover were strategically placed for ease of use and located one on the right-hand side top of the dash-board structure, one on the left-hand forward end of the decking over the auxiliary fuel tank and the last one – making a total of three – located in the right-hand rear corner of the rear compartment. The hand-held, all-purpose

Bromochlorodifluoromethane (BCF) fire extinguishers issued were suitable for all types of fire and were secured using a metal bracket and toggle-action clips.

The reason for having three readily available fire extinguishers is due to the proximity of the radios to the fuel tanks. This is because there is a risk of ignition from the petrol fuel vapours when the radio is switched on. Of particular note regarding these fire extinguishers is that they are/were very good at chilling your beer after a demanding exercise in the desert; just remember to replace them at the QM's Department upon return!

Numerous photographs showing fire extinguishers (x 3) on preserved SAS Land-Rovers can be seen in *Land Rover Enthusiast* (June 2002) and *SAS Panthers in Detail*.

Medical Packs – First Aid Kits

Two medical packs (large and small) were provided on the SAS Land-Rover, the large one known as a FV medical pack and the smaller one known as a troop medical pack. The FV (metal tin) medical pack was secured in the footwell on the commander's/navigator's side of the vehicle against an angle piece at the bottom of the toe board strap, which passes through metal loops at the top and bottom of the toe board and a securing buckle.

The smaller troop medical pack was secured against the tubular supports of the rear gunner's seat by two half-straps connected by press fasteners. Photographic examples of medical packs on preserved SAS Land-Rovers can be seen in *Military Modelcraft International* (1997); *Land Rover Enthusiast* (March 2006); *Military Machines International* (April 2006) and lastly, with several examples *SAS Panthers in Detail*.

However, many period and preserved SAS Land-Rovers have additional Medical Packs on display; this is in the form of the British Army 1944 pattern haversack hanging over the bodywork of the Land-Rover. The shell dressing 1944 pattern haversack is/was a small webbing-based satchel issued to troops to carry shell dressings in the field. The satchel is of a simple design, with a pair of 'weather' flaps and a box-type top flap to protect the shell dressings from the elements.

The lid is secured with two web straps and a pair of brass 'twigg buckles'. The front of the haversack would typically have a large red Geneva Cross on a white circle to indicate that the contents are for medical use only.

The haversack can hold upwards of a dozen of the standard shell dressings, but more often than not; it was used for other essential medical-related equipment. Placing extra medical packs, such as the

British Army 1944 or, on occasions, 1958 pattern webbing pack or pouch outside the Land-Rover truck, can also be seen on scale models of SAS Land-Rovers.

Manila Rope

A length of Manila (sisal) rope (NSN 4020-99-942-5045) was issued and stored on a platform at the right-hand rear corner of the rear compartment of the Land-Rover. Issued one per vehicle and 20-feet in length, the Manila rope proved very durable, flexible, and resistant to saltwater damage, at least in the long term. The rope (AKA rope towing, hook and eye, 20 feet in length, complete) was often used to safely extract vehicles if the winch vehicle / chain was unavailable.

Should the Manila rope not be sufficient for vehicular extraction, a Tirfor winch was available and remained so until required. A Tirfor winch is a heavy-duty pulling machine used to lift and pull heavy loads. These Tifor winches can be used with unlimited lengths of wire rope, which is very useful when extracting a Pinkie from a deep wadi!

A preserved SAS Pink Panther 10 FG 61 (chassis number 251-13989D) has been (perhaps) retrofitted with a PTO Winch. However, this is not confirmed in period and in-theatre photographs of 10 FG 61 when it was previously NATO green in colour.

Interestingly, this notable SAS Land-Rover was subject to a YouTube restoration with Seb Morgan Restorations, *circa* 2021. Presented in a series of 67 Bitesize videos, these videos provide a detailed, up-close, and (very) personal view of the restoration of an SAS vehicle.

Of particular interest regarding the issuing of the Manila (sisal) rope and as a result of FVRDE trials, it was generally accepted that the tow rope was to be (revised and later stowed) in / on the front spare wheel. Indeed, this rope was later changed to the more robust 4-ton 'wire and chain' kinetic energy rope that could fit the front towing eyes with fitted shackles. There is an excellent photo of preserved SAS Pink Panther 10 FG 67 with a similar piece of equipment on page 55 of the magazine *Classic Military Vehicle*, Issue 249 (February 2022), on the front spare wheel too!

It is perhaps interesting to note that many preserved SAS Land-Rovers and scale models show the Manila (sisal) rope, either on the bonnet (perhaps to give the appearance of being recently used) or between the front tow lifting eyes (lifting and towing rings) of the Land-Rover.

And lastly, a KERR type was also listed as being stowed between the Land-Rover's tie-down eyes on the front bumper. A KERR rope is a kinetic energy recovery rope designed to allow British forces to provide fast and effective recovery of armoured vehicles through kinetic energy transfer from the towing vehicle to the trapped vehicle.

In short, it allowed quick and easy deployment for rapid recovery without needing specialist vehicles. Photographs of preserved vehicles 10 FG 34, 10 FG 57, 10 FG 84 and 10 FG 94 showing this method can be seen in various publications, namely *Land Rover Enthusiast* (November 2000); *Land Rover Enthusiast* magazine (June 2002); *Classic Military Vehicle* (July 2002); *Military Machines International* (April 2006) and lastly, *SAS Panthers in Detail.*

Moreover, another example of rope storage can be seen in the *Land Rover Genuine Parts* catalogue (June 1989), where the rope is neatly curled up on the front-mounted spare wheel as per FVRDE trials! Nice.

Camouflage Net

Camouflage, cover and concealment demand creativity, resourcefulness, intelligence, and a bit of luck. The selection of the right ground position is critical at every level. A key principle of camouflage in any environment involves quickly blending in with the natural ground and vegetation without disrupting the terrain's visibility.

To this end, a camouflage (Desert GS, 24 x 24 inches) net was issued and stored over the engine bonnet/hood and secured to the rear top surface of the bonnet by two straps and buckles. The net was designed to bolster the survivability of SAS personnel and protect; moreover, conceal personnel and equipment from observation by enemy forces by using terrain-specific colouration. This was done by draping the net(s) over the vehicle and simulating the colour palette and shadow patterns by matching the camouflage netting colour with the spectrum of the surroundings that were commonly found in the particular theatre and region the SAS were operating in.

Constructed of a lightweight, breathable material, it provided excellent concealment. Moreover, it was designed to break up the shape, shine, outline, and shadow of equipment instantly and allow undetected movement underneath by casting patterned shadows that broke up the characteristic visual signature of the Land-Rover – the cammo net was (and still is) a vital piece of equipment in any soldier's inventory.

In addition to the camouflage, disguise and concealment requirements of the net, the cammo net was also used to provide shade while in the searing heat of the desert sun. When deploying the camouflage net effectively, it would mean that when draped over the vehicle, it could give the impression of an outlying rock formation from an aerial observation, when perhaps in an lying up position (LUP) and concealed from enemy ground and aerial observation.

There are many published photographic examples of camouflage nets on preserved SAS Land-Rovers, perhaps the best being *Wheels & Track*, Issue 9 – 'SAS Land Rovers: The SAS Pink Panther and Its Predecessors' and in particular, the back page, where we see preserved SAS Land-Rover 10 FG 31 in full glorious colour. Moreover, further photographic examples can be seen in *SAS Panthers in Detail.*

Binoculars

Binoculars have been an integral part of military operations for decades. They are used for various reasons, including surveillance, combat, reconnaissance, hunting and training. Therefore, the essential features and characteristics desired of the issued binoculars were durability, robustness and performance in the required conditions in which the regiment were operating.

The skilful use of these binoculars – where visual superiority was mission-critical – allowed for greater target acquisition, identification, and real-time on-the-ground assessment. Stowage for the binoculars was located on the right-hand top surface of the vehicle's dashboard structure. The high-precision binoculars issued at the time to the SAS Regiment would have been previously field- tested, fitted with the best glass, coatings, and housings found in any binocular of the late 1960s and allowed for SAS soldiers and their positions to remain hidden and challenging, longer-range targets, to be zeroed in.

The stowage consisted of a fabricated vertical standing L-shaped strip steel bracket with two spring clips near the top to grip the attachment on the binocular case. Photographic examples of binoculars on SAS Land-Rovers can be seen in *Wheels & Track*, Issue 9, 'SAS Land Rovers, The SAS Pink Panther and Its Predecessors', *Land Rover Enthusiast* (June 2002); *Military Machines International* (April 2006) and lastly, *SAS Panthers in Detail.*

Rear Pannier

To the rear of the SAS Land-Rover truck is a distinctive (and perhaps synonymous) bespoke canvas bag (NSN 2540-99-809-9030). Which, when used, would provide for more space and be used predominantly for the storage of, amongst other items, the following: an extra bivouac (x 1), cushion(s), seat vehicular (x 2) or Jerrycans (x 8). The canvas bag, when in use, was mounted on the rear pannier board. Which, in turn, was supported by a hinged platform at the bottom and by straps to the top of the rear body panel, and the pannier cover is secured by straps.

When deployed and used in the horizontal position, this hinged platform (AKA baseboard assembly pannier or rear pannier board) was supported by two steel struts underneath and a chain at either end. When not used, the hinged platform could be easily folded up and secured by hooking up the nearest chain links over the bolts on the rear mounting board and securing it with wing nuts. The pannier board also acted as a method to which the rear ERM was attached.

The ERM was affixed to a metal mounting plate that came complete with a discreet, centrally mounted number plate light and fixings to secure the actual ERM to the rear pannier board. It is worth noting that this metal mounting plate (NSN 2590-99-810-1692) for the vehicle registration number could be folded down flat when not used. For example, this was done when the rear pannier board was folded up against the rear of the Land-Rover to reduce profile or when the pannier bag was not fully loaded with Jerrycans or water containers.

Excellent and official photographs of not only the rear panner board but also the ERM (10 FG 35) affixed to a metal mounting plate can be seen in the official publications of the *User Handbook (Desert Version) for the SAS Land-Rover* (August 1969) on page 7 and the *Technical Handbook for the Truck, General Service, SAS, ¾ Ton, 4 x 4, Rover II* (February 1970) on page 4 and lastly, Pat Ware's book entitled *Special Forces Vehicles 1940 to the Present Day* (Pen & Sword Books, 2012) on page 62. An in-service and rare 'period' photo of 10 FG 63 with the rear pannier board down can also be seen in the magazine entitled *Military Modelling* (December 1972 and January 1973) by Colonel John Stubbs.

Moreover, photographic references of preserved SAS Land-Rovers and in particular, the rear pannier board, canvas bag, and folded down ERM can be seen in publications of the magazine *Off Road and 4 Wheel Drive* (March 1989) on page 39; *Classic Military Vehicle* (July 2002) (10 FG 35, 10 FG 80 and 10 FG 97); *Land Rover Owner International* (August 1995) (10 FG 69); *Military Modelcraft International* (September 1997) (10 FG 69); Military Machines International (April 2006) (10 FG 97); *SAS Panthers in Detail* and lastly, *Special Operations Landies in Detail*, which features 10 FG 34 and 10 FG 97.

Radios

Communication is critical in any environment, not least on deployment, and radio networks are/were vital in facilitating essential command and control. The Regiment maintained this through voice transmission to enable communication and situational awareness at all echelons and across all phases of the deployment. Therefore, interested parties felt it necessary to have a comprehensive range of radio solutions for the newly appointed Marshall of Cambridge Land-Rover truck to maintain an effective communication loop.

This essential, modern platform requirement was met using three supplied radios to each vehicle, namely the Larkspur Type A123 Radio (AKA the Mk. 123), an A43 Type Radio, and the third set, an A41 Radio. Larkspur equipment remained long in production and it is perhaps interesting to note that in the year the Larkspur program was launched (1962), a horse named Larkspur – an Irish Thoroughbred and sire – ran in the Derby at Epsom and promptly won. This fortuitous win by Neville Sellwood, the jockey, was considered by many as an early sign of a successful introduction of military station radio to a post-war modern British Army. SAS Pink Panthers did not need the fitted for radio (FFR) 24-volt electrical system generally found on British Army Land-Rovers to run these smaller radio installations. The type A41, with its waxed card Crompton Parkinson (dry) battery (and spare NSN 6135-99-901-2229), was designed to be a portable 'Manpack' so it could be removed from the vehicle when needed.

Larkspur was the name officially applied to the tactical radio sets issued to the British Army sets and eventually – by common usage – wrongly applied to virtually any radio equipment used by the British Army. Constructed in robust hermetically sealed light-alloy enclosures – a measure that was essential to ensure durability and reliability when operating in tropical or high-temperature climates – and fitted with Plessey type (Mk. IV) connectors. The Type A43 Larkspur Station Radio was a manpack/ground to air VHF/UHF (240/300 megahertz) combined with a 6-pre-set crystal controlled channels set which was used to communicate with aircraft (ground to air) but could also be used for ground-to-ground communications.

Moreover, it could be used as a beacon for local friendly aircraft assets. However, this depended on the aircraft's altitude and distance, varying from 4 to 100 miles. Maintenance of the A43 Station Radio was relatively simple, as the principal Larkspur sets were modular in design. Moreover, they were sized to fit a standardised range of vehicle mountings.

Storage for the Type A43 (battery) operated radio was provided by an open box fibreglass mounting fitted to the centre of the forward face of the rear compartment forward bulkhead. The radio is then secured in the box (NSN 2540-99-809-0722) by means of a strap with an adjustable buckle and toggle fastener. Another open box – also fibreglass – mounting is also provided for the battery charger and is located immediately under the Type A43 radio mounting and is secured by a strap, an adjustable buckle and toggle fastener.

The power supply for the battery charger is taken from the vehicle's primary electrical system using a five-pin socket mounted on the rear compartment forward bulkhead. Of particular note is that the Type A43 metal case was connected to the positive supply when connected to the charger, so it had to be safely isolated from the vehicle – which was negatively earthed – hence the fibreglass cases already described. On a point of safety, whenever filling up the Pinkie, switch off all the radios! The Type A123 (AKA the Mk. 123) radio set was perhaps the most important, as it was a high-frequency radio capable of Morse code transmissions and offered a broad portfolio of frequencies that could survive through the often disadvantaged line of sight.

Storage for the Type A123 radio is provided by means of two studs and nuts located on the hinged decking over the left-hand auxiliary fuel tank. Mounting holes are also provided for the aerial at the outside edge of the decking immediately to the rear of the radio set itself. Again, the power supply is taken directly from the vehicle's primary electrical system via a four-pin socket on the forward face of the rear compartment bulkhead adjacent to the battery socket.

Extended operation of the Type A123 radio, when using the vehicle battery while the Land-Rover was stationary, would often drain said battery; it was therefore advised to 'run' the engine to recharge the main battery of the Land-Rover. Moreover, it was also advisable to charge radio batteries while the Land-Rover was at speed/travelling due to the drain involved in charging batteries. Due to the extremes of temperature experienced in the desert, Larkspur batteries would often suffer in the cold of the night, especially if not fully charged before dusk and the cold setting in.

It is perhaps interesting to note that at the Royal Signals Museum in Blandford Forum, Dorset, and particularly in their *History of Signalling in 100 Objects*, the Land-Rover SAS Pink Panther is listed as number 66 out of 100. As part of the build up to the Royal Corps of Signals centenary in 2020, the museum worked with the corps to identify 100 objects which have formed part of the history of signalling in general and the corps in particular.

With a history and information sheet available for visitors to the museum. SAS Land-Rover 10 FG 59 (on loan from the National Army Museum) is on display because it carried, at the time, state-of-the-art radio communications systems, namely the Type A123 Radio, an A43 Type Radio and the third set, an A41 Radio.

In addition to the Station Radios previously described (A41, A43 and A123) being fitted, there is an excellent example of an SAS Pink Panther on the historic military vehicle circuit with later equipment

Clansman PRC-351 and PRC-353 (24 volt) radios having been fitted, namely preserved SAS Land-Rovers 10 FG 34 and 10 FG 51. Clansman was/is the name of a combat net radio system (CNR) used by the British Army from *circa* 1976 to the early 2000s when the Bowman communication system replaced it.

Here, one can see the Land-Rover body wings being fitted with the now scarce equipment-extensions (AKA radio trays). A TU-AAM wing box is also fitted on the Driver's side and a base frame, with the later Clansman PRC Station Radio on the left side. VRC stands for vehicle radio communications, and TU-AAM stands for tuning unit, automatic antenna matching.

Anyway, these changes to Clansman were a vital adoption for compatible communications with interested outside parties. These external retrofit bodywork changes resulted in the Theodolite Tripod being located at the top of the bonnet and in front of the cammo net. Moreover, the NATO Service Spades or Shovels GS, being relocated to fit on the driver's side TU-AAM equipment-extension.

In short, the Clansman combat radio system that was developed by the Signals Research and Development Establishment represented a considerable advance over the existing Larkspur radio system and proved to be far more flexible and reliable in addition to being far lighter in weight; a crucial factor when the vehicle was already grossly overweight and laden with mission-critical gear.

To accommodate these retrofits, the Theodolite's Tripod would have been mounted across the bonnet rather than on the vehicle's wheel arch; photographic evidence on a preserved SAS Land-Rover can be seen in the book *SAS Panthers in Detail,* pages 15, 25 and 26. Indeed, an excellent example of an SAS Pink Panther fitted with the later Clansman radios, in particular, the 320 HF, 351 VHF and 344 UHF sets, is preserved SAS Pinkie 10 FG 51 (chassis number 251-13990D).

Interestingly, these later fitments of specialised equipment would highlight the differences in terrain-specific pink camouflage, as these would have been painted with a different mix of paint and several years later. Of particular note concerning these communication improvements and plastic, model making is that TrueScale Miniatures in their accurate interpretation of the SAS Land-Rover (Model No. TSM 144327), is that they too have shown the differing communications set-up but, sadly no Equipment Registration Mark.

Examples of communications systems on preserved SAS Land-Rovers can be seen in *Wheels & Track,* Issue 9 'SAS Land Rovers'; the magazine *Off Road and 4 Wheel Drive* (March 1989) on page 41 (10 FG 69); *Land Rover Owner International* (August 1995) (10 FG 69); *Military*

Modelcraft International (September 1997) (10 FG 69); *Land Rover Enthusiast* (November 2000) (10 FG 97); *Land Rover Enthusiast* (June 2002) (10 FG 94); *Military Machines International* (April 2006) (10 FG 34 and 10 FG 97) and *Military Machines International* (July 2011) (10 FG 57). And lastly, several examples are shown with regard to the VRC-351 and VRC-353, the ever-reliable *SAS Panthers in Detail*, in particular on pages 15, 25, 26, and 50 showing preserved SAS Land-Rover, 10 FG 34 in all its glory.

Finally, I highly recommend visiting the Royal Signals Corps Museum based at Blandford Camp, Blandford Forum in Dorset, England, where one can see both Larkspur and Clansman radios in all their glory. Indeed, 10 FG 59 is also on display!

With regards to equipment-extensions for fitment of the TU-AAM wing box, there is a period and in-service photograph of 10 FG 90 on the ramps on page 13 of *Wheels & Track*, Issue 9. Moreover, an unidentified SAS Land-Rover Pink Panther (perhaps on Exercise or Operations) can be seen on page 91 of Military *Machines International* magazine – the Archives Xtra section (July 2011).

An excellent colour photograph of 10 FG 34 can be seen on page 29 of *Land Rover Enthusiast* (November 2000) and with a further appearance on page 10 of *Classic Military Vehicle* (July 2002). Moreover, on the back cover of *SAS Panthers in Detail* and at high speed, 10 FG 34 can be seen at a military vehicle show with its TU-AAM wing box and extended antenna on full display. And lastly, in *Classic Military Vehicle*, Issue 249 (February 2022), the reader can see on page 54, preserved SAS Land-Rover, 10 FG 51 with vehicle equipment-extensions nicely fitted; a great reference point for scale modellers, should you wish to make an alternative and updated TAMIYA or Kit Form Services version SAS Land-Rover.

Seating

Various seating options were available on the SAS Land-Rover Pink Panther. The driver's seat is standard and fitted in the same manner as that of the basic Land-Rover truck of the time and was equipped with a (safety) seatbelt (NSN 2540-99-809-0708) known as a 'belt, automatic safety'. Once you've posted yourself through the missing door slot, the commander's seat comes standard, complete with a seat belt. However, in this instance, it is bolted to the hinged top of a toolbox, which places it in a slightly elevated position compared to the driver's seat. Sitting in the commander's Seat gives you the sensation of being perched on the Land-Rover's chassis rather than inside the vehicle or truck. This setup provides optimal observation and easy access to the GPMG, making it a crucial feature.

This is particularly evident when observing the vehicle at any angle. This raised position gave better visibility and enabled a firm grip on the GPMG at high speed. A functional grab handle / rail was provided on the left for the commander. It was essential when traversing at speed on the dunes. The toolbox provided a variety of essential maintenance tools and equipment to keep the vehicle moving and was hinged at the forward face and secured by a toggle fastener at the rear.

The seats of the commander, driver and rear gunner were upholstered with a synthetic leather material known as Rexine. This material was commonly used in the motor industry, bookbinding, and upholstery business. It was made of cloth coated with a mixture of cellulose nitrate, camphor oil, pigment, and alcohol, which was then embossed to give the impression of leather. Interestingly, cellulose nitrate is a low-explosive substance also used as the fuel in firearms rounds.

The rear gunner's seat consisted of a narrow centre seat squab and backrest. Which in turn was fitted to a supporting frame, mounted on sliding runners with a spring-loaded notched lever locking handle. The runners were mounted on a frame with tubular legs, securely bolted to the Land-Rover floor to the rear of the auxiliary fuel tanks. Interestingly, the seat back frame is hinged, thus allowing the seat frame to be folded down over the seat.

Further seating arrangements were available, and these were a single upholstered item that fitted neatly to the lid of a stowage compartment, which was located behind each rear wheel-arch. The 'cushion, seat vehicular' as they were known in the *CES* and with a NSN of 2540-99-809-9025, came in pairs and, when not in use, were stored alongside the Jerrycans in the canvas carrier bag on the rear carrier board. The seats were sponge / foam-filled on a wooden (boarded) base, came with lashing points, and would rest on top of a Jerrycan laid flat with the cushion.

I have seen several in-service (1980s) examples and preserved SAS Land-Rover Pink Panthers at classic military vehicle shows, where the spare seat cushions (x 2) have been casually draped over the side of the vehicle to give the appearance of recent use, which is a nice touch. This practice of hanging seats over the bodywork has also been replicated in plastic model interpretations. It is a really nice finish to the final diorama and adds extra realism.

There are many photographic examples available that showcase the seating arrangements of the SAS Land-Rover Pink Panther. In several pictures, the Rexine appears to be painted and showing signs of wear and tear over the years. This 'weathering' effect has been replicated in various scale models I have encountered. Some excellent examples of these models are Glen Bowen's TAMIYA SAS Pink Panther in *Model Military International* (June 2006); Paul Cawte's *SAS Land-Rover in AIRFIX Model World* magazine (November 2015); and Kev Smith's SAS Land-Rover in TAMIYA *Model Magazine International* (March 2021).

Published photographic references of seating arrangements on preserved SAS Pink Panthers include the following: *SAS Land Rovers, Wheels & Track,* Issue 9; *SAS Panthers in Detail; Military Machines International* (April 2006), pages 45 and 49; *Military Modelcraft International* (September 1997), pages 37 and 38 and finally, *Military Machines International* (July 2011), page 85.

Lastly, an interesting article by James Taylor and Neil Mitchell on the fabrication and fitting of seating can be found on pages 125 and 126 of *Land Rover Enthusiast* (June 2004) interesting Project Pink Panther series.

Cooking Equipment

Cooking equipment was provided using a small square cooker fitted with a single burner. It was the British Army's standard No. 2 Mk. 2 portable cooker (NSN 7330-99-125-1802). The cooker issued to SAS Land-Rovers was a pressurised petrol-fuelled portable stove for cooking rations (or locally sourced food) in the field and had its own windbreak as part of the case. Maintenance tools were attached to the side of the windbreak, and a fuel funnel was supplied for filling.

When time permitted or what 'Routine' you were operating on. A tasty hot meal consisting of a large all-in stew (all-in lob) could quickly and easily be prepared in a single large lower pot (NSN 7330-99-125-1804). A smaller, delicious (fresh rations permitting) fried breakfast (full monty or egg banjo) could be made on the top lid (NSN 7330-99-122-2771) or used to place (twenty-four-hour) ration pack tins/cans in boiling water to heat them through, etc. Just remember to puncture or dent the tin; otherwise, it resembles a multi-directional Claymore and, to the uninitiated to the noise, making a contact report!

It's worth noting that two of the tins included in the '24 Hour Ration GS' were highly popular among soldiers. One was processed cheese (AKA cheese possessed) and the other was the 5-ounce bacon grill, which tasted like a tub of candle wax without the opportunity of chewing on the wick! When the ration assassin made the 'all-in lob', the golden rule was not to ask what was in the stew and just scoff as quickly as you could using your wooden 'racing spoon'.

From the mid-1970s, the basic ration pack was the '24 Hour Ration GS' or just plain compo rations to the soldier (Tom) in the field. This ration pack (AKA the brown box of death) contained enough calories to sustain a soldier in the field for one day and was available – according to the menu sheet, DOS Form 494, Revised 1975 – in four different selection (A–D) menus, known colloquially as the 'four blessed menus'.

Interestingly, a four-man ration pack and a ten-man ration pack were also available. The four-man pack was for use in armoured fighting vehicles and was designed for crew feeding with four rations in one box. From memory, there were slight variations in components, no pudding, but an extra savoury pouch and extra beverages. In addition to the delicious food supplied, there was also the useful feature on the '24 Hour Ration GS' box, of a target and range card printed on the side.

Aside from the main meals, there were snacks and ingredients to make a warm '*Frappé Mystique a la* Hereford' (AKA cofftea – an exquisite beverage resembling neither tea nor coffee). There's nothing better than having an international cofftea roast out of a 1944 pattern mug from which you have recently shaved from!

Additionally, there was a flavoured powder cold drink (AKA screech powder, as it removed the enamel from your teeth or on occasions, it was called agent orange or jungle juice). Also included were chewing gum, toilet paper (AKA cumfy bum!), biscuits fruit AB that resembled dead flies in the shape and texture of a paving slab (AKA the combat Garibaldi), a book of matches that more often than not didn't work, water purification tablets that made the water taste like a council swimming pool, the obligatory Mars Bar with an unusual white patina, a detailed menu sheet, cooking instructions (AKA the Poisoner's Handbook), and a handy can opener. Of interest with regard to compo rations, if you ever wanted to know what the letters AB stood for on the biscuits AB in the ration pack, it stood for alternative bread.

The ubiquitous can opener was a small folding 'stamped' metal tin opener issued in a small greaseproof envelope. Interestingly, these tin openers were based on the Second World War P-38 tin opener that was issued with canned United States military rations from its introduction in 1942 and consisted of two hinged pieces of metal and a hole at the end.

These little can openers could arguably be viewed as the first multi-tool issued to soldiers and were hugely popular, as they served as both can openers, beer bottle openers, and improvised screwdrivers and could be used as a knife to cut things like paracord (parachute cord, AKA 550 cord). In addition, the small punched hole at the end allowed the can opener to be carried on a dog tag (ID) chain or later key ring back at camp. Or if you wanted to be really Gucci, attached to your wooden racing spoon.

The contents of the '24 Hour Ration GS' varied depending on what menu had been issued. In theory, each soldier was supposed to be issued a different menu for each day, but in reality, would generally get issued one menu for the duration of the field training exercise (FTX) or Operation. Additionally, seasoned SAS troopers often took extra rations or flavourings as space dictated, Tabasco sauce and curry powder being two such examples. There are numerous period and in-service photographs of SAS Land-Rovers with food hampers on top of vital equipment in the Pinkie.

Moving back to the portable cooker and away from compo rations and tin openers, these two stainless steel metal containers were collectively known as a 'dixie', which comes from the Hindi word 'degchi', meaning a small pot. Interestingly, the (military) slang term 'dixie bashing' comes from the British Army, where a soldier would be required to clean the cooking pots after a meal had been served and was often used as a (minor) punishment for soldiers on an infringement of duties and that didn't warrant being recorded on their company conduct sheets (AFB 121).

As the portable cooker was petrol fed, care had to be exercised when using these cookers as the leather gaskets often dried out if not used regularly. Petrol would leak from the pressure pump and often without warning, ignite, burn your eyebrows off and cause what was colloquially known as 'the slop-jockey's flame thrower' and is quite spectacular to observe – the German (Wehrmacht) word *'Flamenwerfer'* springing to mind!

Whoever was the duty 'cabbage mechanic' (cook) and despite a heat shield being fitted, the fuel tank would get uncomfortably hot when used. This would perhaps more realistically explain why three (x 3) readily available fire extinguishers were issued and fitted to the Land-Rover and needed replacing from the quartermaster's stores upon return to Hereford rather than the risk of ignition from fuel vapours from the main tank, should the radio be switched on!

Stowage for the cooker (fuel funnel and accompanying tools, etc.). Moreover, 'dixie' equipment was provided and readily available to the left-hand rear corner of the rear compartment (as per the layout in the *SAS Landrover (Desert Version) User Handbook* on page 13). And consisted of a tray to which equipment was secured employing a strap with a toggle fastener.

An excellent and scarce photographic example of the 'Dixie' cooking set in position on the Land-Rover appears in the Land Rover Enthusiast magazine, June 2002, on page 9. Where we see preserved SAS Pink Panther, 10 FG 94 (chassis number 251-14087D) fully kitted out and with the all-important and scarce 'period' leather holding strap and carrying handle for the two pans visible. Nice.

Once cooked, one of the longest serving items of equipment in the British Army is then used – the humble rectangular 'nesting' mess tin – in regular service use since 1944! Having 'nesting' mess tins allows the two containers to be placed together, taking up less room in a soldier's rucksack and thus offering some protection to whatever foodstuff might be stored inside them. Each mess tin has an aluminium alloy handle, which folds out to make a safe grip for the tin – the metal used is a poor conductor of heat, so even if the main container gets hot, the thin wire handle remains cool to the touch.

These wire handles are secured to the body of the mess tin by an aluminium plate and four rivets. Having fine dined on menu B, the mess tins were cleaned by a bit of grass and damp soil, then rinsed off with rainwater from a Mozzy-infected, three-week-old puddle. Nice!

Interestingly, while serving in the BAOR and the Green Army, I distinctly remember mess tins were often 'banged' together while running hither and thither, shouting 'GAS GAS GAS'. Fortunately, after the all-clear was given, the late Wolfgang (Meier), 'The Bratty Man' (AKA the unknown legend of the Cold War and the man who knew the Soltau-Lüneburg Training Area better than any map), would surprisingly turn up in his blue Mercedes van – making better progress than the Chieftain tank that had just trundled past – and start selling wondrous food items made from a dead horse and bag of old potatoes. Wúnderbar! I'm sure that Wolfgang was the chief instructor at the School of BATCO, because he knew where we were before we even did!

Tentage – Lean-To Crew Shelter

Throughout history, armies have relied on tents for shelter and admin. Indeed, the Roman Legion's smallest unit, a Contubernium, consisted of soldiers who shared one tent. Military tents must be robust, mobile, and adaptable to various situations, similar to those encountered by the SAS. In addition, the fabric used in constructing tents should be waterproof, breathable and flame-retardant, making them suitable for extreme weather conditions.

Each SAS Land-Rover Pink Panther was fitted with an SAS purpose-designed bespoke lean-to crew shelter (AKA shelter, portable) and was cleverly designed to give shelter at night, act as a windbreak and provide protection from the scorching midday sun for SAS crews. These shelters were also designed to blend in with the surroundings as they were dyed by the SAS before tasking, making them an essential camouflage tool that broke up the vehicle's shape, shine, shadow silhouette and movement.

The bespoke lean-to-crew shelter was lightweight and manufactured by 39 Command Workshops REME, based in Bridgend, Wales. It didn't require cumbersome tent pegs or a multitude of poles when deployed, like its close relative, the Cover, Tank and Bivouac, whose design was quite similar and used in military applications to assist in the repair of armoured vehicles and provided shelter to tank or vehicle crew members while working or at rest.

However, the SAS lean-to-crew shelter had several unique features that distinguished it from other (similar) shelters, including its lightweight design, easy deployment, and durable construction. For example, the Lean-to Shelter could easily be raised to a height of 6 feet and lowered without the need to remove it from the Land-Rover's bodywork. Additionally, it could be enlarged by easy attachment to another crew's lean-to when on deployment. Ingenious.

Of note, it was secured to the top of the cargo compartment wall on the Land-Rover using turn button fasteners. While in transit or an operational emergency, it could quickly be rolled up and secured by supplied webbing straps, known as 'Strap Securing for Shelter Portable for Truck GS ¾ ton 4 x 4 Rover 9 SAS Modified' on the official RAOC/ REME Workshop Indent Form, the G1045 dated 22 January 1968.

With possibly only twenty-seven portable shelters (Desert Modified) originally produced for the SAS Regiment and at a cost per unit of £5 (material £3 and labour £2) there is believed to be only one original lean-to SAS crew shelter known to be in existence, and that is with 10 FG 57. Discovered at an auction house in Hereford by the original owner and restorer of 10 FG 57 Alan Bucknell, and at a price of just £8 in the early 1990s, this is truly a rare piece of SAS Pink Panther memorabilia.

However, thanks to British Army bureaucracy and the workload at 39 Command Workshops REME, the shelter was not made available until several years later. Pattern-style replicas of the SAS Land-Rover shelter are available at cost but SAS Pink Panther Register enthusiasts have been known to fabricate these specialised Lean-to Shelters using existing military canvas tents to recreate the exact panel structure and look. Incorporating aged tentage definitely lends an impressive level of patina and credibility to a showcased SAS Pink Panther, 10 FG 67 being one such excellent example. Open-source photographic examples of the Lean-to (SAS desert modified) Shelter attached to the Land-Rover, can be seen in a variety of magazines and books, namely, *Classic Military Vehicle* (July 2002); *SAS Panthers in Detail*; and lastly, *Military Machines International* (April 2006 and July 2011).

Further Equipment

In addition to the equipment previously listed, other items of importance were also carried on the truck. For example, TACBEs (search and rescue beacon equipment), silk maps, complete sets (x 3) of personalised 1958 pattern webbing, rucksacks (x 3), water bottles, rocket launchers (1966 LAW), M16 Armalite Rifle, torches and survival knives.

An excellent and further reference point for extra equipment used and stowed aboard the SAS Land-Rover can be seen in the *Complete Equipment Schedule (Service Edition)* (April 1969) (British Army code number 34178). The (now scarce) *CES* is designed as an aid to the identification of components, parts or assemblies of parts of the equipment and to provide information necessary for demanding spares associated with the SAS Land-Rover.

Search and Rescue Beacon (SARBE)

The TACBE – TAC(tical) BE(acon) – (with antenna) was a search and rescue beacon (SARBE) unit that was issued to aircrews (yellow) and special forces operators (green) and operated on a two-channel radio frequency. One is a distress frequency, and the other is the line-of-sight frequency for contacting the inbound helicopter or rescue party in preparation for extraction. On the unit's primary channel, you would pull a pin, and it would become a beacon that transmits a pulse that can be DF'ed (direction found).

A photographic example of a TACBE (SARBE) with preserved SAS Pink Panther (10 FG 97) can be seen in the magazine *Combat & Survival*, Volume 1, Issue 9 (December 1989), on page 53. It is perhaps interesting to note that in documentation seen by the author, the Mk. III SARBE, manufactured by Burndept Electronics Limited, Erith, in Kent, was field tested and proved so accurate that no line corrections were required from the ground party involved in the tests. Indeed, the Mk. III SARBE was picked up by the aircraft (an RAF Handley Page HP.67 Hastings) at a distance of 40 miles, and voice communication was established at approximately 8–10 miles.

Silk Escape Map

In addition to the standard maps and charts issued for the area where the SAS Regiment was operating, silk (double-sided) 'escape and evasion maps' were also provided as standard issue. They were printed to help SAS soldiers evade capture and escape to neutral territory and could be used in conjunction with the SARBE unit.

Often measuring 41 x 30.5 inches (104 x 77.5 centimetres), these maps needed to meet a number of operational requirements. As such, the maps (AKA fabric charts) issued were lightweight, legible and informative while simultaneously being compact enough to carry around and covering a sufficient operational area. Silk (or its equivalent) was the perfect fabric for these maps because it is lightweight, can be folded up really small and doesn't rustle when you come to use it. In addition, the fabric (silk/rayon blend) maps could endure the most arduous SAS conditions and would not disintegrate if immersed in water.

Fabric Charts (maps), at a scale of 1:100,000, were often marked as 'RESTRICTED' and 'FOR OFFICIAL USE ONLY' in red writing. These were issued to aircrews, pathfinders, and special forces and were sealed to prevent fraying. Interestingly, later versions of these maps included printed information on edible plants and cooking instructions in the area of operation.

1958-Pattern Webbing

The 1958-pattern webbing (webbing in Latin meaning weighs three times as much when wet!) set was the mainstay of the British Army throughout the Cold War. The equipment was introduced to meet the requirements for an improved pattern of carrying equipment for use in temperate and tropical climates, such as a jungle: the '*Ulu*'.

It is perhaps worth noting that members of the British Army were likely introduced to the 1958 pattern webbing through an article, 'A New Look for the Infantry', published in the British Army magazine *Soldier*, Volume 13, Issue 10 (December 1957).

The feature showcased an infantryman from the Royal Inniskilling Fusiliers (1881–1968), outfitted in the latest battle gear during training at the School of Infantry in Warminster. The magazine feature described the improvements made from the previous pattern, such as a larger pack and wider shoulder straps for better weight distribution, in addition to quick-release straps that were added to enable the user to adjust or even jettison the pack in a matter of seconds.

The equipment was designed to enable the fighting soldier in the field to carry ammunition, rations, personal clothing and necessities. The 1958 pattern (AKA patt. The 1958 WE, the WE standing for web equipment) items were made of a rot-proofed, pre-shrunk and water-repellent lightweight material and were dyed to British standard camouflage colour No. 15. Although allegedly water-repellent, in numerous independent tests conducted throughout usage with the

HM Armed Forces, results indicated that 1958 pattern webbing would absorb almost four to five times more water than the nylon equivalent and on occasions prone to freezing as a result of the amount of water content and altitude the user was operating in.

Interestingly, the Mk.1 set of 1958 pattern, which was introduced in 1959, was so successful that it remained in production for more than thirty years. Indeed, it is still in use today with the Army Cadet Force. However, over time, many components were updated, and the design was improved to enhance operational and user experience. An example being the third issue of pouches had belt hooks that were angled, making it possible to mount the pouches at the side. This late modification feature made it more comfortable for soldiers to sit in armoured personnel carrying vehicles like the FV103 Spartan, FV603 Saracen and Land-Rovers.

The metal fittings were principally manufactured of light alloy with a dull protective finish which should not be removed. Quick-release fittings were used wherever possible to give quick access to the contents of the pouches, etc. Of note is that early to mid-pattern webbing had a problem; it could not easily be decontaminated under nuclear biological chemical (NBC) conditions. Unlike the Butyl-Nylon Bergan, which could be easily scrubbed down to remove chemical and radiological particles.

The 1958 pattern webbing and, on occasions, suitably tailored 1944 pattern webbing one often sees draped over in-service and preserved SAS Pink Panther Land-Rovers consists of the following components: 1958-pattern belt, ammunition pouches (left and right), pouches, rear (a pair forming one item, known as 'kidney pouches'), straps utility (two) and yoke.

The webbing gear was attached using a combination of traditional wire 'c' hooks and straps with metal hooks and loops that secured each piece to the belt or yoke. Interestingly, the famous 1958 pattern water bottle (canteen) and its carrier were not initially included in the set (1959) and had to be retrospectively added. In fact, not until the early 1960s was this seen.

The 1958-pattern bottle (holding two pints of liquid) was initially produced from toughened green nylon (plastic) and was the first mass-issued plastic water bottle (canteen) in service with British Armed Forces. Although the bottles were green, the cups that fit over the top half were always produced in black. The green bottles (and black cups) were later superseded with all-black versions from the mid-1960s onwards. Consequently, green version water bottles (NSN 8465-99-973-6665) are now quite rare.

Using a nylon (plastic) cup prevented the user from burning their lips when drinking (cofftea) hot liquids. However, it meant soldiers couldn't use the cup to melt snow for tea. The solution to rectify this problem was simple: use the older pattern (1944 metal cup) and swap them over and heat directly! Then, just put some black insulation/ carpet tape (AKA black nasty, jungle tape or bodge tape) around the cup where your lips contact the metal and vigorously clean with sand or a green pad to get the soot off the base caused by the foldable Hexamine Cooker! Simples.

The metal handles on the water bottle's (canteen) mug are securely attached with riveted plates and interlock, providing stability when holding it. If you look closer at the 1958 pattern water bottle's carrier, you'll find a small pocket sewn into the underside of the carrier's canvas lid. This pocket is designed to hold the twenty-four-hour ration pack water purifying tabs. It's a clever feature that you may not have noticed before. However, one major criticism of the water bottle carrier is that it can shrink when wet, making it difficult to extract the bottle and locate the eyelet over the early pattern turn-button fastener.

Examples of customised webbing items designed by the Regiment for specialised equipment related to the 1958 pattern (AKA patt. The 1958 WE – 1958 web equipment) include a survival and emergency gear pouch, Armalite magazine pouches, and an altimeter pouch (could also carry a compass) designed in the mid to late 1960s, all of which were extensively used in the following decade by the Regiment and in-service with the SAS Pink Panther Land-Rover. Those 'kit anoraks' amongst us who would like to learn more about 1958 pattern webbing, I recommend checking out Simon Howlett's book *Modern British Webbing Equipment* (published in softcover in 2009). It's full of helpful information and quality illustrations. This book from the Europa Militaria Series (No. 35) covers the evolution of British webbing equipment, from the 1958-pattern gear to modern modular designs.

For example, the personal load-carrying equipment (PLCE). This authoritative and informative publication is ideal for reenactors, SAS Land-Rover custodians, and scale model makers.

The National Army Museum, Royal Hospital Road, in London, has a nice example of 1958 pattern webbing in their (Study Collection) archives with an accession number of NAM. 1983-04-2-10. Interestingly fitted with a 1944-pattern water bottle and first aid shell dressing. Photographic examples of 1958-pattern and 1944-pattern webbing on preserved SAS Land-Rovers can be seen in a variety of open sources, namely *SAS Panthers in Detail, Land Rover Owner* (August 1995) and *Military Machines International* (July 2011).

Map Cases

The SAS and other military strategists rely on maps to identify enemy positions, plan operations, and manage logistics. Accurate directions regarding time and location are crucial for successful missions. Maps display the terrain, including mountains, valleys, and plains, as well as waterways and artificial features like trails, roads (MSRs), towns, boundaries and buildings. Moreover, military campaigns, operations, and exercises require maps for effective planning. However, maps are delicate and need protection from damage. To ensure their safety, map cases are used to store and safeguard them, along with the instruments used on them. Additionally, map cases provide a weatherproof way of viewing maps.

The SAS Regiment used various sizes of map cases, depending on personal preference and the task at hand. Infantry versions were available, while larger ones were used for artillery spotting and survey gathering. Although map cases have a generic look, they need to be durable, easy to use, and able to hold extra equipment like chinographs and pencils.

Most map cases were foldable, portable, and had neck or shoulder slings made of cord or leather. Once opened using the metal fasteners, the map was visible through a celluloid or Perspex panel. This allowed for annotations with a chinograph pencil without damaging the paper copy of the map underneath. However, the early celluloid could melt if it came into contact with mosquito cream, which is common in jungle environments. Therefore, a warning label was visible, cautioning users to keep insect repellent away from the plastic.

According to the *SAS Landrover (Desert Version) User Handbook,* a navigation bag was supplied and fitted to the front surface of the rear compartment forward bulkhead behind the front left-hand seat. Indeed, I have noticed that many preserved SAS Pink Panthers and scale SAS Land-Rover models feature map cases to make them look more authentic. For instance, the July 2011 issue of Military Machines International has a photo on page 88 that shows an original map holder on preserved SAS Pink Panther 10 FG 57. Nice.

If you want to explore various types of map cases, I suggest visiting both the IWM's and National Army Museums' online collections. Both are highly recommended.

Bergan – GS Rucksack

These rucksacks were developed in Norway before the Second World War, and variations of them were used by all sides in the conflict but mainly immortalised in the film *Heroes of Telemark* by the Norwegian

Resistance. Of particular note, the use of the Bergan is often associated with the SAS and commandos, who extensively used them due to the pack's large size, capacity and comfort.

Interestingly, the rucksack is named after its inventor, Ole F. Bergan (1876–1956), who invented the metal-framed carrying system in 1908 (Patent No. 20547, dated 1909). The Norwegian army later adopted the use of Bergans from 1913 onwards.

The Bergan, now known as Pattern '42 (P42) Bergan Rucksack, was built around a metal frame that allowed the weight transfer between shoulders and hips, improving the soldier's comfort and agility. The Bergan has a large canvas body with a flap that buckles over the top; there are two pockets on either side and a longer, thinner one across the front, all secured with webbing straps and metal buckles.

Of particular note is that the design of the P42 allowed for different amounts of equipment externally to be carried. This was quite ahead of its time in terms of design, etc. The metal frame cleverly holds the main pack rigid and allows it to be worn high on the back, allowing the shoulders to carry greater weight. The frame's structure also curves around slightly at the front to stabilise the load.

The second rucksack one often sees on SAS Land-Rovers is the GS rucksack. Like the canvas one previously described, it had a metal frame (heavy) and was designed to sit above the kidney pouches of the 1958 pattern webbing set. However, the GS rucksack was made of green butyl nylon – the same material as the S6 Respirator haversack (Mk. 2 and Mk. 2A) – and had a larger capacity than the Norwegian version previously described, similar in design and with a central drawstring. The larger version is often called the SAS Bergan, merely by association rather than issued nomenclature. This particular rucksack was very robust – it had to be to withstand countless parachute insertions.

Photographic examples of 1944 pattern rucksacks and GS Bergan's being draped over SAS Land-Rover Pink Panthers can be seen on SAS Pink Panther (10 FG 97) – over the rear pannier, in the magazine *Combat & Survival*, Volume 1, Issue 9 (December 1989), on page 53 and *SAS Panthers in Detail*.

Weapons

Several other weapons were carried on the SAS Land-Rover, each bringing a distinct skill set. Namely, the Lee-Enfield No. 4 Mk. 1 sniper rifle, chambered for the 7.62 x 51 millimetres NATO round, designated L42A1, the Springfield Armory (Armoury), M79 Grenade Launcher and the M16 Rifle. And lastly, the Browning 9 millimetre (L9A1) HP.

Lee-Enfield Sniper Rifle – L42A1*(T)

The Lee-Enfield sniper rifle (NSN 1005-99-963-3786) was/is a bolt-action sniper rifle chambered for the 7.62 x 51 millimetres NATO cartridge rather than the traditional .303 cartridge. Indeed, the Lee-Enfield rifle went through a bewildering number of updates during its operational service life, partly due to its designer's tinkering with the design and partially to fix problems that were becoming apparent as the rifle saw more widespread operational use over the years.

The British government approved the L42 Lee-Enfield in August 1970 after undergoing various modifications by the Royal Small Arms Factory in Enfield. These changes, among others, included improved internal rifling, a free-floating barrel assembly and enhanced optics support.

When loaded with its ten-round squared profile detachable box magazine, the L42A1, as it was designated, proved both accurate and reliable, especially when fitted with a telescopic (L1A1) sight (NSN 1240-99-963-2063), and then became known as No. 4 Mk. 1*(T).

The Lee-Enfield L42A1*(T) was designed with an easily changed rifle butt. It came in four sizes, bantam, short, normal and long, so the SAS sniper rifle could be tailored to fit them to aid in accuracy. The bolt operation is smooth, the case ejection positive, and the brass is ejected down and very close to the rifle to aid in collecting empty cases when leaving a final firing position. The L42A1 was the last model in a long line of bolt-action rifles that used a rear-locking action designed by James Paris Lee for the British Army. Finding a boxed (transit chest/case) and 'matching numbers' Lee-Enfield L42A1*(T) is a collector's dream.

Interestingly, there is a book written by Peter Laidler (with Ian Skennerton) about the Lee-Enfield (T) Sniper Rifle. What I particularly like about this book is that it is written from an armourer's perspective. The book is now quite rare and is entitled '.303 No.4 (T) Sniper Rifle'. Of note is an interesting chapter devoted to the L42A1 (7.62-millimetre) model, the very weapon the SAS would have used with SAS Land-Rover Pink Panthers.

Should you wish to go a stage further in your knowledge of the Lee-Enfield Sniper Rifle, Peter Laidler has also written a book on the telescopic sight fitted to the rifle. Entitled *An Inside View of the Snipers Rifle Telescope*, this book is a must for collectors wanting to quench their thirst for Lee-Enfield sniper rifles.

M79 Grenade Launcher

The M79 grenade launcher (AKA the thumper, blooper or egg launcher) is a single-shot, shoulder-fired, break-action (rifled) grenade launcher that fires a 40 x 46-millimetre grenade resembling a huge bullet.

Reliable, easy to use and lethally effective, the M79 can fire various 40 millimetre rounds, including explosive, smoke, buckshot (grain metal pellets) and illumination cartridges.

All of which breached the range gap between the hand grenade and the light mortar. However, its single-shot nature was a severe drawback. Reloading after every shot meant a slow rate of fire and an inability to keep up a constant volume of fire during a firefight – an average rate of fire being six to eight rounds per minute dependent on the user's skill. The upside of the M79 was that you didn't have to expose your body to throw it – a mini mortar.

The M79 grenade launcher resembles a large-bore, break-action, stubby, sawn-off shotgun. However, it is simple in design and use, consisting of fore-end assembly, receiver group, with a short 14-inch barrel sight assembly, stock and lastly, sling swivels. The stock, usually made of wood but also manufactured in fibreglass, is attached to the rear of the stubby butt, that ended with a rubber recoil pad that absorbed some of the weapon's recoil. The front sight is a fixed blade, and the rear sight on the M79 is a folding ladder-style leaf sight. When folded, the leaf sight acts as a fixed sight at close range.

The M79 grenade launcher is renowned for its unique design, tailored to meet the exacting demands of firing at a high angle and precisely delivering grenades to targeted areas. Additionally, the swivel-mounted trigger housing allows users to easily access the single-action trigger, even while wearing gloves.

An excellent example of an M79 Grenade Launcher can be seen online in the IWM, Lambeth, London, weapons and ammunition category with a catalogue number of IWM FIR 9260, where it goes on to say, 'The M79 was heavily used in the Vietnam War and several hundred were purchased by Britain – largely for special forces use'.

Readers interested in the M79 Grenade Launcher would be advised to read Gordon Rottman's seminal book, *US Grenade Launchers*. With full-colour artwork, published in 2017 by Osprey and running to eighty pages, this book on the M79 provides you with all the necessary knowledge.

To view pictures of the M79 grenade launcher utilised by the SAS Regiment, refer to Colonel B.M. Niven's book, *Special Men, Special War: Portraits of the SAS and the Dhofar* (1990). This publication, released in hardback and later paperback, features superb photography and is an excellent resource. You'll also find some photographs of early Pinkies too!

Browning 9 Millimetre (L9A1) HP

The L9A1 Centrefire self-loading pistol was the designation for the British military version of the post-1962 Hi-Power Browning

9 millimetre, and period SAS Brownings were stamped with the inscription 'PISTOL AUTOMATIC 9MM L9A1/FN 1967' on the left side of the slide. For information, it is a single-action, semi-automatic pistol fed by a thirteen-round magazine. Interestingly, almost twice as many rounds as its contemporaries, the Luger (eight rounds) and Colt M1911 (seven to eight rounds). This increased load capacity offered more immediate firepower.

Thanks to this innovative staggered stack magazine design, thirteen rounds could be held without making the pistol grip too large or uncomfortable to hold. With an effective range of approximately 50 metres, this weapon was favoured by all specialised units.

The L9A1 was upgraded with the more ergonomic Mk. 2 ambidextrous safety and grips, moreover a handy lanyard ring. Indeed, I distinctly remember back in the day that Pachmayr grips to reduce recoil and improve control were often later fitted by the Regiment's REME Armourers. Of particular note, the Browning Hi-Power remains one of the most influential pistols in the history of small arms, and despite it being replaced in the British military by the 9-millimetres (Gen. 4) Glock 17 in 2013, it remains in service throughout the world even today.

Should you wish to expand your knowledge of the L9A1 (Mk2), may I suggest reading the book *The Browning High Power Automatic Pistol Book* by R. Blake Stevens. The first edition was published in 1984 and has since been reprinted over the years; a limited-edition book (2014) is available that covers all the necessary information required, a trifle expensive but well worth the investment. Readers interested in the Browning HP may like to visit the Leeds Royal Armouries, particularly their 'study collection' with an object number PR.9273. Also, the IWM in London has a Browning HP in its collection, with a catalogue number of FIR 10812. Both are worth viewing.

M16 Rifle

The SAS Pink Panther also carried the AR15/M16 rifle, officially known as the Rifle, Calibre 5.56 millimetres, M16. The M16, also referred to as the Black Rifle, was an automatic rifle that used a 5.56 x 45-millimetre calibre and had a twenty-round magazine. It could operate in either semi-automatic or fully automatic modes of fire. While the rifle initially used twenty-round magazines, thirty-round ones were later introduced, and the stock was plastic (polymer) to reduce weight.

The M16 is a well-balanced and accurate rifle that is lightweight and easy to handle, especially compared to the heavier SLR. Although it lacked the power and range of the 7.62-millimetre rifle, it was more controllable. The magazine release button was conveniently placed, making magazine changes quick and effortless, and the rifle's conventional layout meant that any stoppages were immediately noticeable and rectified.

The AR-15/M16 was designed to have only three major sub-assemblies, which makes cleaning and maintenance much easier. However, the M16 was falsely advertised as a 'self-cleaning weapon', despite requiring frequent cleaning due to jungle grime, desert grit and increased fouling from new ammunition.

It's interesting to note that the term 'AR' actually comes from the name of the gun's original manufacturer, ArmaLite, Inc. The letters stand for ArmaLite Rifle and not 'assault rifle' or 'automatic rifle'. It's worth mentioning that the name/term 'Armalite Rifle' has evolved into an umbrella term for this type of semi-automatic weapon.

Interestingly, in the book *With the SAS and other Animals* by Andrew Higgins (Pen & Sword Books, 2011) – a book about the author's life as a veterinary officer while on secondment to the SAS in 1974 – he mentions not only using the M-16 Armalite at the ranges but also the Browning 9 millimetre and driving in the (painted for sand camouflage) Pink Panther!

If you're searching for photographic references of the M16 in active service with the SAS, you can locate them in *Who Dares Wins* by Tony Geraghty (1980) and *This Is the SAS: A Pictorial History of the Special Air Service Regiment* (1982). The IWM in London also has an exceptional photographic display of an early AR15/M16 rifle in its collection, referencing/catalogue number IWM/FIR 6328. An ideal source for model makers or SAS military vehicle reenactors.

Moreover, to expand your knowledge of the 'M16-Black Rifle', you may want to read the *Vickers Guide AR-15*, Volume 1, Second Edition (2020). This extensive 648-page book covers the origins of the AR-15, including early ArmaLite and Colt prototypes, as well as the M16A2 and lesser-known advanced combat rifle trial prototypes.

Rocket, 66 millimetre, HEAT, L1A2B1 – Light Anti-Tank Weapon (LAW) – (AKA M72)

The shoulder-fired LAW 66, L1A2B1, was/is a portable, lightweight, unguided 66mm short-range anti-tank weapon designed to engage and penetrate tanks and other fighting vehicles. This was a one-shot disposable rocket launcher system and came in a simple fibreglass tube with controls on the top and instructions (pictogram style) to the body of the launcher. When the inner tube is extended and the trigger armed, the sights automatically extend, and the shoulder-stop drops down; the launcher is then placed on the shoulder, and the electric trigger is pressed. As a result, the olive drab '66 rocket launcher can neutralise bunkers, buildings and other fixed positions with devastating consequences. Note that sights are little used during point-blank bunker-clearing attacks.

When needed, the rubber button on the top of the weapon is depressed to fire. Then, the launcher fires a 66-millimetre HEAT (high explosive anti-tank) rocket – keep clear of the rear when firing said weapon, as there is a substantial back blast. In a combat situation, after firing, it was required that it be destroyed to prevent an enemy from collapsing the tubes to make it look like a discarded and unfired weapon; then filling it with explosives and shrapnel and leaving it as a booby trap for the unwary.

I have often seen L1A2B1 examples at military shows, correctly displayed with its muzzle cover and carry strap. Both rare and nice! The National Army Museum, Royal Hospital Road, in London, has an excellent example of a '66 Rocket Launcher (*circa* 1971) in their (Study Collection) archives with an Accession Number of NAM. 1979-07-126-1. As does the IWM, Lambeth, London, with catalogue number IWM FIR 9467 in its online weapons and ammunition category.

Right Angle Torch

The standard British Army torch – a torch that had been waking up the wrong Oppo, in the wrong Basha, at the wrong time – was an almost direct copy of the excellent US Army TL-122 (1937–1944) flashlight (torch) series. The main body of the torch is made of a heavy-duty olive drab green plastic, with a handy metal belt clip riveted to the rear of the torch that could easily be clipped to uniform or part of a vehicle or radio and was therefore suitably robust for military use.

In the angled head of the torch, the main reflector magnified the light from an incandescent bulb. The torch used two 'D' type cell batteries and came with coloured filters (red and green) for signalling. Just remember that whilst using a red filter is excellent for maintaining your night vision, when map reading, it degrades the visibility of the contour lines on the map. The manufacturer's details – General Electric Company (GEC) and Linpac of England being two such companies that manufactured them – were embossed and located on the end cap.

A superb example of a right-angle torch can be seen in the National Army Museum's digitised collection, with the accession number of NAM. 1995-07-27-1, complete with a green filter. Photographic examples of right-angled torches on preserved SAS Pink Panthers can be seen in *SAS Panthers in Detail* and the March 1989 edition of *Off Road and 4 Wheel Drive* magazine; *Military Machines International* (July 2011) and lastly, *Classic Military Vehicle* magazine (January 2022) showing different coloured lenses.

Clothing

Various clothing can be seen in period and in-service photographs of the SAS Regiment, which is often nicely replicated by present-day custodians of restored SAS Pink Panthers and model makers in their dioramas. Much of the military clothing and stores seen in period and in-service photographs would have been tested and subsequently passed by the Stores and Clothing Research Establishment (SCRDE) based in Colchester.

Interestingly, the SCRDE role, amongst others, was to research the application of new materials to service requirements of clothing and stores and to design, develop and prove new clothing items and PLCE of all types for military use. Indeed, in documentation seen by the author, a member of the SCRDE, was deployed overseas in 1965 for field trials along with 6,000 pounds of equipment and stores. This short article explores what clothing was available at the time and worn while on operations.

Shemagh

The Shemagh scarf is traditional headwear in the Middle East. It is also known as a Ghutrah and Keffiyeh or by other more localised names. It is worn on the head or around the shoulders. It is a piece of square fabric, usually either 42 x 42 inches (107 x 107 centimetres) or 49 x 49 inches. (125 by 125 centimetres). Primary used as a headscarf, it has a variety of other uses too. For example, it can be used as an air filter in a sandstorm. If there's smoke in the air, a damp Shemagh can reduce smoke inhalation and allow you to breathe better.

Their additional functions vary but can be used as dust wipers, sweat mops and field towels. Often seen in shades of green, brown or desert yellow, it can be used as a camouflage outdoors if you wrap it around your head and face or pull it over you. A Shemagh is reasonably tough and also long. Therefore, when you roll it together, it can be used as an improvised rope or belt. And lastly, in a first aid emergency, a Shemagh can be vital if used as a bandage to stop the bleeding and protect the wound. It can also be used as a sling for a broken arm or a sprained wrist.

Photographic examples of the de rigueur Shemagh (green and black, red and white) being used as a headdress by members of the SAS operationally can be seen in Philip Warner's 1971 seminal publication entitled *The Special Air Service,* Colonel B.M. Niven's excellent photographic book *Special Men, Special War: Portraits of the SAS and the Dhofar* and Tony Geraghty's book *This is the SAS: A Pictorial History of the Special Air Service Regiment.* And lastly, on John Sear's YouTube video entitled 'Pink Panthers'.

Denison (Windproof) Smock

The (now iconic) Denison smock was a camouflaged coverall jacket initially issued to members of the Parachute Regiment (b.1 August 1942), Special Operations Executive (SOE) agents, the Glider Pilot Regiment and other specialised air-landing regiments to wear over their battle-dress uniform during airborne assaults of the Second World War. This camouflaged smock jacket was designed to be worn over the paratrooper's 1944-pattern webbing equipment but under the X-Type parachute pack and harness. Its primary function was to prevent the wearer's equipment from snagging while emplaned or during an operational jump.

Unfortunately, and even to this day, although described as windproof, it certainly wasn't waterproof! The Denison smock was manufactured from loose-fitting, yellowish-sand coloured, heavyweight twill material, allegedly hand-painted with a broad, mop-like brush appearance utilising non-colourfast dyes in broad pea green and dark brown stripes in a brush-stroke manner. It had a zip fastener made of steel, knitted woollen cuffs, four external pockets secured with brass snaps (two on the chest and two below the waist), two internal pockets on the chest, and epaulettes secured with plastic battle dress buttons.

The Denison windproof smock was significantly modified for the 1959 Pattern variant, retaining the full-length zip and knitted woollen cuffs, but the flannel lining of the collar was changed from khaki to a lighter green. However, the most visible difference to the eye was the shift in pattern variation and colours of the camouflage.

Excellent photographic examples of the Denison (windproof) smock being worn by members of the SAS operationally can be seen in Colonel B.M. Niven's excellent photographic book *Special Men, Special War: Portraits of the SAS and the Dhofar* (1990) and Tony Geraghty's book *This is the SAS: A Pictorial History of the Special Air Service Regiment* (1982).

And lastly, those readers interested in the Denison Smock would be well advised to read Bruce Wilson's epic 204 pages, large format and a hardback book entitled *'Denison' British Airborne Specialist Clothing from WWII to the Present Day* (published by Military Mode Publishing and in collaboration with the Airborne Assault Museum). A superb read.

Shorts and Shirts

Several short trousers and, on occasion, long-trousers; moreover, shirts were used by SAS members ranging from jungle to tropical khaki ones. Traditionally, they were made from olive green cotton, but from the 1970s onwards, these fabrics were often replaced by polyester or poly-cotton blends.

The trousers were often cut in a typically 1960s manner with a short rise, tight seat and narrow leg openings. Side adjusters, deep pockets and pocket(s) to the rear were fitted to each hip, and both shorts and shirts can often be seen in published and private period SAS photographs of the time. Indeed, notable aspects of Regimental attire of the period include the '72 pattern assault vest' or just plain 'SAS vest', officially known as 'pack lightweight, combat'. This vest or jerkin was designed to be lightweight and breathable butyl-nylon construction, specifically for use in tropical environments such as the jungle and desert.

Sunglasses/Sun Goggles

The arid deserts such as the SAS operated in were dusty, bright and often fly-infested locations. All three factors can easily cause eye problems and irritation for soldiers venturing into those environments. Numerous veils, masks and headdresses (*Shemaghs*) have been used to relieve these problems for millennia, and the Regiment was no exception. Wearing goggles/sunglasses was paramount in the SAS, not only to look good but also to aid driving skills and to avoid unnecessary eye injury.

Of particular note, concerning issued sunglasses (spectacles, tinted), most would have leather corner pieces where the lenses meet the arms; this is an absolute must-have to prevent any light and dust from entering from the side. Interestingly, in the period and official documentation seen by the author, there is a recommendation that RAF Mk. 8 Goggles (with tinted laminated eyepieces) be issued to SAS members, but, at the time, they were unavailable. However, there are period and in-service photographs where SAS members can be seen wearing these goggles. When asked about it decades later, it was revealed that these individuals had made private purchases or, in some instances, inherited them!

Prolonged exposure to the sun, heat, ultraviolet (UV) rays, and dust and debris has a lot of harmful effects on the eyes. Light-coloured eyes are especially prone to the cancer-inducing harmful effects of UV rays. Indeed, coloured-tinted lenses effectively prevent conjunctivitis. Actinic conjunctivitis is an inflammation - ocular photosensitivity reaction – of the eye contracted from prolonged exposure to actinic (ultraviolet) rays.

The Land-Rover's overly exposed bodywork demands that eye protection (goggles) be worn at all times. Therefore, SAS members were constantly told never to underestimate the severity of the weather; it can change without warning. For example, as the wind sails across the desert, it picks up truckloads of tiny sand and animal faeces particles, creates whiteout conditions, and lowers visibility to just inches in front of your eyes. Symptoms often experienced due to these conditions were redness and swelling of the eyes. Therefore, the SAS Regimental Medical Officer (RMO) would often advise pre-deployment to protect your eyes from these environmental factors.

You can find great examples of members of the SAS Regiment wearing sunglasses (goggles) in several publications. These include Philip Warner's book *The Special Air Service*, Colonel B.M. Niven's photographic book *Special Men, Special War* (1990), Tony Geraghty's book *This is the SAS: A Pictorial History of the Special Air Service Regiment*.

Type D Survival Knife

SAS soldiers would often carry a Type D Survival Knife (also known as Type 127) in addition to the machete issued with their Land-Rover while travelling. Initially issued to pilots of the RAF – in their aircraft ejection seat survival pack – and, in this instance, the SAS. The Type D 'Wilkie' Survival Knife was a well-made, solid and versatile (almost bombproof) heavy-duty knife. Hence, it is often referred to by its nickname of 'tree slapper' – as opposed to the machete's byname of 'tree beater'! Initially manufactured by the Wilkinson Sword Company (hence 'Wilkie') for British special forces, it is still considered one of the best practical survival and field knives ever designed. Other companies, over the years, have often reproduced it as the 'MoD survival knife'. Unfortunately, although replicating the original form and dimensions, it is, in my opinion, usually much cruder and has nowhere near the quality of the original design, balance or feel.

Later examples are often seen with the NSN of 5110-99-127-8214 on the blade, either with or without the maker's mark or date. Interestingly, they were initially designated as a 'Knife, Survival. Type D' – and then latterly as simply 'Hand Tool, Edged. Non-powered'. Note that on the Type D Knife, the knife's hardwood grip plates (the Scales) are noticeably protruding, as at -15°C and below, holding exposed metal will increase the chance of frostnip or frostbite (even wearing gloves or mitts) and interestingly not contrary to popular belief to facilitate custom shaping for a bespoke grip; although I have seen this done.

Note also that the spine or back of the (unfullered) blade – opposite the cutting edge – is thicker than the blade, thus making it safe to place your flat hand above for improved control and added pressure. And lastly, note how the Type D Survival Knife's pommel has a lanyard inlet similar to the vehicle-carried and issued machete.

If you have an interest in military survival knives, I recommend that you read Ron Flook's hardback book titled *British and Commonwealth Military Knives* (Airlife, 1999). Although it's no longer in print and hard to come by, it's definitely worth the effort to find a copy. I highly recommend it.

NATO Camp Bed (Cot) and 1958 Pattern Sleeping Bag

The SAS Regiment used the standard NATO camp bed and the design of the NATO camp bed has largely remained unchanged since the mid-1940s and consists of a stretched piece of canvas, about 6 feet long, placed over a simple four-piece metal frame with male and female connectors. The camp bed's main body hinges in the middle, folding neatly to form a compact, roll-type package that can be stored and transported when strapped together using the provided buckles – remember, it is only the infantry that sleeps on the ground!

The 1958-pattern sleeping bag was certainly innovative for its day, offering a welcome change for those who had previously only slept under loose blankets or army greatcoats. Made of green nylon, with a long central and noisy zip and a sprinkling of down feathers – down feathers being fine thermal insulators, the 1958-pattern sleeping bag (AKA green maggot or gonk bag) also featured a hooded section, providing a handy wrap-around thin pillow and keeping the user's head warm. It was also issued with a sleeping bag liner, which no one ever used, as you would often get tangled in it if you wanted to exit quickly.

However, these bags – known as bouncing bombs because they resembled Barnes Wallis's bouncing bomb when packed – had their limitations. The down feathers inside them were easily disturbed and, more often than not, would wear thin or end up in the wrong part of the sleeping bag, often escaping from the nylon material and leaving a trace of where the bag/soldier had been.

Additionally, there was always a shortage of bigger (taller) sizes at the Quartermasters, resulting in taller soldiers having to make do with bags that needed to be longer for them. Of particular note was that the base had a waterproof layer, allowing it to be placed directly onto wet ground. Interestingly, it was the first military sleeping bag in the world to have this feature and a much-welcomed and now much-replicated feature, too!

By the end of their service, many SAS soldiers had replaced their issue 1958 pattern bags with better quality and more modern examples from camping shops in Hereford, as civilian sleeping bags had far outpaced – both in design and material – their military equivalents, which were several decades old by this stage.

Chapter Four

EQUIPMENT REGISTRATION MARKS

SAS LAND-ROVERS

'Some people live an entire lifetime and wonder if they have ever made a difference in the world. A Veteran doesn't have that problem.'
President Ronald Reagan

In this chapter, we will be discussing registration plates (ERMs) for SAS Land-Rovers. Although some readers may find this topic dense or uninteresting, I would like to apologise in advance. The following information can help readers better understand British Army registration plates – ERMs. I hope you find it useful. I am particularly interested in UK civilian registration plates; hence, my wish to discuss ERMs.

As previously mentioned in an earlier chapter. The registration number plates or ERMs to give them their correct military term, and in the case of the FV18064 SAS Land-Rover Pink Panthers, the ERMs allocated were 10 FG 30 to 11 FG 01, respectively. The serial letters FG in the middle indicate the financial year the Land-Rover was purchased / ordered, 1967–1968. And were – where appropriate - on display at the front and rear of the vehicle itself. Interestingly, the FG series of ERMs signified the beginning of an era and the death knell for certain other vehicles in service with the military.

One of the vehicles included in this series was the Volvo Bandvagn 202 (Bv202E) 'Snowcat' – an all-terrain articulated and tracked vehicle designed to transport troops and equipment through snow or boglands. A consignment of (453) BSA motorcycles, Contract No. WV7856, with ERMs of 64 FG 30 – 68 FG 82, and several Austin 1100 Saloons were also equipped with the FG series of ERMs, which served in the military for several years before being replaced by the Ford Cortina Mk. IV and Hillman Hunter.

Furthermore, the FG series introduced the Morris Minor Traveller (45 FG 13, 63 FG 87 and a left-hand drive 00 FG 83 being good examples). The Woody (AKA 'tactical traveller' and officially 'Car, Utility, 4 x 2') succeeded the bench-seated and now-dated Hillman Husky. On the Land-Rover side, the 88-inch lightweight was introduced, 71 FG 97 and 72 FG 88 being two examples with its cutaway wings for lightness and a smaller profile for air portability.

Returning to the SAS Pink Panthers, note how the ERM is split with a double letter comprising two numerals, two letters and two numerals, for example, 10 FG 30. These pair of letters, which interestingly began with BA – all the letter 'AAs' having been allocated to the RAF – gives an indication of both to the accounting year (or years for slow-filling numbers), when the contract was placed for the vehicle and, broadly, the type of vehicle (so individual vehicles may be a few months to a couple of years younger than the ERM implies).

For example, early ERMs allocated to the RAF were 00 AA 01 onwards and 00 BA 01 to the British Army. However, an interesting point is that early (pre-1949) Army vehicles were allocated 00 YA 01 ERMs. The MoD played a crucial role in providing clarity to this system by using letter codes for particular vehicle types and perhaps areas of responsibility. It's this uniqueness that makes the ERM system so intriguing and worth exploring. For example:

- XX LV XX = leased vehicles (*circa* 1986 onwards)
- XX MA XX = military attaché (*circa* 1959 onwards)
- XX MS XX = military sales (*circa* 1969 onwards) – overseas contracts and exports etc.
- XX PB XX = public buildings (*circa* 1982 onwards) – Department of Environment (DoE) vehicles
- XX SP XX = special projects (*circa* 1967 onwards) – research and development vehicles
- XX TC XX = transportable containers or box bodies
- XX TG XX = towed guns (*circa* 1982 onwards) – Royal Artillery
- XX TM XX = trailer mounted (*circa* 1982 onwards) – mainly generators etc
- XX TP XX = temporary plates – akin to civilian (red and white) trade plates

An excellent example of dedicated ERM usage is 01 SP 13 – the SP, in this instance, denoting special projects and was used predominantly for research and development vehicles. The Equipment Registration

Marks of 01 SP 13 to 01 SP 17 were allocated to Forward-Control 101 Land-Rovers for the emerging Swingfire missile system of the mid-1960s.

An informative article by Pat Ware appears in the April 2010 edition of *Classic Military Vehicle* magazine on pages 48–50, all showcasing not only the 101 Forward-Control Land-Rover but also XX SP XX ERMs. Next time you are at a military vehicle show, getting number plate (ERM) spotting, it's a great hobby!

Of interest regarding ERMs is that double letters were issued more or less sequentially, though there were gaps and exceptions. Generally, letter pairs lasted longer in the early years than later – so BA, for example, was used on 'A' (armoured) vehicles between 1950 and 1955, BB on 'A' vehicles between 1955 and 1957. BC, on the other hand, lasted only for 1950 and 1951. But it was allocated to 'B' (soft-skinned) vehicles, and clearly, they were bought in considerably greater numbers than 'A' vehicles.

However, in the late 1960s, for example, the sequence had reached F, with FA applied to 'A' vehicle contracts from 1967–1968, FB, 1968-69 and FC 1969–1970. FC, FD, FE and FF were also allocated to 'A' for succeeding years up to 1972–1973, while 'B' vehicles, over the same period, were FG for 1967-68, FH, 1968–1969 and FK 1969–1970, FL and FM were also allocated to 'B' vehicles (for 1970–1971 and 1972–1973).

As previously mentioned, vehicle registration plates (ERMs) were usually allocated at the time of the original contract, in 10 FG 30 to 11 FG 01's case, 1967–1968, almost an entire year before contract completion and delivery to the SAS Regiment in Hereford in 1969 and in many cases, for a variety of reasons, even later.

Also of note is that the Land-Rover model year at that time in Solihull ran from September to the end of July the following year, August being omitted for the work's annual two-week holiday and then for staff getting the production assembly lines ready for the new model coming through.

It's important to note that British Army trailers have a separate registration process. They often use the ERM code of 'TM' and are not required to display the towing vehicle's ERM. In contrast, civilian-registered trailers must display the registration number of the towing vehicle.

British Armed Forces vehicles were not exempt from displaying registration plates. Accordingly, new vehicles arriving at any given camp, naval port or air station would have already had their ERMs affixed to the vehicle and would be black in colour and with the lettering/characters white, silver or grey. Moreover, they would (should) have conformed to the set specifications of the day as to the width, height, spacing of the font and margins, etc. Of interest regarding pressed metal ERMs is that there would not have been a silver border around the plate, which is often seen on vehicles attending military open-air shows.

The silver border one sees on renovated military vehicles is a civilian registration plate anomaly and is produced by registration plate manufacturers for older vehicles requiring a number plate where the vehicle was manufactured before 1972. Interestingly, post-1972 civilian vehicles, saw the introduction of reflective plates that we see today on civilian vehicles being introduced white at the front and yellow at the rear but with black characters rather than silver, grey or white.

Reflective registration plates have become compulsory on (almost) all vehicles manufactured after 1 January 1973. Also of note is that armoured vehicles such as tanks and some other vehicles, the ERM would have been painted directly onto the vehicle itself, often using a stencil. Getting a period registration plate (ERM) manufactured for your military vehicle today is particularly difficult; what with all the legislation attached to purchase and display of such an item and the silver border/frame is a small price to pay to obtain a pressed-metal authentic-looking 'period' number plate or ERM.

Those SAS Land-Rover Pink Panthers that are used on (UK) public highways, have to by UK law, in addition to being DVLA registered, be insured, use road legal tyres (not sand tyres!) and have a civilian registration plate correctly displayed on their vehicle. However, Pink Panther owners do not need to get an Ministry of Transport (MoT vehicle roadworthiness test) if the vehicle was first registered more than forty years ago and no substantial changes have been made to the vehicle in the last thirty years.

Whether or not your SAS Pink Panther is MoT exempt, the SAS Land-Rover must be roadworthy. Therefore, as with other similar classic vehicles (be they military or civilian), it is good practice to voluntarily undertake an MoT as these vehicles are a definite traffic-stopper of a machine and attract attention wherever and whenever they travel. Indeed, this was evident when they were being driven back to camp (often in convoy – AKA in army parlance, packets).

Before any UK road use of your Land-Rover SAS Pink Panther, I would recommend you seek further advice and guidance from the DVLA and their regularly updated website. This is especially important if your SAS Land-Rover has never been issued a civilian registration plate or recently had a ground-up restoration (a comprehensive overhaul of the vehicle, often involving disassembly and rebuilding).

This advice is also crucial if your vehicle was found in a barn or discovered in Africa! However, if that vehicle is used on private property – such as at a military show – then its original ERM may be affixed on it; that plate then becomes classed as a 'Show Plate'. Show plates is a term widely used that encompasses any number plates that does not follow the legal standard for vehicle registration plates set by DVLA regulations. For example, the wrong font or the illegal spacing of letters and numbers is done, perhaps to suit the vehicle it is on.

I have often seen at *classic military vehicle* shows UK road registration plates on military vehicles that are illegally spaced in such a manner as to give an impression of an ERM that may have been on the vehicle before it was de-mobbed. An excellent example of this is the Series 1 SAS Land-Rover with the ERM of 66 BS 14, this particular and super rare Land-Rover (known as FV18006) was built to special forces reconnaissance and patrol specifications on an 88-inch wheelbase and equipped with twin Vickers K.303, a Bren Light Machine Gun .303 by the driver and a .30 calibre Browning Machine Gun on the rear tailgate.

This particular SAS Land-Rover, part of the famous Dunsfold Collection, has a DVLA age-related registration number plate of 929 XUR and the military 'style' character spacing as 92 9X UR. Of note with this superb renovation is that it appears in several publications (for obvious reasons). In particular, it is featured in the *Land Rover Monthly* magazine's free 2022 calendar in March. Interestingly, the registration plate issued by the local vehicle licensing office of YNP 969G to SAS Land-Rover 10 FG 57 is also an age-related plate. The 'G' suffix or year indicates a vehicle registered from 1 August 1968 to 31 July 1969. We can tell it was registered at the Worcester Local Vehicle Licensing Office from the letters NP. Incidentally, Worcester is not too far from Hereford!

The UK's Suffix registration plate system ran from 1963 to 1982. Before 1963, registration marks were dateless – they did not carry any easily recognisable year identifier. Suffix registration plates made the age of the vehicle easily known by simply attaching a year-identifying letter to the end of the registration plate. For example, this began with the letter 'A' in 1963, and a new letter was issued each subsequent year until 'Y' was reached in 1982.

After 1982, when the suffix letters had been depleted, the system changed, and prefix number plate registrations were introduced. Interestingly, five letters of the alphabet were not used in the suffix number plate system; for example I, O, Q, U and Z were never issued. 'I' and 'Z' were reserved for Northern Ireland, 'O' was obviously thought too closely to resemble zero, the letter 'Q' was used but only on certain vehicles where their date of manufacture was in doubt or unknown and lastly, 'U' appeared to look too much like 'V' for use on suffix car registration plates.

To obtain an age-related registration number, the DVLA can only recognise a vehicle as a reconstructed classic vehicle, if it meets specific and laid down criteria. For example, it must be built from genuine and period components from more than one vehicle that is over twenty-five years old and of the exact specification as the original vehicle.

Ideally, and when available, the appropriate vehicle owners' club (Land-Rover) for the vehicle type ('marque') must also inspect the vehicle and confirm in writing that it has been inspected; only then will the DVLA assign an age-related registration number (plate) to the vehicle based on the youngest component used. In other words, a true reflection of the marque and period of manufacture.

SAS Pinkie 10 FG 34 has often been spotted displaying its civilian registration plate of SMW 111G, again with the Suffix Plate or Age Identifier plate of 'G', which indicates a vehicle manufactured between the dates of 01 Aug 1968 to 31 Jul 1969. The letters 'MW' would indicate it was first registered in the Wiltshire area, and the Swindon Local Vehicle Licensing Office used the area identifying letters of 'MW' from 1926 to 1974.

Another SAS Pinkie with the ERM of 10 FG 67 has the appropriate 'period' civilian registration of SCV 802G. The letters 'CV' would indicate it was registered at the Truro Local Vehicle Licensing Office in Cornwall, as Cornwall Licensing Authority used the area identifying letters of 'CV' from 1928-1974. Moreover, on occasions, 10 FG 55 can be seen with its age-related civilian registration plate affixed, that being UBD 398G. The identifying letters of 'BD' are from Northampton.

Of particular note regarding ERMs and civilian registration plates is the SAS Land-Rover Pink Panther with the ERM of 10 FG 31, which has the civilian registration plate of AEV 814S. The suffix plate or age-identifier plate of 'S' was issued between the dates of 1 August 1977 and 31 July 1978, some nine years after the original manufacturing date, and the letters 'EV' would indicate it was registered at the Chelmsford Local Vehicle Licensing Office.

Interestingly, 10 FG 31 can be spotted in the MoD publication *SAS Land Rover (Desert Version)* on page 13. Although the ERM is just visible in the booklet, the vehicle is being used to identify where equipment such as grenade stowage, tow rope location, and fire extinguishers are positioned on the Land-Rover.

Essex Licensing Authority used the area identifying letters of 'EV' from 1928–1974. However, this is a 1977-1978 registration plate!

Clearly, the S-Suffix on the registration plate might seem like an anomaly for a 1968/1969 vehicle, as the S-Suffix indicates 1977/1978. However, until 1983, newly registered ex-military vehicles used to get current-year letters, and it would appear that this vehicle was sold out of Service in 1978. However, after August 1983, ex-military vehicles sold out of Service would get an appropriate year letter relating to the vehicle's year of manufacture or quite possibly a Q-prefix, especially if the vehicle's history was perhaps not complete.

An excellent example of a Q-prefix registration plate on an SAS Land-Rover in the public domain is the SAS Pink Panther with an ERM of 10 FG 69 and perhaps regarded as the first Pinkie to have been restored. Indeed, there is a superb photograph of Q33 CPE (10 FG 69) on the front cover of *Soldier* magazine on 8 August 1988.

Another example is that of ERM 10 FG 97, this particular vehicle has the civilian registration plate of Q887 JKO. Both Pinkies are in superb condition and are proudly displayed regularly at shows and reunions up and down the country.

DVLA issues 'Q' registration numbers to vehicles whose age or identity is in doubt. Unlike standard registration plates – which can identify a vehicle's entire history from the date of the manufacturer to where it was first registered - Q-plates identify to observers that certain aspects of a vehicle's history are unknown, or a temporary import. Interestingly, Q-plates have been in use since around the 1930s, and while some think the letter Q stands for 'query' or 'questionable', it is used in this manner simply because the letter 'Q' is not used in the vehicle registration plate system of the United Kingdom.

The DVLA will only consider an appeal against a 'Q'-plate if made within twelve months of the original application. Moreover, Q-plated vehicles can be more challenging to insure as it is harder for insurance providers and underwriters to calculate the risk if they need the vehicle's complete history to go on.

There are certain types of vehicles that will be issued with Q-plates, and they include (amongst others) former MoD vehicles whose history cannot be released, as they are classified, or they are vehicles without a VIN, possibly removed or the VIN damaged – both of which are (possible) classic indications of an SAS Land-Rover Pink Panther's heritage!

To simplify the above, when SAS Land-Rover Pink Panthers were sold off by the Army, their purchasers needed to obtain a civilian registration mark (Plate). This would enable them to be used on public roads. Normally, they have been given a G-suffix mark, reflecting their manufacture in the 'G' year, between 1 August 1968 and 31 July 1969.

Initially, these letters indicated calendar years 'A' for 1963, 'B' for 1964 etc. However, from 1 August 1967, when the 'F' suffix was started, the year letter changed on 1 August. Examples of these Land-Rover Pink Panthers being 10 FG 34 became SMW 111G; 10 FG 55 became UBD 969G; 10 FG 57 became YNP 969G and 10 FG 67 became SCV 802G.

It is perhaps interesting to note that when a military vehicle such as an SAS Land-Rover is sold-off through official HM Government channels, then the ERM is lost with the vehicle and cannot be resurrected or sold for profit, unlike a civilian vehicle registration plate. Interestingly, the registration plate (ERM) 10 FG 87 was put up for public auction on the internet site eBay some years ago. The auction was just for the metal registration plate, not the rights associated with the vehicle's registration plate. Of which there aren't any.

The vendor's sales pitch for the ERM of 10 FG 87 was written by the former owner of the SAS Pink Panther it originally belonged to and read (exactly) as follows:

> This is a genuine British Army Number plate that was removed from the front of the Army Land Rover 10 FG 87, which was one of the fleet of 72 specially built Land Rovers that were used by the SAS, referred to as Pink Panthers. I used to own this vehicle and sold it 15 years ago, it went to the US, VERMONT. I found while sorting through boxes of Land Rover Parts in my garage. You can see the pink paint under the green paint on the back of the plate, the back of the plate gets painted as it mounted on the front edge of the bonnet. This is a genuine article ...

What I like about 10 FG 87 is that it has its own dedicated internet website of https://10fg87.org and can be seen with the New York (Department of Motor Vehicles) license plate of GC7 41M with the Statue of Liberty image neatly fitting between the '7 and 4'. The Statue of Liberty image on the registration plate indicates the plate was issued between July 1986 and December 2001. Indeed, this exact license plate would have been issued (in this format) between May 1999 to 28 February 2001.

Collectively known as Liberty plates, they are constructed of aluminium and embossed with dark blue serial numbers/letters on a reflective white plate, with red stripes at the top and bottom. In addition, a red Statue of Liberty graphic is screened in the centre with the words 'NEW YORK' in dark blue centred at the top. It can also be viewed on the website (https://10fg87.org) in a superb photo outside the Marshall of Cambridge art deco headquarters, sporting its correct ERM of 10 FG 87.

There is a great photo of an SAS Long Wheel Base (109) Land-Rover Series 11A widely available on the internet and in Pat Ware's book entitled *Military Land Rover: Development and in Service* (May 2007) on page 93, that is seen driving in muddy conditions and presented in the original deep bronze green (AKA Land Rover Bronze Green LRC001) and shod with desert tyres. What makes this photograph particularly interesting – in addition to the fact it is fully kitted out with all the Marshall of Cambridge additions – is that it can be seen with a registration plate (765 GC) known as a 'trade plate' rather than an issued military-style ERM.

Note also, the colour scheme of the Land-Rover, the European theatre colour change (duller and two-tone green and black) was post-delivery, which again would suggest an early photograph in the life of an SAS Land-Rover. And lastly, the driver's headwear – note it is not a sand/beige coloured beret, nor has he got the obligatory (slug balanced) moustache!

Details of ERM were not only kept on the DOS Form 419B but also, and this is where it gets interesting, on the vehicle record book (AB 562), which was a handy medium- sized booklet that included the following information to be meticulously maintained at all times, ERM, chassis number, contract number etc., servicing, inspection, mileage, fuel records, record of technical inspections, workshop repairs, overhauls and record of authorised modifications. These scarce books hold a wealth of information for the collector and historian alike. Maintained on a month-by-month and year-by-year basis, it shows the life cycle of the SAS Pinkie.

Chapter Five

THE SAS PINK PANTHER IN POPULAR CULTURE

'Even the most beautiful days eventually have their sunsets ...'
Anonymous

In the satirical and allegorical book *Animal Farm* (1945) by George Orwell (AKA Eric Arthur Blair, 1903–1950). He wrote, 'All animals are equal, but some are more equal than others'. This famous quote could perhaps be rewritten as 'All military vehicles have a presence, but some have more presence than others.' The Marshall of Cambridge Land-Rover SAS Pink Panther IS the vehicle with more presence than all the others.

With many SAS Land-Rover Pink Panthers becoming available on the civilian market through the MoD auction rooms of Ruddingtons and the British Car Auctions from 1976 onwards. The stable gate had finally been unbolted, the Panther released, and the demise following the subsequent replacement of the Land-Rover Series IIA was inevitable. For information, when the MoD decides whether a vehicle is surplus to its requirements or is beyond economic repair (BER), it is 'CAST' (withdrawn from service). It then makes its way to one of the approved disposal companies for onward auction and availability to the public. It was, therefore, only a matter of time before Pinkies would attain an almost mythical and legendary status and become ingrained in SAS Regimental history, folklore and popular culture forever.

Sadly, many SAS Land-Rovers ignominiously and, without thought of the historical importance of the vehicle and its military background, ended up at specialist Land Rover breakers and dealers around the country for as little as £100. Having been purchased for spares or being re-fitted and returned to civilian specification and sold as such at a greater profit. Other examples of prices achieved for SAS Land-Rover Pink Panthers can be seen in the October 1976 sale at Ruddingtons in Nottinghamshire. Each vehicle was sold with an auction release note, which accompanied the MOD FORM 666, the MoD certificate of transfer form. These forms included details of the vehicle's ERM, year of manufacture and chassis number.

Lot Number	ERM	Chassis Number	Hammer Price
977	10 FG 65	251-14095D	£460
978	10 FG 48	251-14119D	£460
979	10 FG 31	251-14116D	£460
1098	10 FG 35	251-13970D	£540
1099	10 FG 69	251-14093D	£600
1100	10 FG 72	251-13951D	£600

Indeed, this is neatly confirmed in a mammoth five-page article in the June 2002 edition of *Land Rover Enthusiast*, where well-known Land Rover aficionado John Craddock is interviewed and confirms this. 'They were just old Land-Rovers in those days. We used to buy at £100 apiece as they came through the auctions …' Moreover, these low prices are confirmed in the British Army's *Soldier* magazine (8 August 1988) where the late SSGT Roger Jones REME, purchased his (albeit in bits) SAS Land-Rover (10 FG 69) (chassis number 251-14093D) for the princely sum of £25 in 1981/1982!

Of particular note regarding the June edition of *Land Rover Enthusiast* magazine, 10 FG 94 (chassis number 251-14087D) appears in superb full colour on the front page. Indeed, there are only a few other occasions when SAS Land-Rovers have been given the accolade of gracing the front page of a magazine.

Other notable examples of front-page coverage are *Off Road and 4 Wheel Drive* (March 1989), with 10 FG 69, 10 FG 97, and 10 FG 57 down on the beach and *Classic Military Vehicle*, Issue 14 (July 2002); this time 10 FG 97 on the front cover with the headline of 'Pretty in Pink'. Interestingly, 10 FG 97 (chassis number 251-13968D) does appear on the front cover of a hardback book entitled *The Visual Dictionary of Special Military Forces*, but sadly, the ERM has been obliterated for some reason; still a great picture, though!

If you're not lucky enough to spot an SAS Pink Panther on the front cover of a magazine, you might catch a glimpse in the classifieds section. One example is 10 FG 35 in *Classic Military Vehicle* magazine's May and June 2006 editions. Or perhaps better still, in 10 FG 97's case, be used to promote the Events Page of *Classic Military Vehicle* magazine (April 2006), page 54. Nice!

Little did eager Land Rover scrap merchants and dealers at these MoD auctions realise at the time that only a few years later, these petrol-fuelled beasts would be worth many thousands of pounds and come to represent the holy grail of Land-Rover collectors, modellers, and discerning automotive and military museums around the world! An increase in the prices of SAS Land-Rovers can be seen in the classifieds section of *Classic Military Vehicle* magazine in June 2005, where on page 64, Pinkie 10 FG 51 can be seen with a small photograph and a hefty price tag of £9,000 (ono), an excellent investment in hindsight!

This amazing amalgam, first conceived by operational members of the SAS Regiment working alongside the FVRDE and then superbly finished by Marshall of Cambridge, means that the now few surviving SAS Pinkies of the original seventy-two units produced are now rightly cherished by their respective owners. The stable gate is well and truly closed, locked, and secured – and this time, for all the right reasons. Ask the members of the Pink Panther Register for confirmation!

Chapter Six

THE MARSHALL OF CAMBRIDGE LAND-ROVER

'The boy (David) Stirling is quite mad, quite, quite mad. However, in a war, there is often a place for mad people.'
Field Marshal Montgomery

In the desert, legends are made, and the Marshall of Cambridge SAS Land-Rover is one such legend. However, with a bulwark of secrecy rightly embedded and surrounding the SAS, it makes it almost impossible to fully assess the successful impact, record, and positive outcomes, not only of the SAS Regiment's legendary actions, where its members operated and where they had to move harder, faster and expose themselves to greater risk and rigour but also the covert deployment of the Land-Rover Pinkie.

Consequently, locating accurate accounts, period, original in-service, and unpublished photographs and articles on the Marshall of Cambridge SAS Land-Rover is challenging. Fortunately, for enthusiasts of the SAS Pinkie, there are many noteworthy commercially available books associated with the military Land Rover, and virtually all touch (for obvious reasons) on the SAS Land-Rover in its many guises and, in particular, the Marshall of Cambridge version. Occasionally, SAS Land-Rover Pink Panthers are seen in vehicle auction catalogues or, on occasions, direct from Land Rover dealers themselves.

For example, 10 FG 55 with a (chassis number 251-13950D) was sold by P.A. Blanchard & Co. in 2019, having been in their collection since its release from the military in 1986. This superb example, and I mean superb example, came complete with a copy parts book and handbook, along with a *CES* and illustrated spare parts booklet for the body.

Another auction example can be seen in Bonhams MPH, where they had 10 FG 97 (Q887 JKO – chassis number 251-13968D) in their September 2019 auction. It sold for £47,250 including premium, whereas 10 FG 34 (SMW 111G), this time in NATO green, sold for £34,333 inc. premium. Both these vehicles came with an impeccable pedigree and provenance, as they came from the Barry Pocock SAS Land Rover collection.

Of note is that this particular Bonhams MPH auction sale is mentioned some two months later in December 2019 magazine *Classic Cars* (December 2019). Where, on page 15, the late and well-known motoring journalist, Quentin Willson, mentions that there is 'strong interest in the ex-military and special bodied Land Rovers ...' and confirms this 'gung-ho activity ...' with the sale of an SAS Land-Rover Pink Panther (10 FG 97) for £47,250.

Moreover, in October of 2020, Bonhams, the Auctioneers, had 10 FG 61 (chassis No. 251-13989D) in their auction, which sold for £27,600 including premium. Interestingly, this vehicle was purchased from Land Rover marque specialist Charles Kellogg III's Dare Britannia Ltd in Washington State (America) in July 2018 and then shipped back to the UK.

These auction catalogues are readily available directly from auction houses or internet auction sites such as eBay and Gumtree. They make for great reading and even better reference for collectors and modellers alike, as the photos are up close and personal. Moreover, if one visits the auction house or Land Rover dealer's website, then invariably, there tend to be more photos available to view.

Another example of finding an SAS Pink Panther that has gone through the auction rooms is that of 10 FG 33 (chassis number 251-14118D) – which appeared – shod with desert tyres and offered for restoration – in the monthly round-up of the military vehicle market in the magazine *Classic Military Vehicle*, in particular, March 2013's edition on page 68. Compiled by Nigel Hay and in collaboration with MILWEB – an established marketplace for military vehicles, militaria and deactivated weapons – these pages in the magazine are an excellent reference point for collectors to determine how much military vehicles are worth.

Interestingly, 10 FG 33 is featured, stripped down to the basics, and painted in green with the occasional pink fitting (sand channels and GPMG mounts). These photos and comments of SAS Land-Rover Pink Panthers provide a continuing snapshot of the vehicle's value and history and are worth collecting for your Pinkie scrapbook!

And lastly, while on the subject of auctions, Ruddington Auctions (Nottinghamshire) were at the time contracted to auction off redundant ex-military vehicles and surplus equipment. They were held every eight weeks, and the auctions were publicly advertised in the local and national press.

Sadly, many SAS Pink Panthers were unceremoniously sold-off in this manner over several years. Unfortunately, there is little information to glean from the Ruddingtons' auction catalogue. Besides an ERM, a brief description of the vehicle (odometer reading and its DIS), and lastly, the date it was sold. Sadly, no photographs were printed in these catalogues.

If you happen to find an auction catalogue in which one of the attendees has contemporaneously made notes, then you may have discovered the price realised for an auction lot, and you may also learn the original price for which the SAS Landy was sold for. These auction catalogues can often be found on eBay and are bought by enthusiasts who want to trace the history of their ex-military vehicles. At times, these catalogues can be sold at a premium price.

When military vehicles were sold, the MoD used MoD Form 666, which contained various details such as the ERM, the chassis number, and a vehicle description. This two-sided form was then sent to the DVLA in Swansea.

Of particular note for military vehicle historians is that the DIS details found on the DOS Form 419B relates to the date the vehicle entered service for the first time. For example, upon receipt at an RAOC Depot such as CVD Ashchurch, this date will always either be the nearest January or July of that year. More exact details will be found in the column 'Receipt Voucher/Reference Date'. In 10 FG 35's case, DIS reads 'Jul[y] 1969' (rubber-stamped) with a hand-written note of 17 July 1969.

Another column to note is that of class to and from. This particular column refers to the planned life of the vehicle type. This is based on the age of the vehicle from its DIS and runs as follows:

- Class 1: For the first 60 per cent of planned life.
- Class 2: For the next 40 per cent of planned life.
- Class 3: Over the planned life.

These from and to columns on the DOS Form 419B neatly determined the vehicle's fitness to serve with a Unit. Class 1 was regarded as 'new' and frontline units would be expected to hold and maintain in this Class. Class 2 was for administrative units or those on Garrison duties. Again, rubber-stamped dates would always be either January or July. An example of a class 2 vehicle would be when the SAS Land-Rover was allocated to a Territorial Unit, for the remainder of its 40 per cent planned life, having served (and LAD/REME maintained) in Class 1 for the first 60 per cent of its planned life.

It is interesting to note that on the 'B' vehicle data cards (DOS Form 419B), the chassis numbers are entered continuously – as per the chassis plate – but the letter D has not always been entered on the cards. Perhaps a clerical error by the data entry clerk? Interestingly, the chassis numbers are identical to an enlisted soldier's regimental number. The DOS Form 419B in use at the time of production of the SAS Land-Rover Pink Panther sadly didn't record the colour of the Land-Rover, unlike the Heritage Trust certificate that takes its information directly from the Land-Rover factory ledger.

However, the latter DOS Form 419B (Rev 74) did provide for the colour code to be inserted, and when the forms were revised, it seems that all vehicles used DOS Form 419B (Rev 74) irrespective of 'A', 'B' or 'C' vehicle type as there was provision for identifying the colour in the top right-hand corner – a particularly useful feature for researchers and renovators of military vehicles and this took the form of a two-character code, the first character gives the basic colour and the second the finish.

By noting the change in colour code, a timeline can be established for specific vehicle batches. For example, deep bronze green gloss is '72'. The first character indicates it is 'green' and the second that it is 'gloss'. Olive drab or NATO Green in IRR is 'A6'. Again, the first character indicates 'Army/NATO Green' and the second is 'infrared-reflective'.

Incidentally, 'A' and 'C' vehicle data cards used DOS Form 419A, and these were initially pink in colour. Shame it wasn't available for the 'B' vehicle data cards (DOS Form 419B); now that would have been a nice touch. This colour, pink, was later replaced with a standard Army buff colour. As computerisation became the norm in the British Army, these 'vehicle cards' were sensibly transferred to museums for safe keeping. The majority were donated around the mid-1980s. The 'B' Vehicle cards (soft-skinned vehicles) initially being donated to the Transport Museum in Beverley.

Sadly, this museum closed around 2003, and all 'B' class vehicle cards were then donated for safe-keeping to the Royal Logistics Corps (RLC) Museum, initially in Deepcut in Surrey. Then more recently, at The RLC Museum, based at Worthy Down near Winchester. And secondly, there is the British Motor Museum, Banbury Road, Gaydon, Warwickshire.

The archive of the British Motor Industry Heritage Trust holds the original factory records created by many of the leading British motor manufacturers, including Land Rover. At cost, the archive can provide a certified copy of a vehicle's entry in the original Land-Rover factory ledger, showing the vehicle's specification as it left the production line.

For example, and in 10 FG 65's case, chassis number (251-14095-D), the original colour it left the factory in (bronze green), the exact date of build (24 January 1968), and the date of dispatch (13 February 1968) and the vehicle's destination (Central Army Vehicle Depot (CAVD) Feltham, Middlesex). The CAVD at Feltham was where some (not all) of the Truck, Utility, SAS, ¾ Ton, 4 x 4, Rover II vehicles were receipted and inspected by the MoD before onward delivery.

Note how the Heritage Trust uses a hyphen to separate chassis numbers. The letter 'D' and yet on the original chassis plate of the Land-Rover itself, the numbers are continuous without using a hyphen, and the letter 'D' is then spaced. Please note that the letter D at the end of the series of numbers indicated that significant changes to the vehicle's specification affected servicing rather than the D standing for desert conversion as often quoted.

In addition to confirming key dates, details, and identification numbers for a vehicle, the heritage certificate can be helpful when applying for vehicle tax exemption (road fund licence) or an age-related registration mark or importing/exporting a vehicle such as a Land-Rover.

If you are lucky enough to discover or have an unregistered SAS Pink Panther Land-Rover, another organisation that may be of help is the Invicta Military-Vehicle Preservation Society. Sometimes better known by its acronym of IMPS. IMPS is one of the few vehicle clubs authorised by the DVLA in Swansea to authenticate applications for registering ex-military vehicles for road use. To register an ex-military vehicle, one must confirm the date the vehicle was built; these details can be found in the British Motor Industry Heritage Trust certificate and the 'B' vehicle data cards previously discussed. Both are excellent sources of historical information.

Upon examination of the vehicle and/or relevant photos, they (IMPS) will provide an age-related signed letter on club-headed notepaper that the DVLA will accept as proof of the vehicle's age and a V55/5 form. Vehicles built before 1973 (SAS Pink Panthers fall into this category) should be registered in the historic vehicle taxation class and receive an age-related registration number and a zero-rate taxation fee.

Magazine Articles

This section aims to identify journals, documents and periodical articles representing the history and development of the SAS Pinkie and to provide interested people with an open resource of information. Moreover, a concise reading list that will hopefully expand and develop upon their knowledge of the Marshall of Cambridge SAS Land-Rover.

If one were to read only one of these magazine articles per week, then they would perhaps be much better informed and prepared to overcome the challenges they will face during their 'temporary' custodial ownership and restoration of an SAS Pinkie or possibly the building of a scale model of the now iconic and legendary SAS Land-Rover.

The list below – although not definitive and in no particular order, other than perhaps the date published – is a list I feel may be of interest to readers, vehicle renovators, and modellers alike, as the SAS Pink Panther is covered in superb detail and makes for interesting reading.

Moreover, with full colour photographs and historical vehicle information for reference, get that extra detail in your interpretation of your Land-Rover SAS Pink Panther and, more importantly, get your renovation and model as accurate and sympathetic as possible.

Bibliography, Vehicle History, Public Auctions, Model Builds and Further Reference

Military Modelling (November and December 1972, and January 1973), 'Scratch Built Land Rover'

Scale Modeler (American publication) (October 1976) 'Desert Rover' by Lane Sanders

Military Modeler (Canadian publication) (October 1980) 'S.A.S Land Rover' by Lane Sanders

Wheels & Track, Issue 9, 'SAS Land Rovers, The SAS Pink Panther and Its Predecessors'

Off Road and 4 Wheel Drive (March 1989), 'Pinky and Pinky and Pinky' by Roger Jones

Combat & Survival, Volume, 1 Issue 9 (December 1989) 'SAS Land Rovers' by Anthony Rogers

Land Rover World, Issue 18 (August 1995), 'Cold Metal' by Paul and Andrew Entwistle

Land Rover Owner International (August 1995), 'In the Pink' by Bob Morrison

Military Modelcraft International (September 1997) 'Pink Panther' by Bob Morrison

Military Modelcraft International (September 1997) 'Return of the Pink Panther' by Ian Young

Land Rover Owner (April 2000), 'A Shot in the Dark' by Craig Cheetham

Land Rover Enthusiast (November 2000, June 2002 and March 2005)

Land Rover Monthly (January 2002) 'Behind the Lines' by Bob Morrison

Land Rover Enthusiast (2002–2005) articles cover their renovation of 10 FG 88 – Project Pink Panther

Classic Military Vehicle (July 2002, January 2017 and January 2021), articles covering Pink Panther related titles
Military Armor International, Issue 20 (August–September 2002), 'SAS Land Rover, France'
Land Rover World (January 2003) 'Fight Club – SAS Land Rovers' by Claire Thansriskul
Military Machines International (April 2006) 'Pink Panther' by John Ingram
Model Military International (June 2006) 'Sneaky in Pink' by Glen Bowen
Military Machines International (January 2010), 'Military Roverphile' by James Taylor
Land Rover International (Spring 2010) 'The One and Only Truly Original' by John Carroll
SAS Panthers in Detail: SAS Pink Panthers of the Barry Pocock's and Another British Private Collections (Wings & Wheels Publications, November 2010) Kořán, František and Kautský, Aleš,
Les thématiques Steel Masters (April 2011, France) 'Special Forces 1941-2011' by Emilien Pepin
Military Machines International (July 2011), 'Pink Panther'
Armoured Fighting Vehicle (November/December 2011), 'Serving the Sultan' by Emilien Pepin
Special Operations Landies in Detail: Armed Land Rovers Used by Special Forces de Boer, Jan W., Kautský, Aleš and Kořán, František, (Wings & Wheels Publications, February 2012)
Airfix Model World (November 2015), 'Tickled Pink' by Paul Cawte
Airfix Model World (November 2015), 'Pink But Deadly' by Ian Young
Classic Military Vehicle (January 2017), 'SAS Land Rovers' by James Taylor
Scale Military Modeller International (March 2018), 'Staying in the Pink' by Paul Hargett
Windscreen, Military Vehicle Trust, 'Pink Panther on Patrol' (October 2019)
Land Rover International (December 2020) 'New Model Army' by Adrian Hayward-Wills
Classic Military Vehicle (January 2021), 'A Model Pinkie' by Adrian Hayward-Wills
TAMIYA Model Magazine International (March 2021), 'The Rinky-Dink Panther' by Kev Smith
The Landy Newspaper, Issue 89 (July 2021), 'A Marvel in Miniature' by Adrian Hayward-Wills
Land Rover Yearbook 2022 (November 2021), 'Perfect Pinkie' by Adrian Hayward-Wills
ENGAGE 4 x 4 (November/December 2021), 'Pink Panther' by Ben Branch
Classic Military Vehicle (February 2022), 'Herding Cats' by Louise Limb
Phoenix Scale Modelling (March 2022), 'The Pink Panther' by Lee Powell
Airfix Model World (August 2024), 'Warrior in Pink' by Nick Shuttleworth
Classic Military Vehicle (August 2024) 'Warrior in Pink' by Nick Shuttleworth
Classic Land Rover (September 2024), 'Warrior in Pink' by Nick Shuttleworth
Classic Land Rover (September 2025), 'Green Dragon' by John Carroll
Mixed Grilles (April 2026), 'SAS Pink Panther' by Andrew Montgomery

Chapter Seven

SAS PINK PANTHERS: A CELEBRATION OF PERSONAL OWNERSHIP

This chapter explores why military vehicle collectors collect. For some, it is the tactile and visceral experience of driving an army lorry or riding an RAF motorcycle. In contrast, others enjoy the sounds, feel, and sometimes even the aroma of a military vehicle. Exploring the phenomenon and allure of collecting vehicular memorabilia associated with HM Forces is complex, and there is no straightforward answer. It is a combination of essential factors that each plays an important part.

As soon as you get behind the steering wheel of an SAS Pink Panther, it will get into your blood and DNA and leave an indelible mark on those fortunate enough to have experienced it. For those who do, it will become a responsibility and a privilege. Remember that military vehicle collectors are merely temporary custodians and interim passengers of something that has longevity well beyond theirs.

The SAS Pink Panther, now well beyond its fiftieth birthday (2019), still exudes a timeless military allure. To become a custodian of an SAS Pink Panther is to ensure it gracefully reaches its next milestone. Its collectability is not just a matter of ticking boxes, but a confluence of several precious and potent factors. The first box that is ticked is the design of the vehicle itself. The 1960s Land-Rover conversions were designed in an analogue world where the FVRDE used pencils and paper, occasionally throwing (posting) a hand grenade into the calm world of the design office to capture the needs and wants of the SAS Regiment. This unique process, belonging to a previous age, is a source of intrigue and fond reflection for many, especially Veterans, and contributes to the enduring appeal of the SAS Pink Panther Land-Rover.

The second box that is ticked, and perhaps the most intriguing, is that military vehicles have rich and fascinating stories about what they accomplished during their time in service. For example, where they have been and what they were doing. Of course, some see the cracks in the leather (Rexine), the paint scratches, or the windscreen dents, as imperfections. But, to military fans around the globe, these are a proud record of the vehicle's heritage and add to its allure, character, provenance, and chronicling of its service life.

This creates a material or object biography where the vehicle becomes the narrator, in this instance, the SAS Pink Panther Land-Rover, and highlights the narrative aspect. You don't have to have a personal financial connection with the SAS Pinkie to enjoy the Pinkie; part of the joy of classic military vehicles is imagining the story behind the vehicle when you view it at a military show or read about it in a magazine. This leads to newer forms of writing and stimulates the interest of both the reader and future author. Indeed, this book could be your catalyst!

Box number three that is confidently ticked, is that many of us are driven by our visual perceptions. A particular military vehicle's styling and physical appearance resonate with some people. For others, the vehicle is a simple and overt statement and evokes an array of emotions and memories. Perhaps they served in the military and now, as a Veteran, return and possibly wish to relive those days by driving, operating and polishing the vehicle.

Nostalgia and individualism also play a large part in the appeal of military vehicle collecting, so box four is nicely ticked. For example, perhaps a motorcycle that served in Northern Ireland or a Chieftain tank that played an integral role in protecting forces in the British Army of the Rhine (BAOR). At the same time, others have overcome renovation challenges that are mundane but no less important to the owner. Box number five is an easy and quick box to tick. It's pink, rare and hard, like the *Financial Times*.

Military vehicles with historical importance, ones that pioneered new technology, fought in a particular war, can often become very collectable, and deserve every plaudit we can bestow upon them, especially if they are rare and can compete on a completely different level. It is undoubtedly not about efficiency and speed here, but the experience, exclusivity, and craftsmanship. All of which are universal and timeless.

Owners of military vehicles derive great satisfaction from exhibiting other prized possessions connected to their vehicle at these events and use them to showcase not only the vehicle but also the history of the vehicle (object biography). These in-service photos, vehicle manuals or extra equipment (weapons, cooking utensils, maps etc.) provide interesting flavour and spice to an often static yet tactile display. Driving these vehicles for all to see then takes it to another level, adding excitement and spectacle to the display. For example, the SAS Pink Panther trucks one sees in military vehicle shows appeal to Land Rover admirers and lovers of engineering, design, and special forces history. A colourful history adds to a vehicle's allure. An association with a respected unit, the SAS, is an excellent case in point and auction houses, documentary makers, and Veterans relish that connection.

In conclusion, restoring an SAS Pink Panther is a substantial undertaking that presents numerous challenges. It requires a unique blend of skills that combines skilled craftsmanship with knowledge of military and automotive history. It's not just a repair job per se; it's an instinctual journey to preserve the essence of special forces' automotive history. Additionally, driving a military vehicle, such as an ageing SAS Land-Rover, requires a great deal of skill and manual input from the driver. It represents a bygone military era of the combustion engine where every detonation of the vehicle's spark plug, along with its shake, rattle, and roll, should be treasured and appreciated.

Indeed, it is truly a feast of noise, revs, smells and thrills, all of which are incredibly visceral and special. Its ability to provide intense sensory overload without breaking speed limits or risking a driving licence sets it apart from other specialised collector vehicles. In summary, driving the SAS Pink Panther on a sunny day can make up for multiple days spent in the rain. So, enjoy it while you can, just like I hope you enjoyed reading this book. Thank you.

Chapter Eight

TECHNICAL DATA OF TRUCK, GENERAL SERVICE (UTILITY), SAS, ¾ TON, 4 X 4 ROVER II

Dimensions

Overall length: Pannier Down 216 inches, 548.64 centimetres, 5,486.4 millimetres

Overall width of vehicle: 84 inches, 213.36 centimetres, 2,133.6 millimetres

Overall height – Unladen: 71 inches 180.34 centimetres, 1,803.4 millimetres

Wheelbase: 109 inches, 276.86 centimetres, 2,768.6 millimetres

Track front and rear: 51.5 inches, 130.81 centimetres, 1,308.1 millimetres

Ground clearance: 8.5 inches, 21.59 centimetres, 215.9 millimetres

Weights – Complete Vehicle

Unladen (with oil, coolant and four gallons of fuel (Imperial) or 4.13 (US) and nil armament:

Front: 2,102 pounds (953 kilograms)
Rear: 2,102 pounds (953 kilograms)
Total: 4,204 pounds (1906 kilograms)

Laden (gross):

Front: 2,520 pounds (1,143 kilograms)
Rear: 4,200 pounds (1,905 kilograms)
Total: 6,720 pounds (3,048 kilograms)

Engine

Type: 4-cylinder, in line, petrol, overhead valve, liquid cooled

Make: The Rover Company Limited, Solihull, Warwickshire. England UK

Size: 2¼ litre, Piston displacement 2286cc

Bore and stroke: 77 bhp (57.4kW) at 4,250 rpm

Torque: 124 pounds feet (17 mug (157 Nm) at 2,500 rpm

Compression ratio: 7.0 or 8.0:1

Carburettor: Solex 40PA10-5

Clutch

Type: Single dry plate

Make: Borg & Beck

Diameter: 9 inches (230 millimetres)

Main Gearbox

Type: 4-Speed and Reverse; Manual with synchromesh on third and fourth

Make: The Rover Company Limited, Solihull, Warwickshire. England UK

Ratios: 1st 3.6:1, 2nd 2.22:1, 3rd 1.512:1, 4th 1.00:1 and reverse 3.02:1

Transfer Case

Type: 2-Speed, with front axle disconnect, in unit with main gearbox

Make: The Rover Company Limited, Solihull, Warwickshire. England UK

Ratios: high 1.148:1 and low 2.40:1

Front and Rear Axles

Type: Full floating, spiral bevel drive (at front with enclosed universal joints)

Make: The Rover Company Limited, Solihull, Warwickshire, England, UK

Suspension

Type: front and rear semi-elliptic leaf springs with telescopic shock absorbers

Chassis

Type: Box section frame

Steering

Type: Recirculating ball, with hydraulic telescopic damper
Make: Burman

Brakes

Type: transfer case

Wheels and Tyres

Wheel type: steel disc, well-base, five-hole, rim size 6L x 15
Tyres: 9.00-15, tubed, with sand tread (cross-country tread available and optional)

Tyre Pressures

Road
Front: 15 Ibf/in^2 (103 kN/m^2)
Rear: 40 Ibf/in^2 (276 kN/m^2)

Sand
Front: 10 Ibf/in^2 (69 kN/m^2)
Rear: 22 Ibf/in^2 (152 kN/m^2)

Cross Country
Front: 12 Ibf/in^2 (83 kN/m^2)
Rear: 30 Ibf/in^2 (207 kN/m^2)
Girling, hydraulic, with leading and trailing shoes; parking: mechanical, drum behind

Electrical System

The electrical equipment is standard as for the Land Rover II, except that the registration plate (ERM) and light are mounted centrally on the rear edge of the Pannier Carrier Board, and the additional electrical equipment is fitted for the vehicle's particular role.

The supplementary equipment fitted is as follows:

1. Portable searchlight
2. Normal-ignition only switch
3. Inter-vehicle starter power socket and cable
4. Power socket, radio and radio battery charger
5. Power supply and press switches for the smoke dischargers
6. Power supply and switch for the type E2B illuminated Compass Lamp

Make: Lucas
Voltage: 12 volts (one battery) generator: 12-volt DC

Bodywork
Type: open, modified from the standard model

Angles of Approach and Departure
41° and 26°

Vehicle Performance
Maximum speed: approximately 45 miles per hour (72.4205 kilometres per hour)
Cruising range: approximately 1,500 miles (2,500 kilometres)
Gradability: approximately 33 per cent
Maximum fording depth: 20 inches (50.8 centimetres)
Turning circle: approximately 50 feet (15.24 metres)

Liquid Capacities
Engine sump: (refill 11 pints (6 litres)
Gear box: 2.5 pints (1.5 litres)
Transfer case: 4.5 pints (2.5 litres)
Differentials: 3 pints (1.75 litres) each
Cooling system: 17.5 pints (10 litres)

Fuel Capacities

Tank	Metric Litres	Imperial Gallons	USA Gallons
Main Tank	20	24	90.92
Auxiliary Tank (2 x 40)	80	96	363.68
Expansion Tanks (x 2)	5	6	22.73

Wheels
Type: well-base rim
Size: 6L x 15 inches

Tyres
Size: 9 x 15 inches or 22.86 x 38.1 centimetres

Tyre Pressures

	Front Sand Tyres	Rear Sand Tyres	Front Cross Country Tyres	Rear Cross Country Tyres	Front Cross Country Tyres	Rear Cross Country Tyres
lbf/in²	15	40	10	22	12	30
kgf/cm²	1	2.8	0.7	1.5	0.8	2
kN/m²	103	276	69	152	83	207

Chapter Nine

THE FINAL DESTINATION OF THE LAND-ROVER SERIES IIA SAS PINK PANTHER

'Only those who risk going too far can possibly find out
how far they can go.'
T.S. Eliot

The SAS Land-Rover Pink Panther is a legendary military vehicle that holds a special place in the hearts of many. It is not just a mode of transportation but a symbol of courage, extremes, and resilience. The SAS Pink Panther was designed to operate in the harshest environments. It is a product of the contributions of many people and serves as a cutting-edge reminder of the 1960s engineering at the forefront of special forces design.

Every inch of the SAS Pink Panther has detailed features that captivate and draw your attention, tease your senses, distract, and compel you to look further and elbow its way to prominence amongst the other military vehicles on the parade ground. However, despite its legendary status, many Pinkies did not live to see their entire working lifespan.

For those interested in the fate of these vehicles, a comprehensive list has been compiled in order of their ERM. The list includes vehicles scrapped, lost in action, or donated to local friendly forces. This information has been meticulously gathered to the best of the author's ability in collaboration with the SAS Pink Panther Register and using the vehicle data cards (DOS 419B) from the RLC Museum (Archives and Library), Worthy Down.

SAS Land-Rover Pink Panther – Vehicle Location Data

ERM	Chassis Code	DIS	Date of Disposal	Disposal Location and Entry on Vehicle Data Card
10 FG 30	251-14139D	January 1969	October 1971	Redacted – NCND
10 FG 31	251-14116D	July 1969	August 1976	Ruddington Auctions, Nottingham
10 FG 32	251-13929D	July 1969	May 1976	Ruddington Auctions, Nottingham
10 FG 33	251-14118D	July 1969	December 1985	British Car Auctions, Birmingham
10 FG 34	251-13987D	July 1969	August 1986	British Car Auctions, Birmingham
10 FG 35	251-13970D	July 1969	May 1976	Ruddington Auctions, Nottingham
10 FG 36	251-13999D	July 1969	November 1982	Redacted – NCND
10 FG 37	251-14181D	July 1969	July 1977	Redacted – NCND
10 FG 38	251-14142D	July 1969	May 1977	Redacted – NCND
10 FG 39	251-14167D	July 1969	December 1981	Redacted – NCND
10 FG 40	251-13985D	July 1969	September 1981	Last known entry on card, SAS, Hereford
10 FG 41	251-14100D	July 1969	January1986	Redacted – NCND
10 FG 42	251-14907G	July 1969	July 1977	Redacted – NCND

10 FG 43	251-13986D	July 1969	October 1977	SAS, Hereford – Training Aid
10 FG 44	251-13994D	July 1969	October 1976	Redacted – NCND
10 FG 45	251-14088D	July 1969	March 1982	Last known entry on card, SAS, Hereford
10 FG 46	251-14140D	July 1969	January 1986	Redacted – NCND
10 FG 47	251-13995D	July 1969	January 1986	Redacted – NCND
10 FG 48	251-14119D	July 1969	July 1976	Ruddington Auctions, Nottingham
10 FG 49	251-14179D	July 1969	January 1986	Redacted – NCND
10 FG 50	251-13955D	July 1969	March 1985	Redacted – NCND
10 FG 51	251-13990D	July 1969	September 1986	British Car Auctions, Birmingham
10 FG 52	251-13946D	July 1969	February 1986	British Car Auctions, Birmingham
10 FG 53	251-14094D	July 1969	August 1976	Desert dumped and cannibalised
10 FG 54	251-14081D	July 1969	November 1976	A&AEE, Boscombe Down – scrap
10 FG 55	251-13950D	July 1969	February 1986	British Car Auctions, Birmingham
10 FG 56	251-13969D	July 1969	November 1982	CVD, Ashchurch (location not entered)
10 FG 57	251-13938D	July 1969	March 1986	British Car Auctions, Birmingham

10 FG 58	251-13983D	July 1969	January 1978	Redacted – NCND
10 FG 59	251-13942D	July 1969	March 1982	Last known entry on Card, SAS, Hereford
10 FG 60	251-13952D	July 1969	January 1976	Ruddington Auctions, Nottingham
10 FG 61	251-13989D	July 1969	June 1985	British Car Auctions, Birmingham
10 FG 62	251-13944D	July 1969	June 1985	SAS, Hereford – controlled spares
10 FG 63	251-13948D	July 1969	April 1983	Redacted – NCND
10 FG 64	251-13953D	July 1969	January 1986	Redacted – NCND
10 FG 65	251-14095D	July 1969	August 1976	Ruddington Auctions, Nottingham
10 FG 66	251-13966D	July 1969	December 1981	Redacted – NCND
10 FG 67	251-14101D	July 1969	November 1980	Ruddington Auctions, Nottingham
10 FG 68	251-13984D	July 1969	October 1976	Redacted – NCND
10 FG 69	251-14093D	July 1969	August 1976	Ruddington Auctions, Nottingham
10 FG 70	251-13981D	July 1969	April 1986	Redacted – NCND
10 FG 71	251-13982D	July 1969	August 1976	Desert dumped and cannibalised
10 FG 72	251-13951D	July 1969	August 1976	Ruddington Auctions, Nottingham

10 FG 73	251-13940D	July 1969	December 1977	Redacted – NCND
10 FG 74	251-13949D	July 1969	January 1976	Ruddington Auctions, Nottingham
10 FG 75	251-14089D	July 1969	February 1980	Ruddington Auctions, Nottingham
10 FG 76	251-14098D	July 1969	March 1986	British Car Auctions, Birmingham
10 FG 77	251-14091D	July 1969	January 1986	Redacted – NCND
10 FG 78	251-14134D	July 1969	June 1977	Redacted – NCND
10 FG 79	251-13988D	July 1969	November 1975	Ruddington Auctions, Nottingham
10 FG 80	251-14121D	July 1969	No Entry	No entry on DOS 419B
10 FG 81	251-14169D	July 1969	December 1977	Redacted – NCND
10 FG 82	251-14117D	January 1970	October 1976	Ruddington Auctions, Nottingham
10 FG 83	251-14099D	January 1970	April 1986	Redacted – NCND
10 FG 84	251-14143D	January 1970	April 1986	British Car Auctions, Birmingham
10 FG 85	251-14168D	July 1969	July 1984	Cast vehicle to be used as a training aid
10 FG 86	251-13954D	July 1969	September 1986	Redacted – NCND

10 FG 87	251-14096D	July 1969	December 1985	British Car Auctions, Birmingham
10 FG 88	251-13956D	January 1970	April 1986	Redacted – NCND
10 FG 89	251-14177D	July 1969	January 1986	Redacted – NCND
10 FG 90	251-13967D	July 1969	January 1986	Redacted – NCND
10 FG 91	251-14102D	July 1969	December 1977	Redacted – NCND
10 FG 92	251-14164D	July 1969	July 1985	Redacted – NCND
10 FG 93	251-14078D	January 1970	October 1986	British Car Auctions, Birmingham
10 FG 94	251-14087D	January 1970	March 1986	British Car Auctions, Birmingham
10 FG 95	251-14090D	July 1969	December 1977	Redacted – NCND
10 FG 96	251-14120D	January 1970	October 1986	Vehicle to be used as EXHIBITION ONLY
10 FG 97	251-13968D	January 1970	October 1986	British Car Auctions, Birmingham
10 FG 98	251-14175D	January 1970	December 1977	Redacted – NCND
10 FG 99	251-14183D	January 1970	October 1986	British Car Auctions, Birmingham
11 FG 00	251-14005D	January 1970	April 1986	Redacted – NCND
11 FG 01	251-14161D	January 1970	January 1986	Redacted – NCND

Museums and Websites of Interest Associated with the SAS Pink Panther

Imperial War Museum (IWM)

Website: https://www.iwm.org.uk/visits/iwm-london

The IWM is the world's leading museum of war and conflict. Founded while the First World War was still raging (1917), the IWM is a global authority on conflict and its impact on people's lives. Their collection of objects and stories gives an insight into people's experiences of war, preserves them for future generations, and brings them to today's audiences in the most powerful way possible.

National Army Museum

Website: https://www.nam.ac.uk

The National Army Museum (1960) is a leading authority on the British Army and its impact on society past and present. The museum examines the role of the Army from the British Civil Wars to the modern day. Through their collections, they preserve and share stories of ordinary people with extraordinary responsibilities and explore the role of the British Army and its relevance today. As a part of their collection, they have SAS Land-Rover, 10 FG 90.

British Motor Museum

Website: https://www.britishmotormuseum.co.uk

The British Motor Museum is home to the world's largest collection of historic British Cars; it boasts over 400 cars spanning the classic, vintage and veteran eras. The museum opened in 1993 as the amalgamation of the British Motor Industry Heritage Trust's preserved car collection. It houses SAS Land-Rover Pink Panther, 10 FG 40.

Dunsfold Collection

Website: https://www.dunsfoldcollection.co.uk

The Dunsfold Collection of Land Rovers is a registered charity dedicated to preserving Land Rover history. The collection was started in 1968 by Brian Bashall, who realised that his love of strange prototypes and pre-production Land Rovers was of interest to others. The museum also houses an unrivalled archive of Land Rover brochures, publicity material, manuals, handbooks, photographs, drawings and magazines, and an extraordinary collection of Land Rover models and toys. As part of their collection, they have SAS Pink Panther, 10 FG 45.

Land Rover Heritage Collection

Website: https://www.lrheritagecollection.org.uk

The Land Rover Heritage Collection (LRHC) – Andy and Chris Milsted – set out with a very clear objective with their collection, and that objective was, in their words,

> to capture, preserve and maintain for future generations, an accessible permanent record of the classic Land Rover in the context of seven decades of it being Britain's most loved workhorse; a British design icon.

The collection, based in Somerset, comprises many notable exhibits, including SAS Land-Rover Pink Panthers 10 FG 34 and 10 FG 97, held within the LRHC Trust to ensure their preservation for future generations. The LRHC Trust is also responsible for displaying and exhibiting the collection for the benefit of all. The vehicles in the collection are showcased at classic vehicle events throughout the UK, and some are also featured in print and on screen. The LRHC Trust also makes selected vehicles available on loan terms for publicity and academic purposes.

Royal Signals Museum

Website: https://www.royalsignalsmuseum.co.uk

Telling the story of military communications from semaphore to cyber, the Royal Signals Museum (opened in 1967) houses the national collection of military communications equipment. It vividly tells the story of military communications and the Corps via enlightening exhibitions, including interactive displays. The displays are planned and created by serving soldiers from different units, providing a soldier's perspective of their roles and responsibilities. The museum proudly showcases 10 FG 59.

Isle of Man Motor Museum

Website: https://www.isleofmanmotormuseum.com

Situated on the former RAF Jurby in the sunny north of the Isle of Man, the privately funded Isle of Man Motor Museum was purpose-designed and houses over 500 vehicles. Opened in May 2015, it has become a petrolhead's paradise with something for everyone to enjoy. From unique prototypes to TT-winning motorcycles, early steam cars to 1980s hot hatches, a hovercraft, and even a Soviet Space Capsule are on display. One noteworthy item among their collection was SAS Land-Rover, 10 FG 84, which features on the front cover of this book!

Royal Logistic Corps Museum

Website: https://www.royallogisticcorps.co.uk

The RLC Museum, previously located in Deepcut (Royal Army Ordnance Corps) but now in Worthy Down, Winchester, offers visitors an insightful look into how the British Army has moved, supplied, and sustained itself over the centuries. The museum showcases military history from Agincourt to the present day, including iconic pieces such as Field Marshal Montgomery's D-Day Rolls-Royce, a variety of military horse-drawn and motorised logistic vehicles, uniforms, weapons, medals, and much more.

The museum also houses the essential vehicle data cards (DOS 419Bs) for the SAS Pink Panther Land-Rover, which they graciously permitted me to replicate for this book. These vehicle data cards are easily accessible electronically and can be obtained on a pay-per-view basis.

Ex-Military Land Rover Association

Website: https://www.emlra.org

The Ex-Military Land Rover Association has been serving the Land Rover enthusiast for nearly four decades now. It was set up to promote the operation, restoration, and preservation of ex-military Land Rovers and interest in them.

It supports this aim by promoting events and shows, attending established vehicle shows, and organising association meetings for members to socialise and display their vehicles. It provides members with information, advice, and assistance concerning ex-military Land Rovers and encourages research and the accumulation of documents, photographs, and other relevant material by the Association.

Military Vehicle Trust (MVT)

Website: https://www.mvt.org.uk

MVT is the world's largest group of ex-military vehicle owners and enthusiasts and the only charity dedicated to 'keeping mechanical veterans alive'. Since 1978, the MVT has provided help and support to members and the public, who have preserved thousands of military vehicles after their active lives with the armed forces.

The MVT sets out to achieve its charitable aims by promoting many activities that support members and advance public knowledge and understanding of how historic vehicles have contributed to military heritage. They produce a magazine entitled *Windscreen*, the MVT's prestigious award-winning magazine, published and posted to members six times a year.

Invicta Military-Vehicle Preservation Society (IMPS)

Website: https://www.imps.org.uk

The IMPS (founded 1980) is dedicated to preserving military vehicles of all types, including bicycles, main battle tanks, and vehicles that have been used in both wartime and peacetime. The society's members are actively involved in restoring and preserving military vehicles to ensure their historical significance is not lost. IMPS members are involved in all aspects of vehicle preservation, from sourcing parts and knowledge to the restoration process. They take pride in their work and are dedicated to preserving each vehicle's unique history and character.

Kit Form Service

Website: https:www.kitformservices.com

Kit Form Services (KFS) is one of the most established (1984) 1/24th model truck kit suppliers in the market, and over the last decade, it has also developed a growing range of high-quality 1/24th scale classic British military vehicle kits and accessories.

Kit Form Services (founded by a former REME soldier) manufactures and stocks high-quality polyurethane resin and white metal parts and kits, along with photo-etch detailing sets in brass, stainless steel, nickel silver, and highly detailed waterslide decals made using traditional silk screen printed methods. They do a superb 1/24 scale SAS Pink Panther Land-Rover.

Armorama

Website: https://www.archive.armorama.com

Founded in 2001, Armorama is the largest and most visited site on the internet for scale AFV modellers and is part of the KitMaker Network. This has the coverage of the build by Joe Grafton using the Tamiya SAS Land-Rover Pink Panther together with Eduard Photo-Etch set for the TAMIYA kit and Hussar Productions sand tyres and Legend Productions, SAS Pink Panther stowage and update set.

Brit Modeller

Website: https://www.britmodeller.com

The website https://britmodeller.com has an excellent build of a 1/35 SAS Land-Rover Pink Panther created by someone using the pseudonym 'Heart Failure'. The model was built using the base SAS Land-Rover kit from TAMIYA and the basic set from Legend. I highly recommend visiting this site, as the photos of the model and the build process are genuinely superb.

The Kit Box

Website: https://www.thekitbox.org

The website thekitbox.org hosts the 'Ten Day Challenge' in building two SAS Land-Rover Pink Panthers from two different plastic kit manufacturers, TAMIYA and ITALERI and see how they compare. The modellers are Spencer Pollard and Jonathan Mock. Being part of the Ten Day 'Challenge' series, the build came with several restrictions. First was the ten-day time period in which to build it.

The second, in this case, was that they had to build the model using what was in the box. Additional details could be added, but they had to be made from scratch as no aftermarket accessories could be incorporated. Despite these constraints, both modellers did an amazing job, and the end product of their hard work is superb. Well worth a look.

Kit Maker Forum

Website: https://www.forums.kitmaker.net

On this particular internet forum, there is a fantastic build of an SAS Land-Rover (TAMIYA) by Raphael Golez (AKA cut-n-paste). It is definitely worth checking out, as the SAS Pinkie build is particularly impressive and showcases cut-n-paste's excellent modelling skills. Additionally, he has provided high-quality photos that give a clear and detailed view of the 1/35 scale kit, making it even more enjoyable to admire.

Eduard Model Accessories

Website: https://www.eduard.com

Eduard Model Accessories is a Czech manufacturer of plastic models and fine-scale model accessories; they make some great additions to the SAS Pink Panther. Their range of accessories includes resin and photo-etch conversions, which are perfect for hobbyists who are looking to add more intricate details to their model kits.

Legend

Website: https://www.legend.co.kr

Legend is a company that specialises in producing high-quality plastic model kits and finely detailed accessories. Like Eduard Model Accessories, their range of accessories includes resin and photo-etch conversions, which are perfect for hobbyists who are looking to add more intricate details to their model kits.

S&S Models

Website: https://www.sandsmodels.com

S&S Models (1986), based in Burnham-on-Sea, Somerset, was started by Stewart Crosby and Shaun Matthew; hence the S&S! One of the models that S&S Models is renowned for is the SAS Pink Panther, which is 1/72 in scale. The level of detail in this model is exceptional, and it is highly sought after by collectors and model enthusiasts alike.

WWP Books

Website: https://www.wwpbooks.com

WWP books are an excellent resource for military machine enthusiasts and modellers passionate about improving their final kit's accuracy and detail. The accompanying text is limited but provides essential information on the vehicle's history, specifications, and unique features. The high-quality photographs, taken from various angles and lighting conditions, allow readers to see even the smallest details, such as hatches, rivets, and markings. If you're looking for a softcover book to invest in, *SAS Panthers in Detail* is a great first choice.

Key Publishing

Website: https://www.keypublishing.com

Classic Military Vehicle is a popular publication in the United Kingdom that covers historic military vehicles. The magazine provides coverage of wheeled and tracked military hardware, which has been used in conflicts worldwide. It has been in publication since the turn of the twentieth century, when warfare became increasingly mechanised, up to the Gulf War of the 1990s.

Readers can find in-depth profiles of vehicles, along with readers' restorations and historical features. Regular news, event reports, book reviews and archive photo sections are also included in the magazine. The Pink Panther SAS Land-Rover is often featured in this publication.

BIBLIOGRAPHY

Articles

Anonymous, 'Pink Panther', *Military Machines International* (July 2011)

Branch, Ben, 'Pink Panther', *ENGAGE 4 x 4* (November / December 2021)

Bucknell, Alan, 'Pink Panthers on Patrol', *Windscreen*, Military Vehicle Trust (October 2019)

Bowen, Glen, 'Sneaky in Pink', *Model Military International* (June 2006)

Carroll, John, 'Green Dragon', *Classic Land Rover* (September 2025)

Carroll, John, 'The One and Only Truly Original', *Land Rover International* (Spring 2010)

Cawte, Paul, 'Tickled Pink', *Airfix Model World Magazine* (November 2015)

Cheetham, Craig, 'A Shot in the Dark', *Land Rover Owner* (April 2000)

Edwards, Julian, 'A Scratchbuilt 1 / 32nd Scale S.A.S. Land Rover', *Military Modelling* (November and December 1972, and January 1973)

Entwistle, Paul and Andrew, *Land Rover World*, Issue 18 (August 1995) 'Cold Metal'

Hargett, Paul, 'Staying in the Pink', *Scale Military Modeller International* (March 2018)

Hayward-Wills, Adrian, 'A Marvel in Miniature', *The Landy Newspaper*, Issue 89 (July 2021)

Hayward-Wills, Adrian, 'A Model Pinkie', *Classic Military Vehicle* (January 2021)

Hayward-Wills, Adrian, 'New Model Army', *Land Rover International* (December 2020)

Hayward-Wills, Adrian, 'Perfect Pinkie', *Land Rover Yearbook 2022* (November 2021)

Hebden, Alan and Kennedy, Ian, 'Jet Pilot' *Commando*, Issue 2,263

Hucknall, Simon, *Classic and Sports Car* (January 2024)

Ingram, John, 'Pink Panther', *Military Machines International* (April 2006)

Jones, Roger, 'Pinky and Pinky and Pinky', *Off Road and 4 Wheel Drive* (March 1989)

Limb, Louise, 'Herding Cats', *Classic Military Vehicle* (February 2022)

Morrison, Bob, 'Behind the Lines', *Land Rover Monthly* (January 2002)
Morrison, Bob, 'In the Pink', *Land Rover Owner International* (August 1995)
Morrison, Bob, 'Pink Panther', *Military Modelcraft International* (September 1997)
Pepin, Emilien, 'Serving the Sultan', *Armoured Fighting Vehicle* (November/December 2011)
Pepin, Emilien, 'Special Forces 1941–2011', *Les thématiques Steel Masters* (April 2011, France)
Philip, Craig and Taylor, Alex Taylor, *Inside the SAS* (Bloomsbury, 1992)
Powell, Lee, 'The Pink Panther', *Phoenix Scale Modelling* (March 2022)
Rogers, Anthony, 'SAS Land Rovers', *Combat & Survival*, Volume 1, Issue 9 (December 1989)
Sanders, Lane, 'Desert Rover', *Scale Modeler* (American publication) (October 1976)
Sanders, Lane, 'SAS Land Rover', *Military Modeler* (Canadian publication) (October 1980)
Shuttleworth, Nick, 'Warrior in Pink', *Airfix Model World* (August 2024)
Shuttleworth, Nick, 'Warrior in Pink', *Classic Land Rover* (August 2024)
Shuttleworth, Nick, 'Warrior in Pink', *Classic Land Rover* (September 2024)
Smith, Kev, 'The Rinky-Dink Panther', *TAMIYA Model Magazine International* (March 2021)
Stuart, Michael Crichton, '*G Patrol*', William Kimber, London, (1958)
Stubbs, Colonel John, 'Pink Panther' Military Modelling (1973)
Alain Taou, 'S.A.S Land Rover, France', *Military Armor International*, Issue 20 (August–September 2002)
Taylor, James, articles covering their renovation of 10 FG 88 – 'Project Pink Panther', *Land Rover Enthusiast* (2002–2005)
Taylor, James, 'SAS Land Rovers', *Classic Military Vehicle* (January 2017)
Taylor, James, 'Military Roverphile', *Military Machines International* (January 2010)
Taylor, James, articles covering Pink Panther related titles, *Classic Military Vehicle* (July 2002, January 2017 and January 2021)
Thansriskul, Claire, 'Fight Club – SAS Land Rovers', *Land Rover World* (January 2003)
Timpson MC Major J. Alastair L. and Gibson-Watt, Andrew (editor) *In Rommel's Backyard* (Leo Cooper/Pen & Sword Books, 2000)
Vanderveen, Bart 'SAS Land-Rovers: The SAS Pink Panther and its Predecessors', *Wheels & Track*, Issue 9
Young, Ian, 'Pink But Deadly', *Airfix Model World* (November 2015)
Young, Ian, 'Return of the Pink Panther', *Military Modelcraft International* (September 1997)

Books

Anonymous, *Complete Equipment Schedule (Service Edition) Army Census Code Number 1725, 0766* (April 1969)

Anonymous, *Complete Equipment Schedule (Service Edition)* (April 1969)

Anonymous, *Electrical and Mechanical Engineering Regulations* (February 1970)

Anonymous, *Illustrated Spare Parts List for Body Used on Truck, Utility, SAS, ¾ Ton, 4 x 4, Rover II* (January 1970)

Anonymous, *SLR 7.62mm User Handbook*

Anonymous, *Technical Handbook for the Truck, General Service, SAS ¾, Rover II* (February 1970)

Anonymous, *Truck, General Service, SAS, ¾ Ton, 4 x 4, Rover II* (booklet) (August 1969)

Anonymous, *Truck, General Service, SAS, ¾ Ton, 4 x 4, Rover II* (booklet) (February 1970)

Armaments, Inspectorate of, *User Handbook* (1968)

Bagnold, Brigadier Ralph, *The Physics of Blown Sand and Desert Dunes* (1939)

British Army, *Materiel Regulations for the Army: Painting of Army Vehicles, Aircraft and Equipment*

Challenor MM, Harold Gordon 'Tanky', *Tanky Challenor: SAS and the Met* (Leo Cooper / Pen & Sword Books, Barnsley, 1990)

de Boer, Jan W., Kautský, Aleš and Kořán, František, *Special Operations Landies in Detail: Armed Land Rovers Used by Special Forces* (Wings & Wheels Publications, February 2012) de Saint-Exupéry Antoine, *Wind, Sand and Stars*

Defence, Ministry of, *SAS Landrover (Desert Version) User Handbook* (August 1969)

Doran, Francis 'Geordie' with Morgan, Mike, *Fighting Legend of the SAS* (Sutton Publishing Limited, 2007)

Doran, Francis 'Geordie' with Morgan, Mike, *GEORDIE* (Sutton Publishing Limited) Farran, Major Roy, *Winged Dagger* (1948)

Flook, Ron, *British and Commonwealth Military Knives* (Airlife, 1999)

Geraghty, Tony, *This Is the SAS: A Pictorial History of the Special Air Service Regiment* (1982)

Geraghty, Tony, *Who Dares Wins: The Story of the Special Air Service, 1950–1980* (1980)

Holmes, Richard, *The Visual Dictionary of Special Military Forces (DKP 1993)*

Howlett, Simon, *Modern British Webbing Equipment* (published in paperback, 2009)

HM Government, *Battle Handling (All Arms) Infantry Training*, Volume 1 (1969)

Jenner, Robin and List, David, *The Long Range Desert Group* (Vanguard 36) (Osprey, 1983)

Kořán, František and Kautský, Aleš, *SAS Panthers in Detail: SAS Pink Panthers*

of the Barry Pocock's and Another British Private Collection (Wings & Wheels Publications, November 2010)

Laidler, Peter, *An Inside View of the Snipers Rifle Telescope*

Leger, Philippe Leger, *JERRYCAN: 70 Years and Still in Service* (Heimdal, 2008)

Morgan, Mike, *Sting of the Scorpion: The Inside Story of the LRDG* (Sutton Publishing Limited, 2000)

Mortimer, Gavin, *SAS Combat Vehicles 1941–1991* (Osprey, 2021)

Niven, Colonel B.M., *Special Men, Special War* (1990)

Orwell, George, *Animal Farm* (1945)

Rottman, Gordon, *US Grenade Launchers* (Osprey, 2017)

Skipper, Ben, *Land Rover: Military Versions of the British 4 x 4* (Pen & Sword Books, Barnsley, 2020)

Sprague, Martina, *Machete, Kris and Throwing Iron* (2013)

Stevens, R. Blake, *The Browning High Power Automatic Pistol Book* (First Edition, 1984 and limited-edition reprint 2014)

Taylor, James and Fletcher, Geoff, *British Military Land Rovers* (2015)

Vicker, Larry, *Vickers Guide AR-15*, Volume 1, second edition (2020)

Ware, Pat, *A Compendium of British Soft-Skin Military Vehicles*, Volume 13, Military Vehicles Archive (2023)

Ware, Pat, *Haynes Manual for Military Land Rovers* (2016)

Ware, Pat, *Military Land Rover: Development and in Service* (May 2007)

Ware, Pat, *Special Forces Vehicles 1940 to the Present Day* (Pen & Sword Books, Barnsley, 2012)

Warner, Philip, *The Special Air Service* (1971),

Wilson, Buce, *'Denison' British Airborne Specialist Clothing from WWII to the Present Day* (published by Military Mode Publishing and in collaboration with the Airborne Assault Museum, 2013)

Magazines

Airfix Model World (November 2015 and August 2024)

Armoured Fighting Vehicle (November/December 2011)

Classic and Sports Car (January 2024)

Classic Land Rover (September 2024 and September 2025)

Classic Military Vehicle (July 2002, January 2017, January 2021, February 2022 and August 2024)

Combat & Survival, Volume 1, Issue 9 (December 1989) *ENGAGE 4 x 4* (November/December 2021)

Land Rover Enthusiast (November 2000, June 2002, March 2005 and 2002–2005)

Land Rover International (Spring 2010 and December 2020)

Land Rover Monthly (January 2002)

Land Rover Owner (April 2000)

Land Rover Owner International (August 1995)

Land Rover World, Issue 18 (August 1995)

Land Rover World (January 2003)

Les thématiques Steel Masters (April 2011, France)

Military Armor International, Issue 20 (August–September 2002)

Military Machines International (April 2006, January 2010 and July 2011)

Military Modelcraft International (September 1997)

Military Modeler (Canadian publication) (October 1980)

Military Modelling (November and December 1972, and January 1973)

Mixed Grilles (May 2026)

Model Military International (June 2006)

Off Road and 4 Wheel Drive (March 1989)

Phoenix Scale Modelling (March 2022)

Scale Military Modeller International (March 2018)

Scale Modeler (American publication) (October 1976)

TAMIYA Model Magazine International (March 2021)

Wheels & Track, Issue 9

Windscreen, Military Vehicle Trust (October 2019)

Museums

British Motor Museum, Banbury Road, Gaydon, Warwickshire

Imperial War Museum, Lambeth Road, London

Isle of Man Motor Museum, Jurby, Isle of Man

National Army Museum, Chelsea, London

Royal Logistics Corps Museum, Worthy Down, Winchester

Royal Signals Museum, Blandford Forum, Dorset

The Tank Museum, Bovington, Dorset

Transport Museum, Beverley (closed *circa* 2003)

Newspapers

The Landy Newspaper, Issue 89 (July 2021)

Websites
Armorama: https://www.archive.armorama.com
Brit Modeller: https://www.britmodeller.com
British Motor Museum: https://www.britishmotormuseum.co.uk
Dunsfold Collection: https://www.dunsfoldcollection.co.uk
Eduard Model Accessories: https://www.eduard.com
Ex-Military Land Rover Association: https://www.emlra.org
Imperial War Museum: https://www.iwm.org.uk
Imperial War Museum: https://www.iwm.org.uk/visits/iwm-london
Invicta Military-Vehicle Preservation Society: https://www.imps.org.uk
Isle of Man Motor Museum: https://www.isleofmanmotormuseum.com
Key Publishing: https://www.keypublishing.com
Kit Form Services: https:www.kitformservices.com
Kit Maker Forum: https://www.forums.kitmaker.net
Land Rover Heritage Collection: https://www.lrheritagecollection.org.uk
Legend: https://www.legend.co.kr
Louise Limb: https://www.louiselimb.com
Military Vehicle Trust: https://www.mvt.org.uk
National Army Museum: https://www.nam.ac.uk
Pink Panther 10 FG 87: https://10fg87.org
Royal Logistics Corps Museum: https://www.royallogisticcorps.co.uk
Royal Signals Museum: https://www.royalsignalsmuseum.co.uk
S&S Models: https://www.sandsmodels.com
The Kit Box: https://www.thekitbox.org
WWP Books: https://www.wwpbooks.com
YouTube: Seb Morgan Restorations, *circa* 2021
YouTube: John Sear's video entitled 'Pink Panthers'

Yearbooks
Land Rover Yearbook 2022 (November 2021)

INDEX

A
ADPCON, 20
Ambi-Budd Presswerk, Berlin, 84
Ammunition, 6, 46, 47, 50, 52, 53, 68, 77, 83, 106, 107, 112, 114, 115
Armalite (rifle), 105, 108, 114
Army Strategic Command, 23
Army Air Transport Training and Development Centre (AATDC), 34
Asbestos, 44
Austin Champ, 5
Auxiliary (fuel) Tank, 8, 20, 39, 40, 41, 44, 45, 53, 56, 57, 59, 75, 84, 89, 96, 99, 147

B
BAOR, British Army of the Rhine, 24, 103, 142
Bash plates, (underbody protection plates), 8, 42, 43
Baty, Patrick, 25
Battery, 67, 68, 69, 95, 96, 146, 147
Belgian Army Minerva, 2
Bergan, 107, 109, 110
Blackout Driving Light, Curfew, 53, 54
Blanchard & Co. 39, 134
BMW (Bayerische Motoren Werke AG), 84
Binoculars, 40, 93
Bonhams, Auctioneers, 2, 17, 63, 135
Boscombe Down, 14, 151
Bradbury Lines, 12, 21, 67
Bridging (Convoy) Plate, 78, 79, 80
Bridgestone, (Tyres), 14, 72
British Car Auctions, 12, 131
British Motor Industry Heritage Trust, 137, 138, 155
Bromochlorodifluoromethane, (Fire Extinguisher), 90
Browning, (weapons), 5, 6, 110, 112, 113, 114, 126, 164
Burndept Electronics Limited, (SARBE), 105
Bucknell, Alan, 64, 104, 161

C
Canvas Bucket Mk. 5, 89
Camouflage Net, 92
Carl-Gustaf, (anti-tank weapon), 11, 51, 52
Caroll, John, 140
Chagall, natural fibre Water Carrier, 88
Challenor, Tanky 5, 163
Chertsey, (RARDE), 10, 39
Chevrolet WB, 30cwt, 31
Chronometers, 60
Clansman (Radio), 97, 98
Classic Land Rover, (Magazine), 140, 156, 161, 162, 16
Classic Military Vehicle, magazine, 33, 49, 51, 73, 84, 85, 88, 91, 104, 116, 124, 126, 142, 160, 165
Claymore, 100
Combat & Survival, (magazine), 29, 110, 139, 162, 165
Crank – hand starting, 68
Craddock, John, 132
Crichton Stuart, Michael, 31
Cole (Sun Compass) 11, 56, 63
Commando Helicopter Operating Support Cells, (CHOSC), 30
Complete Equipment Schedule, (CES), 2, 22, 163
Compass, Prismatic, 58, 59
Cooker (No. 2, Mk.2), 40, 100, 102, 108
Cooking Equipment, 100, 101, 102, 106, 143
Cyprus, 24

D
DCI (Directorate of Cataloguing and Identification), 21
Denison, combat smock, 117, 164
Denmark, 24
Dixie Equipment, 40, 102
Doran, Geordie, 33, 75
DOS Form 419B, 12, 18, 19, 20, 83, 130, 136, 137
Drop shackles, 73, 74
DPM, (Disruptive Pattern Material), 24
Duckboards, (wooden), 17, 39, 40, 48
Dunsfold, 1, 2, 26, 155, 166
Dunlop, (Tyres), 14, 72
DVLA (Driver Vehicle Licensing Authority), 1, 2, 14, 125, 126, 127, 128, 136, 138

E
E2B Compass, Type, 9, 40, 54, 56
Engine, 5, 18, 34, 38, 40, 42, 67, 71, 74, 80, 96, 145, 147
Equipment Registration Mark (ERM, Registration Plates), 1, 2, 5, 6, 8, 9, 13, 15, 18, 19, 21, 24, 29, 30, 32, 35, 36, 40, 48, 55, 60, 63, 68, 69, 70, 71, 75, 78, 80, 81, 82, 83, 85, 87, 91, 94, 95, 100, 102, 110, 114, 120, 122, 123, 124, 125, 126, 127, 128, 129, 130, 132, 135, 136, 146, 149, 150, 156, 157, 159
Expansion tanks (Fuel), 44, 147

F
Fabric Chart (Maps), 106
FVRDE, (Fighting Vehicles Research and Development Establishment) 2, 8, 9, 10, 11, 15, 17, 36, 38, 39, 43, 47, 49, 62, 66, 67, 71, 72, 73, 77, 87, 91, 92, 133, 141,
Farran, Roy, 5, 6
Feltham CVD, Central Vehicle Depot (RAOC) 13, 138
Fibreglass, 55, 95, 96, 112, 114
Fire Extinguishers, 2, 40,89, 90, 102, 127
First Aid Kit, 2, 90, 108, 116
Flares (Signal) and Flare Box, 81
Fletcher, Geoff, 80, 87, 164
Flook, Ron 120

G
Galvanised, 36, 70
Gamma (Radiation), 59
Gaydon, British Motor Museum, 137,155, 165, 166
General Purpose Machine Gun – GPMG (x 2), 8, 11, 14, 20, 45, 46, 47, 48, 49, 50, 51, 63, 81, 98, 99, 135
General Service, 12, 13, 16, 18, 20, 41, 44, 45, 62, 68, 76, 83, 87, 94, 144, 163
Geraghty, Tony, 59, 117, 119
Germany, (BAOR), 6, 24, 84
Goodwood, (Speedweek) 2, 17
Green Dragon, (SAS, Land-Rover), 24, 140, 161
Grenades, 63, 64, 77, 78, 112

H
Handley Page HP.67 Hastings, RAF, 105
de Havilland Mosquito, RAF, 30
Hexamine, (cooker), 108
Higgins, Andrew, 114
Hilton CVD, Central Vehicle Depot (RAOC), 13
Household Division, (Guards Regiment), 31
Howlett, Simon, 108

I
Irvine CVD, Central Vehicle Depot (RAOC), 13
Imperial Chemical Industries (ICI), (Imperial Metal Industries), 80
Imperial War Museum, (IWM), 50, 82, 88, 109, 112, 113, 114, 115, 155, 166
Inter-Vehicle Starter Power Socket, 67, 146
Invicta Military-Vehicle Preservation Society (IMPS), 138, 158, 166
ITALERI, 54, 57, 59, 159

J
Jebel (mountain or hill), 7
Jerrycan, 1, 2, 8, 9, 45, 84, 85, 86, 87, 93, 94, 99, 164
Jones, Roger, 64, 78, 132, 139
Joint Air Transport Establishment, (JATE) unit, 14
Jungle, (the Ulu) 46, 82, 101, 106, 108, 109, 114, 118
Jute, (Water container), 88, 89

K
Kinetic Energy Recovery Rope, (KERR), 91
Kit Form Services, (KFS, Models), 98, 158, 166
Kirkpatrick, Ray, 74, 89
Knife, 82, 101, 119, 120

L
Lady Be Good, 32, 33, 34
Land Rover Enthusiast magazine, 44, 45, 49, 53, 56, 59, 63, 67, 68, 70, 73, 75, 76, 77, 78,
Land Rover Heritage Collection, 156, 166
Land Rover International magazine, 140, 161, 165
Land Rover Monthly magazine, 2, 87, 126, 139, 162, 165
Land-Rover, Mk. 5, SAS, 1, 5
Land-Rover Mk.8 Lightweight, 12
Land Rover World (magazine), 139, 140, 162 165
Larkspur, (Radio), 95, 96, 97, 98
Lean-to Shelter, (Tentage), 87, 89, 103, 104
Lee-Enfield, 2, 110, 111
Light Aid Detachment, (REME), 21
Lockheed, Hercules, (C1-30), 76
Long Range Desert Group (LRDG), 31, 32, 66, 85, 164
Long Range Patrol (LRP), 66
Long Marston, 33
Lord Mayor, (Parade, 1972), 34
Lucas Light, 53, 61
Lying up Position, (LUP), 92

M
MacArthur, Douglas (US Army, General), 37
Machete or Machet, 82
Manila Rope, 91
Marshall, David Gregory MBE, 10
Map, Escape, 105, 106
Mayne, Blair (Paddy) 5
Medical Pack, 90
Mess Tin, 103
Mitchell, Neil 64, 78, 82, 100
Morgan, Seb, 91
Morrison, Bob, 87, 139
Mountbatten (Pink), 28, 30, 31
Mortimer, Gavin, 32, 164
Mosquito, (RAF, fighter plane), 30
Motor Transport, (MT), 9, 21, 34, 87

N
National Army Museum, 108, 109, 115, 155, 165, 166
NATO, 12, 14, 17, 20, 23, 24, 26, 28, 50, 54, 59, 76, 91, 97, 110, 111, 120, 135, 137
Niven, B.M. (Colonel), 112, 117, 119
Northern Ireland, 24, 27, 126, 142
North Africa, 30, 88

O

P
Paint for Vehicles, (a publication), 35
Pannier, rear, 6, 8, 12, 15, 33, 84, 93, 110, 144
Persian Gulf, 30
Photo-Reconnaissance Unit, (PRU) 30,
Pierced (Pressed) Steel Planking, 65
Pickaxe, (Pick helve), 76, 77
Pink Panther Register, 38, 61, 64, 77, 104, 133, 149
Pistol, 80, 81, 112, 113
Plymouth Pink, 30
Pocock, Barry 1, 17, 64, 82, 135, 140, 164
Popski's Private Army (PPA), 29, 65, 85, 111, 114
Project 212, (painting and application of) 23
Purkinje, effect, 28
Purkyně, Jan Evangelista, 28

Q
Quartermaster, (QM or just plain Q), 18, 21, 35, 75, 80, 81, 102, 120

R
RAF (Royal Air Force), 10, 12, 15, 18, 27, 29, 30, 55, 105, 118, 123, 141, 158,
Rexine, (seating), 99, 142
Radio(s), 1, 8, 43, 58, 61, 69, 83, 90, 94, 96, 97, 98, 102, 105, 107, 115
RCT, Royal Corps of Transport, 21, 28, 34
Ruddingtons, 131, 132, 136
RAOC, (Royal Army Ordnance Corps), 12, 15, 20, 21, 25, 27, 28, 34, 39, 41, 42, 45, 65, 80, 104, 136

(RARDE,) Royal Armament Research and Development Establishment, 10
REME, (Royal Electrical and Mechanical Engineers), 2, 16, 21, 24, 28, 34, 45, 104, 113, 132, 137, 158
RLC Museum, Worthy Down, 20, 40, 137, 149, 157
Rocket Launcher, 105, 114, 115
Royal Navy, (RN), 15, 30
Royal Signals, 10, 15, 96, 98, 156, 165, 166

S

SALOME (System for the Accounting, Location and Online Management of Equipment) 19
Samarkand, 3
Sand Channels (sand ladders), 65, 66, 67, 89, 135
Sand Tyres, (Balloon Tyres) 11, 14, 69, 70, 71, 72, 79, 125, 158
Sapele, plywood, 44
Saudi Arabia, 30
SCRDE, Stores and Clothing Research Establishment, 116
Search and Rescue Beacon (SARBE), 105
Searchlight, Portable, 39, 41, 61, 62, 63, 146
Seating, 40, 84, 98, 99, 100
Sear, John, 88, 117, 166
Sellers, Peter, 29
Scholey, Pete, 89
Shemagh, 116, 118
Shovels, 76, 77, 97
Sisal, (rope), 91
Skipper, Ben, 32
SLR, Self-Loading Rifle, 49, 50, 51, 69, 77, 113, 163
Sleeping bag, (Barnes Wallis), 120
Smoke Discharger Units (Smoke Pots), 63, 65, 79
SOE, (Special Operations Executive), 117
Soldier Magazine, 128, 132
Solihull, (Warwickshire) 4, 15, 35, 39, 40, 124, 145
Spanner Wagon, 75
Spitfire, (RAF, fighter plane), 30
Stirling, David (SAS Founder) 4
Stores and Clothing Research Development Establishment, (SCRDE), 116
Stubbs John, (Colonel), 29
Stowage, 2, 8, 25, 33, 40, 49, 50, 52, 53, 60, 68, 69, 76, 77, 78, 80, 81, 83, 93, 99, 102, 127, 158
Sunglasses, 118, 119

T

TACBEs, (search and rescue beacon equipment), 105
TAMIYA, 19, 57, 70, 89, 98, 100, 140, 158, 159, 162, 165
Tank Museum, Bovington, 52, 165
Taylor, James, 33, 64, 78, 80, 82, 84, 87, 87, 100, 140
Tentage, 89, 103, 104
Theodolite, 11, 56, 59, 60, 61, 97
Timpson, Alastair, 31
Tirfor (Winch), 91
Torch, Right-angle, 115
Tropicalised, 17, 66
Tripod, 59, 60, 61, 97
Tyre-Bead Breaker, (AKA, separator bead assy), 69
Tyres, 'studded', 73

U

Ulu (The jungle), 106
United States Army Air Force, (USAAF), 33
Utility, 15, 18, 19, 20, 21, 22, 45, 62, 65, 69, 76, 77, 107,123, 138, 163
Unit-Modified, (SAS Land-Rover), 9, 88

V

Vehicle Data Card, 12,13, 14, 16, 17, 18, 19, 20, 27, 34, 39, 40, 41, 83, 137, 138, 149, 157
VESPER (Vehicle Equipment and Spares, Provision Economics) 19
Vickers, Twin machine-gun, 2, 5, 46, 114,164

W

War Diary, SAS The, 6, 62
Ware, Pat, 9, 79, 94, 124, 130
Warner, Philip, 116, 119
Water Container, 86, 87, 88, 94

Webbing, 58' Pattern, 59, 78, 82, 86, 87, 90, 91, 104, 105, 106, 107, 108, 110, 117, 163
Wheeled Vehicle, WV, 9, 10, 16, 17, 18, 19, 20, 23, 41, 83, 122
Wheels & Track, (Magazine, Issue 9) 93, 139
White Helmets, 15
Wilks, Maurice, 4
Wilks, Spencer, 4
Willys Jeep, 4, 5, 6, 8, 31, 62
Willys-Overland Jeep, 4
Willson, Quentin 135
Wooden Wonder (the de Havilland Mosquito), 30

X

Y

Z